HERBERT READ
Formlessness and Form

HERBERT READ
Formlessness and Form
An introduction to his aesthetics

David Thistlewood

Routledge & Kegan Paul
London, Boston, Melbourne and Henley

First published in 1984
by Routledge & Kegan Paul plc
39 Store Street, London WC1E 7DD, England
9 Park Street, Boston, Mass. 02108, USA
296 Beaconsfield Parade, Middle Park,
Melbourne, 3206, Australia
Broadway House, Newtown Road,
Henley-on-Thames, Oxon RG9 1EN, England
Phototypeset in Linotron Sabon by Input Typesetting Ltd, London
and printed in Great Britain by St Edmundsbury Press Ltd,
Bury St Edmunds, Suffolk

Library of Congress Cataloging in Publication Data

Thistlewood, David.
Herbert Read: formlessness and form.

Includes bibliographical references and index.
1. Read, Herbert Edward, Sir, 1893–1968 – Aesthetics.
I. Title.
PR6035.E24Z92   1984   828′91209   83–21180

British Library CIP available.
ISBN 0–7102–0147–8

Contents

Acknowledgments

I am especially grateful to Lady Read for generously allowing me to use Sir Herbert Read's library at Stonegrave House; and I am indebted to Benedict Read for granting me unrestricted access to his father's unpublished notes, manuscripts and correspondence.

I owe my thanks to Howard Gerwing and Christopher Petter of the McPherson Library, University of Victoria, British Columbia, for their unstinting help over the number of years that I have been using the Herbert Read Archive there, and to Dietrich Bertz for sharing his extraordinary understanding of Read's miscellaneous papers, and also for translating certain items of the correspondence of Wilhelm Worringer which revealed Read's debt to this philosopher. Robin Skelton gave me much encouragement when he published my preliminary surveys of Read's work in the *Malahat Review* (University of Victoria BC), and I am keen to express my thanks to him and to George Woodcock, whom I have not met, but whose biography *Herbert Read: the Stream and the Source* (Faber, London 1972) provided much incidental detail as well as unique insights into Read's anarchism. Sandy Nairne presented my survey of relatively recent events in British art education in an exhibition entitled *A Continuing Process* (Institute of Contemporary Arts, London 1981): I am grateful to him and to the many others who, as a result, supplied information about Read's involvement in educational argument and debate. Tom Hudson has been of particular help in this respect. He is a consistent and longstanding practitioner of principles he first found in Read's *Education through Art*, and his example makes Read's theories clear and self-evidently right. Richard Hamilton, too, gave invalu-

Acknowledgments

able assistance here. Though my recognition of parallels between Read's organicism in education and his own organic creative expression may have surprised him, he was kind enough not to deny my arguments, and to encourage me to pursue them further.

I am grateful to Henry Moore for endorsing my account of the evolution of Read's aesthetic criticism in the 1940s, and to Victor Pasmore and Patrick Heron whom I similarly sounded on the question of Read's criticism in the 1950s. Alan Bowness kindly allowed me to quote from letters to Read written by Barbara Hepworth; Sarah and John Roberts granted similar permission in respect of Jacob Kramer's correspondence; and Miriam Gabo and Nina Gabo Williams generously allowed extensive quotation from the correspondence of Naum Gabo. I am grateful also to Colin Sanderson for his comments on passages dealing with Gabo's work; to Terry Diffey for his help when I was sorting Read's scientific influences; to Tom Heron for his memories of the Leeds Arts Club; to Oliver Pickering for his advice concerning Michael Sadler, an early influence on Read's thought; to Josef Hodin for information about Lancelot Law Whyte and the Institute of Contemporary Arts; to Roland Penrose for his recollections of the founding of this Institute; and to Dorothy Morland for granting me access to her private ICA archive.

I owe thanks to Louis Arnaud Reid for his helpful advice about the importance of Alfred North Whitehead; to Valerie Eliot for her comments on my treatment of an early theoretical exchange between T. S. Eliot and Read; to Gerda Niedieck, Richard Sadler, Gerda Ehrenzweig and Eve Whyte for permission to quote from the unpublished notes and correspondence, respectively, of Carl Gustav Jung, Michael Sadler, Anton Ehrenzweig and Lancelot Law Whyte; and to Norman Franklin for permitting me access to the business archive of Routledge & Kegan Paul, of which Read was a director. I have experienced the kindness and co-operation of librarians and archivists wherever I have worked, and I should like to mention, in addition to those whose help I have already acknowledged, David Schoonover of the Beinecke Rare Book and Manuscript Library at Yale University, and Christine Gascoigne of the D. W. Thompson Archive at the University of St Andrews.

I am indebted to Benedict Read, Joseph Rykwert and Stuart Macdonald for their critical appraisals of preparatory MSS; and I thank the Trustees of the British Academy, the officers of the

Acknowledgments

Staff Research Fund of Liverpool University, and the University authorities at Victoria BC for their assistance towards the costs of travelling to and from the centres of Herbert Read research. I am grateful to the following for permission to quote at length from works in copyright: Thames & Hudson for extracts from *Henry Moore* and *Arp*; Sheed & Ward passages from *Form in Modern Poetry*; Lund Humphries for quotations from L. L. Whyte's *Aspects of Form*; Cambridge University Press for passages from A. N. Whitehead's *Science and the Modern World* and D. W. Thompson's *On Growth and Form*; and the Trustees of the Sir Herbert Read Discretionary Trust, for extracts from Read's published essays, and from certain of his major works originally published by Faber & Faber, Jonathan Cape, Thames & Hudson, William Heinemann, Lindsay Drummond and the Freedom Press. I apologize profusely to any one whose help I have unwittingly overlooked, and to the scores of publishers who are too numerous to list here, but whose copyrights are acknowledged in the notes at the end of this volume.

Introduction

Herbert Read's achievements do not submit easily to drastic summary. He regarded himself as primarily a poet; and there is little doubt that, had it been possible to make the barest livelihood from poetry, this would have been his exclusive preoccupation. But his poetic ambitions had to be financed by other means – a decade of full-time employment; subsequently a variety of part-time ventures (editorial positions, publishing consultancies, and so forth); and as much freelance writing and reviewing as he could cope with. Criticizing literature and art became, quite quickly, his predominant activity; and this he pursued with great devotion, intelligence and feeling, hampered by few of the conventions which would have conditioned such work had he had the doubtful benefits of an academic grounding.

It seems fair to say that his criticism was a surrogate for poetry, because it was immediate, unsystematic and spontaneous. Quite possibly its great popularity was due to its being positive, unequivocal, aesthetic affirmation – though to some this was its chief weakness for, subject to the vagaries of emotional response, it could hardly be said to be consistent. Accusations of inconsistency, however, gave him not a moment's anxiety because he took this to be proof that his sensibility was live. His aesthetic thought must be understood as inclusive of romantic and classic sympathies: a prime purpose of this book is to argue that such 'inconsistency', far from debilitating his work, was rather evidence of its vitality.

He embraced contradictions from the start. He was by inclination a romantic, favouring the poetry of Coleridge, Shelley and Wordsworth, Ruskin's criticism and guild-socialist politics. His first serious literary venture, though, was into editing the miscellaneous papers of T. E. Hulme, the self-styled classicist. It may be argued that this initiated Read's practice of adhering to romanticism, while simultaneously respecting the classic – neither being biased towards either extreme for long, nor being intentionally ambivalent, but conducting his criticism in relation to the two polarities.

His early work was a searching for appropriate antitheses, and it was this that was given significant impetus by Hulme. For one thing, Hulme had put forward ostensibly romantic arguments, clouded only by a classic prejudice, that a specifically modern art would be, analogous to Bergson's theory of *Creative Evolution*, of the imagination and illuminated by the science of psychology. For another, he had paraphrased Wilhelm Worringer's arguments about historical manifestations of two separate tendencies in art, the one empathetic and vital and the other intellectual and structured. Quite early in his career, therefore, Read would distinguish between an art of romanticism, responding to 'projected' feeling or emotion, exploiting unconscious leaps of inspiration, and an art of classic precision, apprehending the forms and proportions of universal beauty, theoretically strengthened by the recent recognition of discontinuous processes in quantum science. At first he confined his attention to literary criticism, in which he could balance a natural romanticism and a fascination for the classic idiom imagism. In the field of art criticism, which he entered seriously in 1930, he recognized the romanticism of surrealism beside its classic counterpart, constructivism, and for a decade-and-a-half his conception of modern art in England was of these twin columns advancing – the superrealist (his preferred term) and the abstract.

For a while, identifying with the revolutionary achievements of pioneering modern art, which had been abstract, Read proclaimed classic loyalties: for a while later, however, he became a wholehearted devotee of surrealism. Towards the end of the 1930s he was drawn to a proper critical position, at the centre, supporting both wings of modernism, and occasionally cross-representing them to partisan audiences. He became closely involved with the work of a Hampstead circle of artists, largely because its authors were his friends and it conformed with his preferences, though partly because he realized that modernism would have to survive in Europe in an English form. Because the work of Henry Moore could not be ascribed conclusively either to abstraction or to superrealism, he began to speak of modern art as an axis, with such as Moore's art occupying middle ground. He saw that 'in different psychological states' Ben Nicholson and Barbara Hepworth worked sometimes abstractly and sometimes realistically, and that Paul Nash in particular ranged entirely between both modes of expression. He began to suspect that the English creative sensibility was peculiarly adept at traversing the notional axis; and he was prepared to argue that the extremes of this axis were the equal-opposite poles of a dialectic, and that Moore's art, now occupying a position in advance of the centre, exhibited all the signs of a synthesis or resolution.

By 1952 he had located the various approaches of these English artists within his theoretical pyramid. He had slowly grown accustomed to the constructivism of Naum Gabo, and had also accommodated this, as well as the different constructive art of Piet Mondrian, another cultural refugee in London, within his system. This scheme was not put forward explicitly because it was overtaken by other events (principally, Read seems to have had a sudden aversion for its obvious 'artificiality'). Following the chronological sequence of his writings onward of 1930, however, a dialectic theory may be seen to develop, to depend upon psychoanalytical principles which are mainly Freudian, and to be elaborated in his interpretations of an English avant-garde of art. But the main works in which Read set down such ideas – *Art and Society* (1937) and *The Philosophy of Modern Art* (1952) – present a system of thought not satisfactorily completed. Indeed, the next principal works on art (as distinct from creative education, an intervening, and then continuing, preoccupation), *Icon and Idea* (1955) and *The Forms of Things Unknown* (1960), superficially seem to be concerned with matters quite unrelated: former thoughts have been usurped by a scheme comparing a process-dominant art with growth and formation observable in nature, and accompanying psychological theory is dominantly Jungian.

Such dislocation, though perceptible in Read's major works, is deceptive. There are interconnecting threads in less-prominent publications, in a theoretical collaboration with Lancelot Law Whyte, a physicist, and in Read's establishing, with others, an Institute of Contemporary Arts in London. He had pursued certain anarchistic beliefs which had prompted him to conceive of an ideal community, in which a creative avant-garde would have been

engaged at the forefront of experience, making new perceptions
for diffusion throughout the culture. There is evidence that he saw
in the ICA a microcosm of his ideal community, and that he
proceeded to bring to bear upon its early development a number
of aesthetic, social and even scientific matters appropriate to his
theorizing. The ICA's large-scale expositions of primitive and
prehistoric art came within this category – they embraced principles
of Freudian psychoanalysis, of a collectivist society, and of two
distinct aesthetics, abstraction and superrealism. So too did his
collaboration with Whyte which, geared towards a unified theory
of artistic and scientific organicism, Read believed would result in
a major current of contemporary thought. This harked back to his
earlier admiration for the philosophies of Bertrand Russell and
Alfred North Whitehead, which had helped shape his premature
theories of creative form. In this way in his day-to-day concerns,
if not obviously in his major published works, there is an unbroken
succession in Read's oeuvre. *Icon and Idea* may be seen to have
been a confident assertion of the organicism of art; and *The Forms
of Things Unknown* to have followed the realization that Jungian
psychology was more relevant than the Freudian – so relevant, in
fact, that Read was encouraged to conduct his subsequent arguments in the presence of the Eranos Tagung, an annual convention
over which Jung himself presided.

Jungian theory, according to which collective, hereditable
patterns of perception could be said to effect man's perception
of reality, justified Read's long-standing conception of creativity:
universal principles (of nature and, now, of collective mind) and
individual impulses (the 'projections' of subjective imagery) are
resolved within the artistic event, an extended pattern of awareness.
Read was encouraged by Susanne Langer's belief that the potency
of such events resided in their symbolism; and he was prompted
to elaborate the more-involved hypothesis – authentic art is the
symbolic transformation of experience. Read's final works constitute an extension and a defence of this hypothesis. They also mark
a cyclic return to the dominant predispositions of his youthful self-
education (referring again, for example, to *Creative Evolution* and
its derivatives), to the social (now aligned with the humanist), and
to the metaphysics which provided initial insights into philosophy.

Several of Read's most important publications are collections
of essays written over considerable periods, re-presented out of

chronological sequence, and often unrevised. As such they give occasional impressions of substantial changes in his critical stance. A perception of value in such work is thus more likely to be a matter of sensation than of intellectual appreciation: that is to say, his books are often persuasive in spite of randomness of form. When the parts are examined in a different order, however, following the sequence in which they were first set down, and especially when they are seen beside matters which contemporaneously influenced his thought, the whole presents a vastly changed image – of an aesthetic theory developing far from randomly, leaving a permanent record of its formation. The intention here, therefore, is to trace the gradual *evolution* of Read's aesthetic theory (a metaphor of which, it will be seen, he would certainly have approved) so that changes may be studied in the order of their effectiveness. First it will be necessary to consider key influences upon his self-education in aesthetics and criticism; and in the course of this discussion it will be seen that an early adoption of dialectic logic gave rise to one of the most consistent features of his life's work.

The main episodes of Read's interests are conveniently sequential, and these are examined chronologically, though in chapters which often refer back to formative events. The first deals with contradictory aspects of Read's own aesthetic preferences, and is broadly synoptic of his life (1893–1968). The second examines his earliest philosophical influences and his immature criticism; and the third considers his first vocation (apart from poetry), his literary theorizing. Subsequent chapters describe an abortive philosophy, which he abandoned in the early 1950s; his social and educational criticism; a theory of organicism which affected all his work and especially his theories in their late and most perfected form; and an eventual return to review the archetypes of his own sensibility and intellect.

This is not an apologia for Read – one would be quite superfluous. It is rather an introduction to his work, in that it attempts to reveal a hidden order, and to present a context with which his original readership and audience would have been in contact, but which is often indistinct today.

Chapter 1

Innocence and Experience

The first decade of Herbert Read's life was spent on the remote north Yorkshire farm where he was born; the second, due to changed family circumstances, in the industrial centres of Halifax and Leeds. His earliest recollections were of weather, climate, the land, and the cycles of farm-work; and in later life it became clear to him that the sensibilities of the ten-year-old had developed naturally, that is to say aimlessly, amid a multitude of fascinations for the seasonal activities of the rural community, for the habits and traditions which accompanied the husbanding of animals and land, for the changing patterns and rhythms of the countryside, and for the wealth of experiences which this countryside yielded as he gradually increased the circles of his exploration, of which the smithy, the saddle-room and the stackyard lay near the centre.[1] In the harshest possible contrast his succeeding acquaintance, after the death of his father and the loss of farm-tenancy, was with the features of an education he recognized in the novels of Dickens: at a modest boarding establishment the child's learning was rigorously directed and severely disciplined, serving the single principle of memory-retention. Later, employed as a bank-clerk in Leeds and compelled by poverty to go to work on foot rather than by tram, Read witnessed 'areas in which factories were only relieved by slums, slums by factories', populated by drifting 'drab and stunted wage-slaves', and, he later realized, this environment gradually penetrated an inherited conservatism. He began to take an interest in socialism, giving his attention first to the works of Carlyle, Ruskin and Morris, which collectively provided, as he said, a window through which he not only saw the social realities,

1

but by whose light he also read what had been written about them. While taking Law and Economics at Leeds University, after having matriculated at evening classes, he acquired a comprehensive grounding in social economics and economic history, as well as an insatiable interest in socialist tracts of all kinds; and during the decade after 1910 – the period which embraced his studentship, his military service and return to civilian life, in which he gradually determined to become a poet, essayist and critic – he read widely and apparently indiscriminately (though as he was careful to record the authors who were most effective it is not difficult to reconstruct his interests.)[2] These seem to have been conditioned by dominant intuitions: because of the experiences of infancy (and more especially, perhaps, since they were made prominent by the contrasting, succeeding experiences) Read was intuitively predisposed to respond to ideas which took account of the natural, or which were based upon a pre-eminence of natural processes; and due to the recently acquired socialist beliefs, emerging as a coalescence of anarchism and guild-socialism, he was also likely to respond to theories which reflected this aspect of his awareness.

It was the coincidence of these two factors, the natural and the socialist, in the writings of Ruskin and Morris which originally aroused Read's interest. What seems to have caused Ruskin to be of particular significance, however, was that he wrote authoritatively about a variety of subjects – economics, socialism, botany, ornithology, geology – and seemed to suggest their potential interrelationship. That the artistic held prominence within Ruskin's theorizing made Read widen the scope of his learning to accommodate art; and it was also due partly to Ruskin's example that Read accepted at the outset that aesthetic criticism must be exact. He saw that Ruskin had insisted upon definitions, not merely of philosophical terms such as 'truth' or 'beauty', but of psychological concepts such as 'colour', 'space', 'expression' and 'imagination', and that he had also tried to relate the aesthetic activity to life as a whole. Not intentionally a system-maker, he had not put forward a coherent theory of art; but he had represented the search for truth of perception, and of this, Read thought, there was as much to be learned from Ruskin as from other, more seriously regarded writers, such as Hegel, Nietzsche, Bergson or Croce.[3] Bergson and Croce appealed to his feeling for nature, as, in different ways, did such as Coleridge, Wordsworth, Goethe and Kant; and in the writings of Kropotkin he found an appropriate blending of socialism and natural philosophy. Most works he read easily, 'with a joyous acceptance': the first author, however, to provoke a *crisis* of intellectual development, 'distinct in its impact, decisive in its outcome', was Friedrich Nietzsche. Twenty years later Read observed that it was difficult to recall the pre-Nietzschean state of mind, but that it had been simple, naive and conventional.

> What I found in Nietzsche, of course, was the complete destruction of all my ancestral gods, the deriding of all my cherished illusions, an iconoclasm verging on blasphemy. All of that I might have found elsewhere; there were plenty of strident atheists and persuasive rationalists about in those days. But I found something more in Nietzsche – a poetic force which survived translation, an imagination which soared into the future, a mind of apparently universal comprehension.[4]

This mind had formed a philosophy which was the first real indication to Read that (whereas the writings of Ruskin demonstrated that it was possible to command with equal assurance several disparate fields of knowledge) a system of thought might be holistic. Read recognized the governing concepts of Nietzschean thought to be a natural, evolutionary principle and a principle of human perfectibility; and these in themselves, for a while, were sufficient to fill the void left by relinquished Christian faith. In accordance with these principles he was prepared to admit with Nietzsche that every spontaneous act of human expression or creativity is effected by an 'arbitrary law; and in all seriousness, it is not at all improbable that precisely this is *nature* and *natural*'.[5] Read later came to accept that 'nature' is penetrated throughout by 'law', an observation which became clearer to him with every published advance of science; and he criticized Nietzsche only for suggesting that natural law was arbitrary. What *was* arbitrary, he said, was not the law of nature, but man's interpretation of it: the primary necessity was 'to discover the true laws of nature and conduct our lives in accordance with them',[6] which phrase Read was willing to keep as an aphorism.

This attitude of mind gave rise, in 1918, to his first serious opinions on poetics. These consisted in definitions *towards* a modern theory of poetry, demonstrating a sense of searching for axioms – axioms which, he clearly thought, would be related to certain counterparts in nature. Poetic form was to be determined by emotion requiring expression, stimulated by environmental form and colour. The poet's 'duty and joy' would be to express the exquisite among his perceptions by means which had similarities in nature – unity, rhythm, vitality, exactness, concentration.[7] The whole of this was to be governed and preserved from arbitrariness by the poet's conception of absolute formal beauty, a conception gained either as a result of a long and rich experience of life, or (as in the case of Read himself) through a traumatic, intense and highly concentrated experience (his involvement in the most desperate fighting of the Great War).[8] This theory presents him as having been aware of a solitary critical stance. An eagerness to distance himself from a section of the pre-war avant-garde led him to argue that the imagists (with whose work, in retrospect, his own contemporary poetry was most often aligned) had fallen short of their aim to curb emotional excess, by failing to submit their original apprehensions to the shaping influence of a proper aesthetic judgment.[9] Paradoxically, though, he gained an obvious satisfaction from his now being associated with the much-reduced avant-garde of literature and art which had survived active service in the war. This had created a sense of camaraderie which was to continue indefinitely in relationships with such as Paul Nash and Richard Aldington,[10] and reverberate in his lamentations at the loss of a leader, Thomas Ernest Hulme. And it resulted in a brief literary collaboration with Wyndham Lewis, though this evaporated, gradually, along with friendship.[11]

Read's return to civilian life took him first to the beginnings of a career at the Treasury which, as he rose within its echelons, left dwindling amounts of free time with which to satisfy the demands of an increasing literary reputation. This is chiefly why he transferred, in 1922, to a post in another branch of the civil service, at the Victoria and Albert Museum. Read occasionally was to speculate about what might have been – for example, if practical politics had beckoned, had he not in this way turned his back upon Whitehall; or, earlier, had it been possible to have realized the normal expectations of an eldest son in a fairly prosperous farming family, either to have taken over his father's responsibilities or to have enjoyed an Oxford or a Cambridge education. Would an Oxbridge graduate, unaffected by industrial Halifax or Leeds or the ensuing socialism, have been quite so evangelical in a subsequent critical career? Would the assurance of belonging to an academic tradition have pre-empted that equally characteristic feature of Read's actual achievements, his restless searching for relevant theory to substantiate the sensed conviction? All that may safely be observed, perhaps, is that his attachment to the civil service constrained his politics, preventing any contribution he might have made to socialist thought in the days of the General Strike and of the first Labour governments; there is no reason to suppose that principles now associated with him – those of full civil and personal freedoms within regional and smaller, devolved forms of government – would have affected the works of a career-politician. And, considering the unconventional nature of his life's eventual work, no better preparation could have been gained other than in Leeds, for there the Arts Club (rather than the University) had given him a grounding in Platonic thought, guild-socialist theory, European aesthetic philosophies and, above all, artistic abstraction, which interrelationship, as a practical model of modern life and conduct, had been unrivalled elsewhere, and mirrored theoretically only in the London weekly *The New Age*. It was to this paper that Read contributed many of his first critical essays – several on the work of Thomas Ernest Hulme; and it was at the suggestion of its editor, Alfred Orage, that he undertook to edit Hulme's literary remains, which task (though Hulme had been nothing if not a rebel philosopher) provided Read with the academic respectability for which he had sought.

Read wrote a regular column for *The New Age*;[12] and over a two-year period he attended weekly editorial meetings at Orage's office in Rolls Passage or at the ABC Restaurant in Chancery Lane. He had a frequent exchange of letters with Orage, who recognized certain features of his work – an easily ranging, kaleidoscopic vision; a tendency not to be 'dogmatic, conclusive, final, black-cappish'; and, already, an urge to perceive romantic and classic aspects in any argument.[13] If it was Nietzsche who had sparked Read's poetic imagination and taught him what he might dare to bring within the scope of his thinking, it was Orage who drew attention to innate propensities for making critical judgments, and who helped him considerably to polish his literary style. It was Orage, undoubtedly, who gave him his start as a writer and helped establish his literary standing. He wanted Read to edit *The New Age*, while he himself took what he thought would be a one-year sabbatical absence;[14] and, though Read declined because of commitments to his paid employment and to the Hulme manuscripts, this fact alone, in view of Orage's widely respected opinions, was sufficient to shape a reputation. One of Read's ambitions now was to put this at the service of a Yorkshire Literary Movement. It did not materialize; but it is clear from correspondence with the Leeds poet Wilfred Rowland Childe, and with others,[15] that this would have been no merely provincial venture. Their concerns would have focused upon whether Freud or Jung were capable of explaining the creative unconscious; upon whether a return to classic values in logic and morals would provide more than a partial solution to the great social collapse they believed they were witnessing; upon whether poetic 'ecstasy', or feeling for truth, were the only possible means of resolving apparently intractable contradictions; and upon the probable futility of seeking *exact* symbolic representation of universals, 'the final ends of consciousness being infinite'. It may not be surprising to note, incidentally, that the cultural climate in Leeds which had fostered a close association with continental abstract art before the war now sustained an awareness of dadaist poetry and drama.[16]

Another of Read's ambitions – his main one, it seems, in 1922 – was to define the contemporary possibilities of a metaphysical poetry. This was an attempt to countenance equal and opposite contradictions – emotion and thought as channels of poetic conception; and it was the first tangible effect of his study of Hulme, whose own work had been characterized by a wish to hold apparently romantic values while strenuously maintaining the primacy of classicism. Previously Read had been content to say that poetry – a poetry of this particular time, as of any other – would be directly connected with visual sensibility, consisting in the selection of emotional unities from within the phenomenal world of form and colour. Now, influenced by Hulme, he would say that the causes of emotion were not always concrete, and that, furthermore, there could be few, if any, clear-cut definitions. Emotion might in some sense be impersonal; and emotion might inhere in thought itself and not in its associations. The responsibility of the specifically modern poetic philosopher would be to identify a wide conception – a general stream of thought – that would generate sufficient emotional force for a poetry aspiring to unanimous meaning. (A little later he would say that Wordsworth had been an authentic metaphysical poet, in that his early works, at least, had embodied perceptions of nature together with a sympathy for republicanism, which had been in the mainstream of the thought of his age[17].) The present age seemed characterized by an absence of such unanimism: modern science, however, its material not yet assimilated into a general philosophy, promised to be a sphere for which a sustained metaphysical poetry might be appropriate. To appreciate the discrete phenomena of science and assimilate them to the general culture might well be to create an emotional unity belonging to the new age.

Read had become friendly with T. S. Eliot, through Orage's editorial meetings, and he submitted this outline scheme for his critical appraisal. In this way there began an unlikely exchange of ideas, to be maintained by Read and Eliot, in spite of religious and philosophical differences, for more than forty years. Eliot's immediate response was to question certain of Read's premises. Could it be said positively that emotion-of-thought could be isolated from emotion-of-associations? A philosophical poetry might digest one or more of the sciences, but would it be possible to assimilate them all? Some scientific philosophies, for example Bertrand Russell's, Eliot thought, were, by virtue of an emotional incoherence, unable to serve his conception of poetry. Eliot's advice, if not exactly classic, was traditionalist: the function of a contemporary poetry is to express the whole of feeling, a digestion of all experiences in a mind continuous with all previous minds, and as complicated and as comprehensive as possible.[18] This was quite in keeping with Read's view of the poet's necessarily intensive experience; though not obviously compatible with his belief that a truly contemporary poetry would be metaphysical, nor with his new axiom – metaphysical poetry is the emotional apprehension of (modern) thought.[19]

In this correspondence there were the seeds of several of Read's subsequent ideas. He was already well acquainted with Russell's philosophy, and had been impressed with certain key concepts, especially as they seemed to offer potential relevance, beyond Russell's immediate concerns, to the world of aesthetics. And he was aware that Hulme, had he lived, would have relied upon aspects of Russell's work in his plans for a literary career.[20] What Russell offered was the notion of 'insight' as the first inkling of 'truth' in any process of apprehension. This faculty, he said –

instinct, intuition, insight – was the one which first identified
'beliefs', which would only then be confirmed or confuted by
reason; and such confirmation, in the last analysis, would consist
in agreement with other beliefs no less instinctive. Here reason was
held to be a controlling, harmonizing force rather than a creative
one: even in the realm of logic it would be insight that would first
arrive at what was new. This construct offered Read the means of
describing to his own satisfaction the reciprocal poles of creative
experience: his first book of literary criticism, which he called
Reason and Romanticism (1926), might well have had the title
Reason and Insight.[21] It was his declared purpose to seek some
reconciliation or synthesis of these opposites,[22] which were to
considerable degrees personified, respectively, in Eliot and himself.

For it was clear to him that in moments of spontaneous poetic
creativity there was no obvious, perceptible reciprocation between
impulse and reasoned confirmation, but rather a continuous fusion
of vision and expressed form unquestionably right. On other occasions, much the more usual, a poet baffled for an exact correspondence of vision and utterance, and unwilling to settle for an approx-
imation, had merely to wait an indeterminate time for words to
come, exactly expressive. The only possible explanation, to Read,
of these facts of his own experience, was that 'the mind, given raw
material, will work unconsciously to create'. And the only possible
explanation of the second activity, in particular, was some hypothesis involving prevision and an unconscious matching of prevision
with ready counters, the abstract words constituting the poet's
random capacity.[23] This train of thought took Read straight to
Freud and Jung and to what was to be the predominant feature
of his work throughout his lifetime – its foundation upon an
(occasionally shifting) basis in psychology. And the realization that
Russell's ideas possessed a greater-than-apparent relevance
convinced Read of the importance of seeking a unified conception,
not only holding all the sciences, but also incorporating aesthetics
and other aspects of human conduct. Thus he welcomed, when it
came, what he saw as an enlargement of Russell's philosophy by
one who had collaborated with him, Alfred North Whitehead,
whose aim had been to give shape to precisely such a construction.
A metaphysical poetry, in fact, rooted in a unified philosophy of
science, and respecting, by means of a theory of collective unconscious, the idea of some continuity of mind beyond the individual,

may be seen as Read's more or less deliberate retort to many of Eliot's chief objections.

Whitehead's philosophy, in common with much of Hulme's, was essentially Bergsonian, centring upon an *evolutionary* principle as the key to understanding the development of both mind and matter. Hulme had been among England's foremost apologists for Bergson at a time when he had seemed to offer irrefutable arguments that consciousness, art, culture were evolving in time by processes comparable with those of natural evolution – that is, by proceeding from formlessness (the chaos reigning in the sphere of intuition) to ordered formation (the effects of intellection). Read had taken this to support the idea of cultural *progress*, and for a time it was his prime justification for a belief in the importance of an avant-garde of art. Then he grew disenchanted as he became aware of its mechanistic ramifications. Comparing mind and a regularly extending evolution led unavoidably to this paradox: creativity is ultimately reducible to laws and formulae which, correctly applied, will prohibit true creativity. Whitehead redeemed an evolutionary theory from mechanism, for Read, by drawing upon the most recent advances of scientific thinking, incorporating the new quantum theory, and making clear the modern scientist's conception of a *discontinuous* physics. The progression from formlessness to form, in the physical world, could now be seen to be erratic, and evolution to be patently irregular. A quite convincing analogous relationship, moreover, could be shared by a quantum-leap affected physics and another science – psychology – seeking to analyse the 'leaps' of inspiration and other discontinuous processes of the mind. This at once satisfied Read's predisposition towards natural philosophies, indicated the powerful stream of thought which would characterize the Zeitgeist, and gave rise to another lifelong belief – art is an organic event unfolding, but its eventual forms may not be preordained.

At a time when much critical thought was polarized, therefore, and when there was possibly more antagonism between romantic and classic factions in literature and art than ever before, Read possessed a system of thought by which it was not inconsistent to proclaim the virtues of both or of either. If he *was* occasionally inconsistent, it was because he would fail to make distinction between a spontaneous creativity, in which insight and reason were instantaneously fused, and creativity of a more usual kind, in which

9

there was some lapse affording a more obvious reciprocation. But he was often accused of inconsistency in the sense of supporting now the romantic, now the classic; liking now the lyrical, now the epic; promoting now an empathetic art and now abstraction. And such opposites, to him, were so obviously mutually dependent, as extremes within a *single* creative process, rather than themselves *alternative* processes, that it mattered little to him where, from time to time, his changing aesthetic preference would lie. In his own view his creative sensibility was rarely balanced and never for long:[24] he could legitimately indulge a classic preference and write an eminently reasoned criticism on the one occasion, and then stand for romanticism and give forth an emotional criticism on the next. Thus in his years as a civil servant, when his considerable organizing abilities were being given full scope in bureaucracy, he would advocate a classic attitude of mind. In his poetry he would attempt to impose rigid form upon ideas irrespective of their necessary rhythm, to make, in his own words, 'a form in space rather than in time – not the duration of a rhythm, but a chunk of poetic thought process carved into geometrical shape'.[25] He would justify this by saying that inspiration could only legitimately take its leap at the furthest point established by reason,[26] and that in this case the good metaphysical poet must incorporate the complete rationalist. In this frame of mind he would also contrive to see in Wordsworth's poetry the start of a great classic movement still gathering strength in the twentieth century.[27]

Then in 1931, having left his former employment for a short tenancy of the Watson Gordon Chair of Fine Arts at the University of Edinburgh, exchanging, as he said, an impersonal mode of existence for a very personal one, he found himself possessed for a while of exactly the opposite outlook, maintaining that the classic aspect of creativity was virtually irrelevant. This polar attraction, back and forth, seemed so patently the normal rhythm of a reciprocating sensibility – so patently *consistent* – that he felt it hardly worth the while of explaining. If he needed confirmation of its soundness, he had only to recall the path Richard Aldington's poetry had followed, from the hard, classic precision of imagism towards a 'looseness of structure, texture and idea' which Aldington maintained was a 'conscious tapping of the unconscious'.[28] Read had the greatest admiration for this work but, always a slight step behind in his appreciation, he had met its changes with some suspicion.[29] But then he came to see such transition, when he identified it in the creativity of others, as a necessary prelude to some synthetic activity – not merely a shift of inspiration but a momentous leap forward towards an advanced condition of art. In this way he would see the critic's chief responsibilities to be to reconcile opposing aspects of an individual's creativity, and to encourage a cross-representation of the warring factions in modern culture as a whole.

This is not to say that he found it easy to elaborate such theory. His first significant attempt took two years of effort; and there are indications that at least one publisher was unwilling to accept it, because of incoherence,[30] before it appeared as a short monograph entitled *Form in Modern Poetry* in 1932. This was an attempt to conduct arguments which only someone with Read's special outlook would have agreed were compatible – a belief in the primacy of the romantic principle in art; and an assertion that, in an authentic individual creativity, romantic and classic aspects would necessarily interfuse. He realized that these terms had become hackneyed, and it was also an objective to bring to their comparison a more scientific exactness. Thus he saw a distinction between the 'organic' nature of the former and an 'absolute' condition of the latter; and he suggested that a *personality*, free of repressions (as described chiefly by Freud) could be the only channel through which a properly organic conception might materialize in human creativity. A subsequent shaping and ordering was to be attributed to *character*; though he was unsure whether character was inhibitive in the better sense of its being a 'tempering' influence upon personal expression, or whether it was unnecessary, negative, and to be circumvented. The concept 'personality' was tentative, too: it was initially the *conscious* stream of thought, then *preconscious*, and, eventually, the total flow of all mental impulses that were not repressed. It was here that a conscious sense of character was said to be repressive, and to be eliminated from the creative equation; though throughout his argument Read held a *necessary* opposition of personality and character, maintaining that a vital, creative imagery would result from releasing mental impulses from a prior unconscious repression.[31]

This essay, more than anything else he wrote, is a barely revised transcript of an argument Read conducted with himself. It bears evidence of a turmoil of thought even in one of its principal conclusions – that the dreary quarrel of romantic and classic might be explained as an opposition of two kinds of art springing, respectively, from personality and character – which, in the heat of his argument, he inadvertently transposed.[32] Moreover, he was led into another difficulty: if character, as he had eventually defined it, were formed by the inhibition of instinctive life, it seemed to follow that a full and free personality had to be sacrificed by those who practised an art of order and harmony in the interests of their fixed ideals. He had already staked heavily on the idea that the artist's worth to society resided in his act of constructing such ideals, hypotheses, standards, of which the moral consciousness was constituted.[33] Now, however, he frankly avoided the corollary of his present argument – that an original, creative artist must avoid developing a high moral character – preferring to say that the essence of personality would be its lack of fixed purpose, its mobility, which observation contained more than a little self-analysis. This may be recognized as avoiding an extremely painful self-observation, too, on the part of a highly principled man now doubtful of his own moral standing while his first marriage was in the course of dissolution (which also, no doubt, contributed to the general disorder of his thought).

Such difficulties affected Read's theorizing throughout the brief period in which he considered art to be primarily a matter of *individual* impulses, issuing unaffected by individual repressions, for the good of the individual personality. Before 1930 it had been possible to say that, in the realm of the plastic arts and to a large extent in poetry, significant gains of the twentieth century had been abstract or classic, and these had had general or impersonal connotations. But his change of stance had coincided with recognition of an authentic romanticism in modern plastic art – surrealism – and with an ensuing, growing tendency to see himself as a surrealist; and of course this art was rooted in an individual psychology – Freud's – and was intentionally amoral. He was an active participant in all the main surrealist events in England in the mid 1930s; and he was stung by criticism that surrealism was destructive to maintain that it had quite the opposite purpose in society. This was the first hint of the dialectical theory, implicit in his earlier work, which it was now his published ambition to perfect.[34] This itself underwent constant revision, and at its outset it may be seen to have involved principles not strictly antithetic.

He said all progress was, in Marxian terms, dialectical, a logical succession of thesis, antithesis and synthesis. Realism, one of the poles of his current argument, was passive awareness of the external world, a static thesis. Opposed to this was the mental faculty commonly known as the imagination, but which was recognized 'more scientifically' to be the internal activity of the mind when 'free from the various moral conventions and social taboos which constitute the accepted social reality'. Their synthesis was to be the superreality of art – reality transformed by the imagination.[35] Thus the role of art was to exceed that which had previously been conventionalized, in the process creating temporarily relevant new conventions; like the physicist and chemist, the artist had merely one aim – to discover and describe the unknown.[36] This, though, made art of considerably more-than-individual significance, a conclusion towards which Read had been reaching in a recently given series of lectures published under the title *Art and Society* (1937). It became an issue he felt compelled to discuss with fellow surrealists. While art did appear to be an expression of the artist's personality, and to depend for its success upon his ability to break through the conventions of normality, Read thought it not unreasonable to suggest that in his *greatest* moments an artist might actually escape from the personal and express himself in impersonal and collective terms. These would not necessarily be dry and unemotional: they might have all the phantasy associated with lore and fable – the kind of symbolism some psychologists would ascribe to a collective unconscious.[37]

Between this and the main theme of *Form in Modern Poetry* there is a terminological difference: there 'personality' was a channel of expression and not, as here, a property to be expressed. Otherwise there is a similar emphasis, in an authentic creativity, on some interaction of individual and shared (ideal) phenomena. But there is here for the first time an explicit remark that the subconscious reservoir of imagery, tapped by the artist, might be collective mind. Thus it might be appropriate to speak of the formal ideals of a more-than-individual, 'absolute' or abstract art as being comparable, in significance, to the looser properties of an individual, 'organic' or surrealist counterpart. Furthermore, though the latter undoubtedly would be the more effective in an immediate revolution in social values, the former would probably have a greater capacity for survival, expressly because of its impersonality.

Largely for these heresies Read was expelled from the English Surrealist Group in 1939.

In the late 1930s, then, Read was employing pairs of opposed concepts which he did not propose as simultaneous contradictions. 'Realism' and 'superreality' were action and reaction; and an 'organic' and an 'absolute' art were of alternating value. In 1936 he had made the casual observation that modern art seemed to be a broad, virtually unbroken front stretching from superrealism (his term, now signifying his detachment from the movement) to abstraction, with such as Henry Moore, not readily identifiable with either extreme, in occupation of the centre.[38] He regained this idea, and at a time when he was most fascinated by the prospect of constructing a complete and perfect dialectic, he speculated about an immediate superrealist revolution at one extreme of a notional axis, and an abstract revolution (which had been in progress for twenty years) at the other; and he made sustained efforts to represent the virtues of each to its opposing faction, in order to assist the reconciliation he was convinced would result in an advancement of the general culture.

Since 1933 he had lived in Parkhill Road in Hampstead; and, as before he went to Edinburgh, he was writing art criticism for *The Listener*. At the suggestion of Roger Fry, he had succeeded him as editor of *The Burlington Magazine*;[39] and for the time being he considered himself more a theorist of art than of literature. His model of modern art became a specifically English model, almost unavoidably, as it dawned on him that a European movement might well have to survive for a while in an English form, and also as he realized that his friends and neighbours who were painters and sculptors – Henry Moore, Barbara Hepworth, Ben Nicholson, Paul Nash – possessed shifting sensibilities akin to his own, and were regularly traversing the broad front of modern art – Nash and Moore in its entirety. In the case of Moore, the counter-attractions to superrealism and to abstraction had preceded a tangible advance, establishing his art at the apex of Read's dialectic pyramid, along with that of Naum Gabo, who seemed to Read to have brought to England the results of revolution already attained. The work of another refugee in London, Piet Mondrian, however, though apparently similar to Gabo's in conception, was held to be *entirely* impersonal, and consigned to a less-than-advanced position within Read's scheme, beyond which it was thought unlikely to progress because of Mondrian's 'immobile' creative sensibility.

This system was never fully articulated, though most of Read's preparatory work was published, as a random sequence, in *The Philosophy of Modern Art* in 1952. Read was almost sixty now, and he had clearly intended this to be the summation of his life's work in relation to the plastic arts:[40] in the event, however, it held a much reduced importance for him. It was built upon guesswork about the nature of the creative subconscious, for which, in the 1940s, he had sought justification in a mixture of Freudian and Jungian principles – an interrelationship which was quite unauthorized. This was a system of co-ordinates, in which horizontal factors were the various Jungian mental types, ranging from introversion to extroversion, and vertical factors were the several layers of a Freudian representation of the subconscious, with extraneous elements at the very base – a Jungian collective unconscious – and at the very top Read's own idea of the supra-conscious, an accessible field *beyond* the range of consciousness. It incorporated, in addition, Read's explanation of how mental phenomena might be projected from beneath consciousness into conscious attention; and though he believed in this – it mirrored his own creative experience – it would nöt submit to a rigorous examination such as he would have desired. His use of selfsame co-ordinates to accommodate modern art seemed to be successful, for a while, when confined to the work of his friends, exhibiting as this did a fortuitous ranging between introversion (superrealism) and extroversion (abstraction). But they failed to hold a wider sample, and in particular could not cope with the approach termed 'abstract expressionism', 'tachisme' or 'action painting', when this became apparent as a widespread tendency. This seemed to require to be considered a dialectic advance (as a synthesis of abstraction and the formless imagery of the shallow unconscious); but Read could not contemplate it in anything so obviously devoid of formal organization. In any case, he believed he had witnessed the emergence of a new 'organic' art in Moore's sculpture[41] and a new 'absolute' art in Gabo's constructivism, which two polarities would have determined the nature of a further dialectic opposition. As he was about to proclaim this, however, a *stylistic* analysis became discredited in Read's mind; and its publication was displaced by matters which were to lead towards more appropriate conclusions to his life of criticism.

It was abandoned with some reluctance;[42] but it was seen to have been superseded, not by a single interest but by the ramifications of many, both new and revived. For one thing, he had realized a very long-standing ambition in the shape of the newly established Institute of Contemporary Arts in London, of which he was founder-president. He had desperately desired something of the kind for thirty years – since, in fact, his release from the army in 1919, when he had attempted to found an artists' and writers' co-operative.[43] This effort had been directed into publishing a short-lived quarterly, *Art and Letters*,[44] intended as the first step in an enterprise which eventually would have supported a printing-house, bindery, studio and shop; but the scheme was inadequately funded, ambitions were postponed, and the journal made way for Eliot's *Criterion*. Then he had wanted to help found a Yorkshire Literary Movement which, if he had had his way, would have published a series of chapbooks devoted to the county's ancient linguistic patterns, and contemporary efforts to extend these in all their purity. But his suggestions were again ineffective, for the similar reason that the necessary, hundred one-shilling subscribers could not be found.

In Edinburgh in 1932 he had attempted to create a *Bauhaus*, closely imitating the prototype at Dessau in Germany. He had urged some Scottish philanthropist[45] to offer funds for a central institution, not to replace those already existing in the city – the College of Art, university departments, Academy and orchestras – but to provide for the unification of their functions, appreciational, practical and publicist. He had foreseen an experimental institute, housed in a modern, 'functional' building, having lecture-rooms, music rooms, exhibition gallery, film workshop, and studios for lease: it would have been a 'laboratory' for experimental art, and matters of 'town planning, rebuilding and civic decoration' would have been within its scope. There are no indications that this plan met a positive response; but a few years later he revived it in an English context, when he persuaded the American heiress Peggy Guggenheim to found a Museum of Modern Art in London.[46] Premises were obtained for this enterprise, and detailed estimates of capital costs and running expenses were agreed and pledged; but its opening was postponed at the outbreak of the Second World

War, and the scheme was not revived. So when, shortly after the war, a committee was formed for the purpose of establishing an Institute of Contemporary Arts in London – in which it was successful – it was the culmination of Read's obsessive interest; and it gave him opportunities, for practically the first time, to represent directly to the artistic community certain matters which he believed were shaping modern thought, and which might provide a central, unifying force for all creative effort. This in itself meant that he had to widen his vision beyond a Hampstead circle, even before he accepted the improbable truth that an alternative, valid descendant of European abstraction and surrealism – action painting – had originated across the Atlantic.

Wartime, and the austerities of post-war peace, had caused Read to sort out his political thought; and to give this an outlet he had written pamphlet essays for the *Freedom Press*, and for *Now*, the anarchist magazine published by George Woodcock. He was convinced that the world was in the throes of cultural change comparable in depth and extent to that between the paleolithic and the neolithic, and greater than any such transformation in known history. Among the conditions of success in the present change, he thought, was abandonment of ingrained habits of aggression and competition (and of the assumption that such habits were unalterably 'human') in favour of co-operation, mutual aid, and mutual celebration.[47] In this sense Read saw an Institute of Contemporary Arts as a microcosm of a modern, anarchistic society; and this may explain what might otherwise be seen as the Institute's curious preoccupation, in its infancy, with observing dislocation and transition between the Old Stone Age and the New from every conceivable standpoint.[48]

The third factor to effect the widening of Read's horizon was a decisive conversion to Jungian psychology, offering as it did a convincing basis for believing in a not merely desirable but *inevitable* collectivity in society. Read undertook to edit the whole of Jung's published writings; and this may be understood as the result of his wish to gain access to the many still untranslated.[49] And a fourth factor was the rekindling of his faith in modern science as a determinant of the Zeitgeist, partly because he saw positive virtues in an emulation, by artists, of the mutuality exhibited by an international scientific community, and partly because he had met a physicist and admirer of Whitehead – Lancelot Law Whyte

– with whom he began to collaborate on a unified theory of art and science. This resulted, not in a treatise, but in an ICA symposium, and in the general conclusion that essentially similar pattern-selecting and pattern-creating processes were evident in the fields of physics, biology, psychology and art, bringing them to an identical plane of enquiry.[50] In this way Whitehead's legacy, a theory of formation and transformation, came to be one of the most significant features of Read's late work. His interests – social, political, educational, cultural, aesthetic – were essentially collective or unifying and pregnant with archetypal symbolism; and their patterns were continuously changing, in concert with an 'unfolding' of reality. The most important phenomenon here was human creativity – not merely the passive recorder of a changing reality, but *instrumental* in its evolution.

The philosophy of styles, which he seemed to accept that he had contrived, thus gave way to late concerns which were more properly philosophical, that is, less constrained by preconceived theoretical form. He had returned to the archetypes of his own sensibility, to live and work in the locality of his birthplace; and he had hopes that one of his sons might become a farmer, and repair the link of the chain which had been broken. His knighthood had come in the New Year's Honours of 1953; and he had accepted it, after much indecision,[51] as recognition of the fundamental importance to society of art. And now he enjoyed the first real financial security of his life. These matters combined to help make his late writings more self-assured, more identical with the flow of his consciousness, more *original* and therefore of greater value than much of the earlier work.[52] These, however, remain relatively little known; and this may be due to the fact that he had acquired a reputation as an inconsistent and possibly unreliable theorist, and partly to his self-effacing nature. He had rarely claimed credit for having had an idea, but had been more likely to identify it with someone else's work, which had struck a sympathetic chord. This is why his own writings tended to be eclectic mixtures of references to other authors – Bergson, Hulme, Eliot, Nietzsche, Whitehead, Freud, Jung, and many others – the compatibility of which was sometimes unconvincing. This was damaging, in the views of some,[53] but it was accepted (not always easily) by those who had read him extensively. Thus it was said of him, in the 1950s, that 'the identification of values and the affirmation of value-judgements is an important function, perhaps at the present moment . . . at least as important as logical and verbal consistency'; and 'Read affirms better than he identifies'.[54] And it was put to him repeatedly that there was no need to take support 'by leaning on others not so interesting': it was a vice to drag in such references, spoiling what his admirers most welcomed – a sense of the movement of his thought.[55]

One who had followed the gradual unfolding of Read's thought with the closest attention was Allen Tate,[56] whose written correspondence with him[57] had been only slightly less extensive than Eliot's. Whereas Eliot had tended often to challenge Read's ideas, though, and thus to provide an occasional check against headlong momentum, Tate had been entirely sympathetic. At first encounter he had seen that Read was struggling with a problem which (it is now known) would engage him for the rest of his life: the synthesis of romantic intuition and intellectual order. Tate had had much the same preoccupation, and had realized, also in common with Read, that this problem was insoluble beyond increasing the intelligence of an awareness of it. His view of Read's work thereafter, over very many years, was of just such an increasing intelligence, beginning with the Coleridgean theory of 'organicism', and assimilating to it a large number of insights offered by other philosophers.[58] It is arguable whether Read was as purposeful as this implies, and whether Coleridge did provide an original impetus, for there are strong indications that Read did not explain *fully* to himself his long-standing admiration for Coleridge until the relatively late revision of his theories.[59] But this is irrelevant to Tate's main observation: no other Anglo-American critic of his time had pursued with greater devotion, learning and profundity a single theory of the arts. Maintaining that Read's objective *was* specifically to extend Coleridgean theory, however, supported arguments about consistency. Though Tate was prepared to question the placing, in this tradition, of certain writers (for example, Hulme, perhaps in ignorance of the fact that Read's Hulmean experience had been formative), it was not hard for him to identify a patient substantiation of Coleridge's intuitions. In this way Jung's 'collective unconscious' would vindicate Coleridge's theory of the source of organic form; and Jungian archetypes would be the substance of Coleridge's 'primary imagination'. And the only notable criticism of such association, Tate thought, would be the rather

19

pedantic one – it is unsound to take seriously any enlargement of Coleridge's thought affected by matters he himself could not have known.

Francis Berry was the first to make an extensive, retrospective survey of Read's work, by a process of analysing his major publications;[60] and it is interesting that this post-rational view, on the part of one with sympathies quite similar to Tate's, is intrinsically different from the coeval appreciation. Where Tate witnessed gradual refinement and uninterrupted movement, Berry saw fundamental deviations from a main development, and a progression from crisis to crisis. The most obvious of these were evident in *Form in Modern Poetry*, and in Read's late abandonment of a well-established position; and to Berry these were not the workings of a systematic theorist, but of one responding to his basic impulses as poet. These impulses appeared to have been shaped by earliest experience; and Read seemed to exist, like Blake and Wordsworth, on the strength of childhood. His best criticism, that is to say, was not criticism in an accepted sense, but recognition of kindred sensibility: this seemed equally true of his responses to visual and plastic, as well as literary, forms. In this sense Read's oeuvre was a consistent transmutation of 'the haunting shapes of childhood into literature',[61] his educational theories were concerned with prolonging such innocent vision in the lives of others, and his aesthetic writings were attempts to re-create an immediate vision for those whose continuity with childhood had been lost. In the light of this, the clarity and tranquillity which followed Read's return to Yorkshire, in contrast to the disturbance of thought which just preceded it, bear particular significance. Thus the dialectic, which in 1936 he stated a desire to perfect, is somehow related to an 'artificial' life he had been forced by chance to lead; and his thoughts preserving continuity with childhood, and those conveyed in his late work, are correspondingly 'natural'. It is curious that this dependence was modelled exactly in the life of Olivero, the hero of Read's only novel, *The Green Child* (1935). This has been described as premonition or predestination;[62] and Read himself believed that he was 'lived' by reverberations of his vivid early life. A brief account of the book may indicate grounds for such arguments; but it cannot possibly do justice to one of the finest of modern prose narratives. It is expressed simply, in a style which may be called imagist, containing the acuteness of detail of a well-recalled dream, and, most notably, the sense of aural and spatial reality often associated with such recollection.

The Green Child is a triptych of barely connected parts. In the first, Olivero, a world traveller, returns after an absence of thirty years to the Yorkshire village of his youth, there to find that the beck which ran by the market-place has reversed its flow, and is streaming back towards its source. At first unable to believe the evidence of his senses, and then intrigued, he immediately sets out, though it is nightfall, to follow its flow up into the moors where it had originated. On the village outskirts he passes the watermill, and observes, framed in its window, a horrifying melodrama: a young and sickly woman, bound to a chair, is being maltreated by a rough-looking man. Olivero intervenes, and discovers the tormentor to be Kneeshaw, whose youthful act of wanton destruction (he had deliberately broken a mechanical toy, the delight of the village children) had caused him to break his ties with the place of his birth so long before. The woman he perceives to be one of two 'green children', a boy and girl, who had appeared from no-one-knew-where on the day of his departure: he had not seen them but had read about them, and their existence had fascinated him ever since. There follows first a battle of minds, in which Olivero's superior intellect succeeds over the simple, instinctual mode of his adversary; and then a physical struggle, as a result of which Kneeshaw falls into the mill-race and cannot be rescued. Olivero and the woman find him drowned, at dawn, as they proceed along the stream towards where it had once risen. This had been a marsh: now it is a vibrating diaphragm of quicksand, into which they leap without hesitation.

The second part of the novel is a mixture of travelogue, adventure yarn and political discourse. It deals with the thirty years prior to the traveller's return – his departure from the village, travels in Europe, imprisonment for Jacobin sympathies in Spain, a sea-passage to South America, and a fateful, accidental involvement in revolutionary politics there. It charts Olivero's successful planning of a political coup in the state of Roncador, and his devising for it an ideal democracy and an agrarian economy. And it also describes a subsequent, slow transition from democracy to benign dictatorship, the result of apathy pervading the electorate and its representatives. In order to escape the imprisonment of office,

Olivero fakes his own assassination and makes a leisurely return to England.

The third part is set in the Green Child's homeland, a cavernous underworld, entered by Olivero and the woman Siloen through the source of the stream. This is inhabited by a race of green-skinned people who know nothing of the passage of time (since they have no sky or seasons) and who, though they have a verbal tradition, have no literature. They have an existence ordered in relation to distinct, progressive planes or levels – one for youth, for play and reproduction; another for toil, for food-gathering and for various kinds of manufacture; another for the pleasures of opinion and argument; and the highest for retirement and solitary thought. The main pursuits at all levels are aesthetic – at the lowest, play; at the next, the polishing of rocks and crystals into near-perfect geometric forms; the next, intellectual construction; the last, mathematical contemplation, preparing for death and for purging the body of its lability, becoming petrified and incorporated within the structure of the earth.

Read maintained that to a considerable degree his narrative was automatic,[63] thus implying that (written with a fresh memory of *Form in Modern Poetry*) it was an individual psychological outpouring. Years later, however, he submitted it to Jung, who was greatly excited by its clear depiction of a collective archetype, personified in the Green Child, a compensation for all the things lived and professed in a lifetime.[64] George Woodcock saw the novel as an expression of Read's inner life, as an advanced 'phase of indirection, in which experience, having passed through the stages of immediate recording and autobiographical artifice, is finally transformed, like the bodies of the Green People, into the crystal patterns of art'.[65] He noticed that besides being rooted in Read's memories it also charted symbolically his future, since he too would return home exactly thirty years after his decision to seek a life elsewhere. Woodcock also noted similarities between Olivero and Kneeshaw – their common fascination for the Green Child, for example – and speculated that, in Jungian terms, they represented opposed aspects of Read's existence – the one the traveller, bureaucrat and politician, who had mastered the power of words; the other his dark shadow, the Read of simple and instinctual mode of life, who would have become actual if his path had not suddenly changed when he was ten.

The novel manifests a haunting superreality; and it is this that has claimed most critical attention.[66] But it also contains what may be seen as, in the context of Read's contemporaneous writings, a degree of deliberate introspection. Its principal elements correspond with his view of the creative mentality. The Quixotic adventures constitute the artist's extensive, rich experience: following the stream back to its source is to discover the channels of a personality; the aesthetic underworld is the classic shaping of a character. Or rather the shying away from such a final shaping, for Olivero realized that the Green People's aesthetic sense was fully engaged only when the form of a manufactured crystal corresponded almost exactly with its natural prototype, but narrowly avoided replication. This was evidence of an exerting free-will or spontaneity; and when he reached life's level of habitual discourse Olivero was made to conduct Read's arguments about a broad front of aesthetic sensibility. Approaching the crystal from the side of the senses yielded an appreciation of order created by the senses, and of an apparent ability to quell disorder: approaching from the other side of the mind yielded a distinction between order created by man and the superior order of the universe.[67] Elaborating this, Olivero rose greatly in the esteem of his peers (though he thought it prudent to suppress evidence of his secret store of understanding gained in a prior realm).

Much of Read's novel, particularly the large passages of luminous description, seems undoubtedly to have been automatic; but, seen beside interests which were current, much of it also seems conscious construction. There is an unresolved paradox which opposes two lesser contradictions – the first part of the narrative (a romantic realism), and the last (a classic fantasy); and there is an implication that the life of the traveller, to the extent that it was unaffected by his elemental experience, was artificial. It is suspected that Read retrospectively regarded some of his own accomplishments as, in this sense, artificial. In late life he did not review his dialectic of styles, though he polished considerably a succeeding hypothesis, expressed after he had regained contact with his alternative mode of existence. He then took great pains to revive initial experiences, and, not unnaturally, to discover what had shaped his early, malleable thoughts.

Chapter 2

Empathy and Abstraction

The years between 1912 and 1918 were among the most eventful in what was to be a very varied life. They saw Read's transition from bank-clerk to man of letters; and they witnessed his distinguished service, in spite of a latent pacifism, in the war he felt would end the threat of future war. The horrors of the front were relieved by near-idyllic periods of rest and recuperation, and during these he wrote his first serious commentaries – for *The Guildsman*, *The New Age*, and *Art and Letters*. In this time Read's socialism developed from emotional beginnings towards a coherence he considered eminently practicable; but perhaps the most interesting change was that which affected an early aesthetic outlook. His diary account of this[1] records an almost daily enlargement, clarification and fitting into place of some new argument; though *decisive* change began in 1912, before he kept a diary, when the young man who, conventionally enough, respected Ruskin and Morris, found suddenly that the context of his thought had vastly broadened. It was his good fortune to chance upon the Leeds Arts Club, an association dedicated to 'the free interchange and expression of modern thought', and to placing art and politics, religion and philosophy in a socialist perspective.[2] In these respects it was probably the most accomplished of its kind, excelling in practice even the proceedings of the Fabian Arts Club in London, the formation of which it had actually inspired.[3] And it was here that the village schoolboy, the orphanage pupil, the night-school student, the student of economics, gained his most effective (and, considering his origins, a highly unlikely) education.

This club, as Read found it, was nurturing a surprisingly

advanced aesthetic: abstract drawing and painting were accepted practices, and there were links with Wassily Kandinsky and the Blaue Reiter group in Munich. Evidence suggests that Leeds, as a centre of the English avant-garde of art, was second merely to London; and if only for this reason (that is, without for the moment speculating about lasting effects upon Read) the milieu which he discovered may merit some discursive attention. The Club had been established in 1903 by Alfred Orage, a mainly self-educated man who for some years had combined teaching in a Leeds board school, writing a regular column in *Labour Weekly*, and lecturing for the International Labour Party. He had devoted seven years of spare time to a study of Platonic philosophy;[4] and the natural outcome of all these interests had been to see the Arts and Crafts movement as a medium in which preferred social, industrial and aesthetic principles might be interfused. The Club was intended to embody such ideals: Orage and Arthur Penty (a local architect who was preparing a seminal work on guild-socialism) created the theoretical context, and other members – notably Holbrook Jackson, a lace merchant, and Tom Heron, a silk manufacturer – put theory into practice in model commercial and industrial schemes.[5] When Read joined the Club – still popularly known as the 'Platonic Lodge' though Orage had departed – he found attachment to the belief that many of society's deficiencies were *aesthetic* deficiencies, and commitment to woman suffrage and other principles emanating from the practical socialist experiments.

Orage had gone to London in 1907, to resurrect and edit a defunct periodical, *The New Age*; and in the opposite direction, early in 1912, had come Frank Rutter, the critic and founder of the Allied Artists' Association, to be Curator of the Leeds Art Gallery. As Read began to take an active part in the Club's affairs Rutter, having been invited to be President, had already introduced several of his own predilections, all of which were entirely compatible with the prevailing, corporate sense of purpose. He brought from London an aesthetic hypothesis, a theory of 'significant form',[6] maintaining that it was form itself – lines, shapes, colours, irrespective of pictorial content – which stimulated 'aesthetic emotion' during contemplation of works of art. Club members had for several years insisted on the primacy of quick, expressive sketches over finished drawings and paintings.[7] Rutter now urged that such sketches need not necessarily be pictorial, and he encouraged

25

attempts to represent musical sound and composition by means of reflex painting, and to correlate words with drawings representing nothing other than emotions which the words aroused. These efforts towards a non-pictorial expression began immediately upon Rutter's arrival, though they were considered educational and, at best, preparatory – that is, they were not geared to a specifically abstract style of art. Rutter's achievement, however, was to focus argument and debate upon individual creativity and emotional expression, matters quite outside the narrow conventions of contemporary criticism; and this initiative gave rise to Read's great debt to an acknowledged mentor.[8]

The objectives of Rutter's experiments, of course, were similar to those which were central to Kandinsky's art; and there were, in the city, recent works by this artist to which the Arts Club membership made frequent reference. The collection of Michael Sadler, Vice Chancellor of Leeds University, contained paintings by Gauguin and van Gogh, by Paul Klee and, in 1912, several by Kandinsky, the first of a growing number, which Sadler had bought on a visit to the artist's home near Munich.[9] Thereafter works by Kandinsky arrived in Leeds at regular intervals; and on one such occasion, in 1913, it was apparent that the latest differed from its predecessors by virtue of its complete non-representation.

> The pattern of the composition had broken free from orthodox decoration, as vers libre departed from conventional metre.
> The design, strong in structure and balance, suggested hurtling masses in impending collision. The dominant colours were vermilion, black, purple, sulphur yellow and blood red . . . .[10]

Sadler himself seems to have found such abstraction less interesting than Kandinsky's earlier, pictographic expressionism. He clearly welcomed the expressionist movement in whatever form it took, and also its portents of social revolution;[11] but at the same time he felt that the search for new significance in pure composition was limiting, and would ultimately lead 'perilously near to reducing art to the diagrammatic'.[12] Such arguments as these were often put forth on the monthly occasions when the Club was invited to the Sadlers' home – and there was also a lively opposition. A Blaue Reiter exhibition was planned for England, and an extended visit arranged for Kandinsky,[13] the greater part of which he would have spent with his English patron and in contact with Rutter (who had received his work into the fourth AAA exhibition in London in 1911).[14] It was this climate of opinion, then, which nurtured an expressionist realism, for example in the works of Jacob Kramer and Bruce Turner, young members of the Arts Club, and which encouraged Read to paint a succession of 'futurist works' and some entirely non-representational compositions.[15]

Orage's periodical, meanwhile, was introducing avant-garde European movements – post-impressionism, cubism, futurism – to its English readership; and Read, onwards of 1912, was an enthusiastic subscriber (even contriving to obtain it at the front during the war). Between 1912 and 1914 it reproduced a number of works by the then relatively unknown Jacob Epstein, Wyndham Lewis, Henri Gaudier-Brzeska, David Bomberg, Christopher Nevinson, Edward Wadsworth and William Roberts, notably in a series entitled 'Contemporary Drawings' edited by Thomas Ernest Hulme;[16] and it also carried Hulme's famous pronouncements on a modern art of abstraction, which were contemporaneous with the announcement of vorticism. Walter Sickert fought his rearguard action against the abstractionists here; and while this radical-reactionary engagement was claiming most attention another theory of art – that of neo-realism – was unobtrusively being formed in the context created by the paper. This theory (the origins of which, if the truth be known, were in debates at Leeds), rejecting abstraction *in finished works of art*, was announced in *The New Age* at practically the same time as Hulme's definitive statement. It seemed to be an equally logical and equally inevitable result of selfsame arguments; and in this sense (whereas Sickert's impressionistic realism was seen as a preceding condition within a realism-abstraction alternation) neo-realism was the genuine rival of Hulme's abstraction, and its proper antithesis.

Besides introducing his own ideas into the Leeds Arts Club Rutter encouraged the usual practice of following closely and re-debating the editorial matters of Orage's paper; and the resulting consensus, in the field of art, was the embryonic neo-realism. Kramer, Turner and Read were always prominent in such argument, as were Rutter's friends Charles Ginner and Harold Gilman, members of the AAA, who were occasional visitors from London. Though it was not conducted in its pages, their discussion was none the less a searching for ramifications of *New Age* principles; and as such it was influenced by Nietzschean and, above all, by

Bergsonian theories. The translators of Nietzsche and his interpreters (of whom Orage was one[17]) wrote regularly in *The New Age*; and Hulme, at that time perhaps Bergson's foremost apologist in England, contributed lengthy appraisals of his philosophy – in particular the theory of *Creative Evolution* – as well as his own views of its bearing upon an intrinsically abstract modern art.

According to Hulme's interpretation (which clearly met with Bergson's approval[18]) the only possible explanation of the fact of evolution was to suppose that it was the result of an impulse similar to that which seemed to initiate human mental activity. On both sides of an analogy – concerning the unformed material of physical evolution, and the unformed substance held in intuitive apprehension – there were said to be vast entanglements of raw phenomena; and it was suggested that on the one side a natural-creative impulse, and on the other a mental-creative impulse, would release fragments from their respective states of flux, for reassociation in much simpler natural and mental constructions. Accordingly, human creativity was said to consist in the urge to present to intellectual attention glimpses into the vast, hidden reservoir of intuition – or, in other words, to gain fleeting fragments of imagery, snatched from a dynamic intuition, though transmuted from an original formlessness into forms with which the intellect might come to terms. Such arguments in themselves seemed to Hulme to justify a trading in abstractions, the idiom he believed held prior claims to being refined, rationalized, intellectual;[19] though he had other reasons too for campaigning for abstraction. These were to do with his own intuitive liking for certain archaic forms of art which were faceted, stylized or geometricized, such as Egyptian and Indian painting and Byzantine mosaics, and with the complete lack of appeal which most post-Renaissance art of the west held for him. He had been moved by a power in Byzantine mosaics which he had been unable to explain until he perceived similarities forming in the works of those whom he respected – Epstein, Bomberg and others; and he began to conjecture that the acutest sensibilities of his age were finding relevance in something akin to a pre-Renaissance system of aesthetic values.[20] Holding this belief, he was able to put forward a remarkable hypothesis: western culture was experiencing the first effects of a difficult and painful transition from the damp, romantic decadence of late-Renaissance values to those dry, hard and classic values, the properties of a new age.

Because this passage could not possibly be smooth (the romantic and the classic possessing absolutely nothing in common) those who were responsive to the new climate would have to negotiate the dislocation as best they might – by finding a foothold in the archaic, making use of archaic geometric imagery, before developing this into an abstract language more appropriate to the present age – an age characterized chiefly by the geometry of machinery, mechanical production, industrial efficiency.[21]

According to Hulme's analysis, therefore, it could be said that works of art (of literature as well as painting and sculpture) executed over the preceding two centuries and sympathetic with the then-prevailing romanticism, were irrelevant to the modern sensibility. It could be acknowledged that preparatory stages in the gaining of an authentic, modern means of expression could be associated with the classicizing influence of Cézanne, and with the recognition of archaic forms initiated by Picasso; (and, incidentally, it could be recognized that the critic Roger Fry, who had arranged exhibitions of post-impressionism in London, had been instrumental in bringing such principles into the English consciousness – although the significance of this was considerably reduced by the thought that classicism, archaism, geometricism were 'in the air', and available in any case to all receptive sensibilities.) It could be argued that the work of Hulme's favoured group would be the foundation upon which the next generation would build, and that the tendency he had recognized – the disintegration of the subject as appearing, and its re-presentation in hardened form – would be the crucial factor here.[22] And an interesting supposition of Hulme's, from the present standpoint, is that this development would have stopped well short of *complete* abstraction. No artist, he said, could create abstract form spontaneously: it had to be generated, or at least suggested, during a period of consideration of 'outside, concrete shapes'.[23] Abstract form for its own sake, offering little indication as to the nature of an original intuition, or to that aspect of the outside world from which it had derived, held no attraction for one who, while stressing the utmost relevance of a classic language of forms, maintained an extensive vested interest in Bergsonism.

The Leeds Arts Club membership looked to Hulme's presentations not so much for an explanation of abstraction as for a theoretical account of the creative process.[24] For insights into abstraction those who were interested in this phenomenon, in particular Read, looked to Nietzsche. Read had an unusual freedom of access to Sadler's collection of paintings;[25] and in trying to comprehend non-representational works there he was assisted by Nietzsche's recognition of a specific art-form, the result of an interplay of opposing factors – an inner richness with an outward simplicity, an inventiveness within the bounds of rigid discipline.[26] Read also found value in Nietzsche's having postulated two distinct types of art – the one Apollonian, this art of pure form, and the other Dionysian, corresponding with the term 'romantic'; and he accepted all of this as an indication of how dialectical law might work in the realm of art. The Leeds circle generally did not see the space between romantic and classic as a barely negotiable divide (as Hulme did) but they found a rather gentle succession, even an interpenetration. Sadler, for example, perhaps surprisingly, was expounding affinities between the writings of Nietzsche and Ruskin,[27] which undoubtedly helped Read progress beyond the conventional matters of his earlier reading. Sadler, too, recognized romanticism in those aspects of modern industrial life (which Hulme thought specifically classic), criticizing Ruskin only for failing to see in factory chimneys a form of beauty he had perceived in medieval towers, or for refusing to accept that 'strength and power (might) show themselves in the great arms of travelling cranes, in the gossamer beauty of scaffolding, in the gaunt severity of . . . mill sheds and in the intense and silent power of dynamos and turbines'.[28] While respecting a great deal of what Hulme had to say, therefore, Read had no reason to relinquish an enjoyment of romanticism, or to expunge it from his art. He came to write in his diaries about the intellectual demands of an aspect of his work he called 'design', which were balanced by those of an intuitive expression, 'colour';[29] and it was in this related way that Bergson was a major influence upon Read, and upon the proceedings of the Leeds Arts Club, while Nietzsche was the occasional provider of decisive insights. Thus Read would say that Bergson had shaped and directed his theoretical development, while simultaneously acknowledging that, at its outset and for at least five years, Nietzsche had been his most effective teacher.[30]

Their two philosophies had superficial similarities. Both lent themselves to *dialectical* conjecture – on Nietzsche's part about an antagonism of classic and romantic art, and, on Bergson's, about an opposition of intellect and intuition; and both eventually could be called upon to support the idea of aesthetic experience as a *dynamic process*, seeking if never quite attaining perfection. Thus the collective approach of the Leeds group combined personal or individual concepts – such as impulse, intuition, imagination – with a universal principle of dynamism. It was flexible enough also to accommodate various aspects of other philosophies which were essentially dialectical, evolutionary or morphological; and in scope and consistency, except with regard to two important matters, it had much in common with the composition which had been blended by Orage's editorial skill. The two exceptions were the conservative philosophy[31] and the preference for an art of exclusively classic precision which Hulme, in particular, considered perfectly compatible with a Bergsonian allegiance; and in 1914, when *The New Age* gave expression to a controversy concerning the supposed attributes of a specifically modern art, it was precisely these last ideas which were used to support arguments that only an art of abstraction could capably reflect the spirit of the age. The principal protagonists in this debate were Charles Ginner, who spoke for neo-realism, and Hulme, whose commitment was to the geometric abstraction he had recognized particularly in the work of Epstein and Bomberg (and, except when it was *entirely* non-representational, in the work of Wyndham Lewis[32]).

Ginner's view was that all the great advances of art had been effected by individuals, making immediate and unprecedented apprehensions of the natural world around them, transposing their discoveries into images, each of which, though recognizably 'realistic', conveyed a sense of the artist's emotional condition in the presence of his subject-matter. Art which, in his opinion, exhibited a distance from nature (which included post-impressionism, cubism, and the 'official' art of the Royal Academy) he considered to have lapsed into repetitive formulae; and he put forward the suggestion that an art of the present, like its counterparts of other ages and cultures, might only be thought *specifically* modern if it fulfilled this role of immediate discovery and realistic transposition.[33] Hulme was sharply critical, partly of Ginner's *natural* principle of authenticity, and chiefly of his assertion that cubist and other abstract expressions were academic derivatives of the original achievements of Cézanne, and therefore inherently degenerate. He described an axial theory which linked the extremities realism and abstraction and encompassed two other attitudes to art – a willingness to abstract perceptions from nature, perhaps exercising the right to be selective; and a willingness to engage in some reciprocal, imaginative activity, to shape natural form according to conceptions gained elsewhere. The late work of Cézanne seemed to Hulme to conform exactly with this latter tendency: his *Bathing Women*, for example, contained a deliberate, constructive composition and a wilful distortion of form which were neither realistic, nor purely decorative, nor merely selective. Only such art as this could lay claims to an immediate relevancy, because art born of other attitudes (in particular, the readiness to trade in exact representational images, though also, to some extent, the desire to manipulate pure form for its own sake) would be tainted by preconceptions. Recognition of a necessary reciprocation between nature and imagination, effective in the act of creative development, would ensure an absence of such preconceptions, most of which Hulme held to be characteristically imprecise, emotional, romantic. It was his prejudice (it may be clearer now than it was in 1914 that he and Ginner differed mainly in their prejudices) that an art of the moment should, on the contrary, be classic, precise and geometrical.[34]

During the following three years, while reserving his opinion that continental abstractionists had driven into a blind alley, Ginner came to align with Hulme in one of his principal arguments – that the vorticists' desire for dynamic composition, and their concern, by this means, to express 'some abstract or philosophical idea', did in fact bear evidence of vitality. He now recognized that in England two kinds of art, a vigorous, intellectual abstraction and a new realism, the result of a largely intuitive approach to subject-matter, were travelling side by side; and he suggested that artists, instead of indulging in mutual recrimination, ought to attempt to synthesize the best characteristics of the two. Thus he foresaw that the emotional attachment to nature, as well as the sound appraisal of natural colour on the part of the new realists, and the formal precision and strong sense of purpose of the abstractionists, would combine to create an advanced condition of English art.[35] This Read instantly accepted as a profound encapsulation of matters he believed important;[36] though he maintained that the necessary synthesis would be less likely to result from any group effort than from an individual percipience. He had accepted the

Leeds argument that evolutionary stages in the development of human consciousness were always individual achievements.[37] Thus, being evolutionary, individual creativity could be said to be subject to dynamic laws analogous to those of nature; and also, dedicated as it was to 'progress' or 'perfectibility', it could be said to counter the existential purposelessness found, for example, in Nietzsche. As he learned not to be entirely uncritical of Nietzsche, therefore (or, for that matter, of Bergson[38]), Read gained convictions he would hold, more or less consistently, for the rest of his life. An evolution of consciousness is the chief purpose of existence. It is achieved aesthetically, that is, by submitting individual mentality to the effects of *vivid experience*;[39] and this is assimilated and subsequently transmitted in unambiguous forms of art emerging from the resolution of abstraction and its antithesis. Various strands of his general reading, once unconnected threads – Kant's *Critiques*, Goethe's theories of morphology, Schelling's relational theory of art and nature, Croce's *Aesthetic*, Hegel's *Dialectic*, the natural-anarchic theories of Kropotkin, and the works of the English romantics Coleridge and Wordsworth (to which Read felt an attraction he could only explain, in the case of Wordsworth, by noting that he, like himself, had been of northern yeoman stock) – these might now be interwoven with the general beliefs.

Read had witnessed the prevailing arguments with some detachment, because of the war: now, however, he began to be drawn back into fuller participation. He received a remarkable letter, in which Jacob Kramer, with whom he had corresponded throughout hostilities, took pains to describe the matters which gave rise to his idiosyncratic imagery; and this account was compatible with the view of creativity given by Ginner, though in the slightly modified form – emphasizing an individuality – which Read preferred. Perhaps recalling the debates at Leeds, Kramer took it for granted that Read would say the degree of *expression* in a work of art was the measure of its greatness; and it was his wish to maintain that this fundamental property was more a 'spiritual' than an intellectual phenomenon. But whereas Ginner spoke of two opposed types of art, and of creative resolution as an activity in which realists and abstractionists would be concerned to learn from one another, Kramer perceived an essential antagonism affecting his *individual* mentality. When 'spiritual' and intellectual faculties were brought to bear upon the shaping of a work of art, he said, a struggle invariably ensued, and he was conscious of the great efforts needed to reduce detailed representation of subject-matter to the smallest amount consistent with conveying a recognizable image, whilst carrying the greatest possible weight of 'spiritual' expression.[40] In other words, he was aware of a dialectical opposition conditioning his creativity, and he realized that his aesthetic preference was inclined towards one of the polarities (he was, as Read paid tribute almost fifty years later, an expressionist, unfortunate in that he had worked in a cultural climate in which he had not been understood[41]).

'I should say', wrote Kramer,

> that when you have attained power of perceiving two distinct and separate entities, and furthermore, when you know that the spiritual element is in the ascendancy, it will culminate in a completeness which incorporates both in a manner which is calculated to produce an entire oneness; and in that way both elements are mutually dependent and merge with one another.[42]

Read did not quarrel with this explanation, but he did engage in a terminological dispute, urging Kramer to substitute 'intuition' for 'spirituality'. Where Kramer had said he endeavoured to permeate representational form with spiritual feeling, Read would have had him say that his art forms came *from* an intuitive understanding of his subject. Read insisted that the artist's consciousness – the consciousness of any artist – would receive a nervous impulse, or an intuition, from the chosen field of his perception; and that Kramer's priority would be to put forward an embodiment of this impulse relatively unaffected by intellectual reasoning. In such an event the work of art, conforming with a chiefly Bergsonian scheme, would be 'merely a plastic utterance by certain skilled means of the expression or mental intuition'.[43] Furthermore, Read asserted (exhibiting now an aspect of his Nietzschean influence) the work's claim to realism would at best be likely to be partial, residing in the degree of accuracy with which a feeling comparable with the original intuition could be re-created in an observer: there could be no *undiminished* reality outside the mind. He wrote himself this memorandum: it is

a fallacy to imagine that you distinguish the spiritual from the

actual. The actual is . . . the intuition; and when we posit
something real we are making a judgement, an abstraction of
the intuition . . . . The beauty of a thing is not indwelling in
that thing itself but in the image of the thing in your mind.
Beauty has no absolute existence except in the mind.[44]

Holding such beliefs, Read would identify wholeheartedly with
those artists, particularly Ginner and Kramer, who thought their
responsibility was to convey intuitive feelings in recognizable
forms, that is their *aesthetic* apprehensions of reality, whilst also
accepting that others might wish to manipulate form and design
without referring to perceived reality, that is largely for decorative,
even *ascetic* purposes.[45] Read himself had pursued such abstraction
in his own painting, while simultaneously enjoying an emotional
attachment to neo-realism; and he agreed with Ginner that to
synthesize the two extremes was the next great task of contemporary art. Though he abandoned this objective in his painting, he
did for a while concentrate upon achieving a corresponding condition in his poetic works, or, more precisely, in his poetic theorizing.

In an intentionally dogmatic essay, which just preceded the
important exchange with Kramer, Read gave evidence of an exact
relationship he saw between an aesthetic of poetry and its counterpart he would describe to the painter. Form, he said, is determined
by emotion which requires expression. Emotion is a sensuous
response to environmental form and colour. There follows, in the
creative process, a series of intuitive impulses which are sorted by
the intellect according to the individual's appreciation of absolute
formal beauty. Presumably he believed that such an appreciation
might result from a practised correspondence with nature, during
which its universal principles might gradually become revealed.
However they became known, a growing understanding of them
would affect each further unique response. Then the created form
would possess, and possibly communicate, what Read termed an
'exact emotional significance': properly derived, it would bear an
unbroken relationship with the emotional quality of the original
vision, and as such it could not be predetermined without sacrificing unity or vitality.[46] In 1918 Read thus possessed aesthetic
axioms of poetry which could, when the need arose (as, for
example, in the discussion with Kramer), be transferred with little
difficulty into the realm of plastic art.

Upon his demobilization Read obtained a post at the Treasury with Arthur Greenwood, who had taught him economics at Leeds. He came to live in London and to mix with writers, including Ezra Pound, who published regularly in *The New Age*; and through his friendship with Ginner and Kramer he gained access to the activities of the avant-garde of art, which included Epstein, Lewis and Bomberg. With Frank Rutter (who had been dismissed from his post at the Leeds Art Gallery, ostensibly because he had purchased a painting by Pissarro[47]) he began to edit a monthly review entitled *Art and Letters*. In the course of this work he met T. S. Eliot and Richard Aldington; and in this climate in the years just after the war his literary activity gradually increased, though the interest in art did suffer a temporary neglect until in 1922 he was granted transference from the Treasury to an assistant-keepership at the Victoria and Albert Museum. It may be imagined that Read, for a time, would reconsider and rework the predominant themes of 1914 and before: this thought is supported by the fact that he now read Bergson's *Creative Evolution* for the first time in its completeness. Read's debt to Bergson was to be acknowledged often, and it was summarized best in this autobiographical passage:

> He gave validity to such terms as consciousness and intuition
> – terms upon which, I already then perceived, any philosophy
> of art must rely. (I should perhaps say any philosophy of
> romanticism, but that is a distinction which . . . makes no
> difference.) 'Art lives on creation and implies a latent belief in
> the spontaneity of nature.' Sentences like this showed that
> Bergson himself was aware that art had some evidence to offer
> for his theory; and when he comes to define intuition, by
> which he means 'instinct that has become disinterested, self-
> conscious, capable of reflecting upon its object and of
> enlarging it indefinitely', he uses the aesthetic faculty as a proof
> that such a process is possible. 'Our eye perceives the features
> of the living being, merely as assembled, not as mutually
> organized. The intention of life, the simple movement that
> runs through the lines, that binds them together and gives them
> significance, escapes it. This intention is just what the artist
> tries to regain, in placing himself back within the object by a
> kind of sympathy, in breaking down, by an effort of intuition,
> the barrier that space puts up between him and his model.'[48]

Observations such as these made Read wish that Bergson had put forward his own aesthetic theory.

Much of Read's later work may be recognized as a striving to complete this system of thought, and indeed his first tentative act was to try to clarify the scientific analogy. The least attractive aspect of conventional evolutionary theories, at the heart of much that had been discussed before the war, had been their danger of tending towards the mechanistic or deterministic. This had not worried him particularly then, for a recent loss of religious faith had left him a bleak rationalist; but rationalism in its turn was displaced by other matters of faith – beliefs that creativity is an evolution of consciousness, by stages, proceeding upon vivid intuitive experience, and that its genuine direction may not be preconceived – and these had demanded a way out of the closed system of predetermined events. Thus he welcomed, when it was published, Alfred North Whitehead's concept of evolution[49] which, in common with recent general advances of scientific thought, was less remorselessly sequential. And when, in 1921, Orage persuaded him to accept the quite arduous task (six months' hard labour, it was called – and this in addition to his regular employment) of contributing the weekly two-or-three-thousand word *Readers and Writers* column to *The New Age*, it was this more satisfying concept of evolution that shaped his efforts.

He noted, with an obvious enjoyment, that in modern scientific thought there was no support for arguments that the past is a continuous stream emerging in the present moment of sense awareness, or that the future is an unavoidable consequence of present phenomena; and he quoted Whitehead to his *New Age* readership:

'The past and the future meet and mingle in the ill-defined
present. The passage of nature, which is only another name
for the creative force of existence, has no narrow ledge of
definite, instantaneous present within which to operate. Its
operative presence must be sought for throughout the whole,
in the remotest past as well as in the narrowest breadth of
any present duration. Perhaps also in the unrealized future.
Perhaps also in the future which might be, as well as in the
actual future which will be.'[50]

The most interesting feature of this scheme – as opposed to others in which the immediate present was held to be an almost arbitrary stage within an evolutionary progression – was the store that was set by *synthesis*. In Whitehead's hypothesis could be divined the idea of past and future (analogously romantic formlessness and classic formation) resolving themselves in the present constructive act. This placed unequalled significance upon the activities of the immediate moment (rather than upon a more or less distant future); and it made a view of creative evolution, thus reinterpreted, much more convincing in Read's eyes. Some idea of why this should have been so is gained on realizing that he was also temporarily preoccupied with the philosophical writings of Benedetto Croce, and on noting that he took the essence of Crocean thought to be the recognized importance of a particular motive in giving value and energy to the aesthetic activity – a motive in the form of a passion, an interpenetration of intuitive and intellectual knowing.[51]

In this way, therefore, echoed as it was in their different concerns by Croce and Whitehead, the idea which characterized, more than any other, this spate of Read's work was that of an essential synthesis conditioning all aspects of creativity. In place of a gradual transmutation of intuitive formlessness into intellectual form, he saw an interfusion of the two rising 'through the lyric, beyond the dream, to intelligence and thought – from the symbols of things to the vision of reality.'[52] And while maintaining a strategic allegiance to both romanticism and classicism, he could be critical of any undue emphasizing of the one at the expense of the other – he would criticize, for example, a suggested pre-eminence of pure intuition in the creative process[53] or in the matter of defining beauty.[54] 'It does seem to me', he wrote, 'that Beauty ... is a quality of moral action as well as of significant form';[55] and intuition interlocked with moral understanding became his tactical definition of the creative motive. There is an urgent need for a present classicism, he also suggested, 'a balance that avoids emotional and rational excesses'; and he adopted this definition of genius – 'to contain in oneself opposite extremes and to occupy all of the space between them'.[56]

Orage tactfully advised against the over-stressing of this theme, especially when it was brought to bear, in effect adversely, upon the work of a poet whom he happened to admire;[57] but in general he was impressed with the quality of Read's contributions to his paper – so impressed, in fact, that he entrusted him with what he considered to be a major literary undertaking. Thomas Ernest

Hulme had been killed in action, at the age of thirty-four, in 1917. His manuscript material was with Ethel Kibblewhite, whose home in Soho had been a centre for all who responded to his views. She asked Orage to edit the manuscripts, and he passed them on to Read.[58] The material consisted of a great mass of disordered notes and papers in a tea-chest, and Read spent two years interpreting and sorting, with only Hulme's relatively few finished articles to guide him. At the outset he published in *The New Age* fragments he thought representative of the whole, and then he compiled a volume of collected writings.[59] This, though reasonably extensive, was quite a small proportion of Hulme's output; and it seems fair to say that while Read sought a proper representation he also clearly exercised his own preferences in the matter of selection – he considered the residue of papers insignificant,[60] though this included, for example, an elaboration of the 'Tory Philosophy'[61] Hulme had held in paramount importance. The work Read did select, however, included an interpretation of Bergson's *Creative Evolution*, a theoretical discourse which was an admixture of Bergson and Hulme, Hulme's theory of modern art, and, in skeletal form, his plan for a book on modern art and aesthetics; and with each of these Read held substantial agreement. In this sense, therefore, the resulting publication was an exposition, through the intermedium of Hulme, of much that Read himself believed in. As such, it marked the culmination of his own initial theoretical development.

The first representative samples of Hulme's writing, trailed in advance of the more comprehensive collection, were in two parts – the Bergsonian analysis (the basis of many of the pieces Hulme himself had published), worked so carefully as to suggest that it was in its final form; and a series of jottings from a day-book, expressed in the careless language of immediacy, which convinced Read that Hulme had been about to surpass the original Bergsonian ideas.[62] In the former phase Hulme had been thinking of the process of artistic creation as one of discovery, disentanglement, simplification. An artist was said to dive down into the flux of inner life, the stream of formless apprehensions, and to return with a disengaged 'new shape' which he would endeavour to fix in conscious attention. He could not then be said to have invented this, but to have discovered it; and Hulme's belief was that, properly expressed in fresh metaphoric language or form, it would provoke a general conviction of validity or truthfulness. Hulme saw the vast majority of people bound by the conventionalizing effects of intellection – this functioning not that phenomena might be understood, but more that they might be acted upon. An artist, though, was a special being who, by some freak chance, possessed in one of his senses (but, curiously, in not more than one) an ability to circumvent the normal needs to action. In this *disinterested* fashion he could bring forth perceptions in forms not necessarily prepared for use; and by a certain tension of mind – by an interfusion of intuitive and imaginative capacities (or, as in Read's understanding of Croce, by virtue of a 'passion') – he could force his discoveries, in something near an original freshness, into the common awareness. In widespread use these would become devitalized: thus, aphoristically, everyday language could be called a museum of the once-living metaphors of poets.[63]

In his subsequent, more idiosyncratic thoughts, Hulme appeared to have been trying to eliminate any mechanistic traces, apparently-inevitable legacies of the concept 'evolution', from his essentially Bergsonian scheme. Mainly for this reason (though partly, no doubt, for reasons of style) he had seemed prepared to forgo a central principle of 'purposeful' dynamism, and to substitute the idea of an existential chaos, containing only fragments of organization and these distinctly hard. He had used the term 'cinders' both to characterize the existential medium and to describe the philosophical fragments which his efforts had dislodged: another term, 'counters', had described what remained of these after the polishing effects of intellectual use, and had also signified their being shifted and traded, in use, as in a board game.[64] Thus he had sought a view of the world in which the only realities were *partitions* of experience;[65] and his classic prejudice had informed him that only in the fact of *consciousness* was there any unity within prevailing chaos.[66] Read was obviously heartened that Hulme had become critical of a scheme ultimately reducible to laws; but at a time when Whitehead's concept of nature had provided saving grace for an evolutionary theory, Hulme's late notes offered little more than moral support. Hulme, of course, had not had the benefit of recent scientific philosophy: there is evidence, however, that he had been aware of its drift, and had been determined to keep a philosophy of science and a philosophy of mind quite separate.[67] And in any case it is difficult to imagine how scientific thought more specific than Bergson's might have coexisted with his classic style.

An insight into how his classicism had arisen was given in his papers. He was quite emphatic: he first came to believe, for reasons unconnected with art, that Renaissance attitudes were becoming less and less relevant, and he began to prepare a thesis about a predicted return to pre-Renaissance systems of thought. This was confirmed for him when he saw Byzantine mosaics, and realized that their simple geometricism might be a feature of a reinstated culture. He then recognized its re-emergence in the painting and sculpture of a few contemporaries; and he began to theorize about a coincidence of matters which now affected art – a return to archaic formal values, a classic reaction, and a change from realism to abstraction.[68] Looking for a reasoned account of the phenomenon abstraction, he came across references to the work of the German art historian Wilhelm Worringer, whom he subsequently met at the Berlin Congress on Aesthetics in 1911. He was so impressed with Worringer's essay *Abstraktion und Einfühlung* (which, published in 1908, had been influential in Munich and elsewhere, but which was entirely unknown in England[69]) that he pressed it virtually without modification into the service of his seminal lecture on *Modern Art and its Philosophy*, given in London in January 1914,[70] that is, just preceding the crystallization of vorticism. It was a paraphrasing of Worringer that Read found in Hulme's manuscripts; and it had a resounding effect upon his theoretical development. During his first two years at the Victoria and Albert Museum Read learned German, ostensibly because of the vast amount of material in the archives there, untranslated and unused. The first result of his new learning, however, was his translation of Worringer's ensuing thesis *Formprobleme der Gotik*.[71] Read began a long friendship with Worringer, whom he came to regard as his 'esteemed master in the philosophy of art';[72] and for forty years he was to restate, in his turn and with little modification, Worringer's distinction between an art of devised abstraction and an art of reflected realism. He later was to accept the greater involvements of Worringer's arguments, in particular as they related to the regional peculiarities of art, and as they gave an explanation of expressionism. Before he learned German, however, Read's appreciation was confined to those arguments construed by Hulme.

There are two essentially different tendencies in art. There is one, typified in Greek art and in modern art since the Renaissance, which might generally be described as 'vital': there is another, to be seen in the Egyptian, the Indian and the Byzantine, which evokes descriptions such as angular, hard and geometric, and in which (according to Hulme's only significant addition to the theory, which may be seen as his contriving to fit it with the modern art of his preference) representations of the human body are often effected with 'stiff lines and cubical shapes'. An art of vitalism, naturalism or realism (using these terms in their widest sense, but excluding the slavish imitation of nature) – such an art provokes an empathetic response. It is objectified self-enjoyment, and its value lies in an observer's ability to project into it his own emotional response. It seems obvious that this art may only occur in a people whose relation to the world admits of a feeling of pleasure in such contemplation. Geometrical art, on the other hand, most obviously exhibits no delight in nature and no striving after vitality. The dead form of a pyramid and the suppression of life in a Byzantine mosaic demonstrate the results of a quite different impulse, an impulse produced by a feeling of alienation before the hostile face of nature. Vital art belongs to the tendency to empathetic realism, geometric art to the tendency to abstraction. While a realistic or naturalistic art is the result of a happy, pantheistic relationship between man and his surroundings, an abstract art results from man's indrawing.[73]

Read thus received from Worringer, by means of Hulme's notes, a reasoned distinction between the tendencies realism and abstraction which was to prove adequate to his future needs. In common with many of the theories to which he was attracted, the principal arguments related to nature. An art of realism was the product of man's willingness to realize self-enjoyment objectified in nature (an observation to which Ginner and Kramer had been drawn in their accounts of their own creative processes); and abstraction was an attempt to establish independent, stable values before a harsh and fluctuating nature. Read's own extension of the theory allowed that in the twentieth century, the excesses of nature having been understood or tamed, the artist's attitude was probably no longer entirely to be conditioned by an accident of geography, but was more likely to be formed by hereditary or psychological factors. And if the circumstances were such that appropriate determinants might come to the fore, it could be argued, then the artist's adoption of an abstract or a realistic idiom might not be wilful but involuntary. For the moment, however, a matter of psychology, which Read was ill-equipped to elaborate, was to be regarded as a loose thread, perhaps later to be bound within a coherent theory.

The extent of Read's early ambition to such a theory is unclear. He may already have been conscious of a desire to supplement Bergson's theories; or, had he not edited Hulme's papers, he might have been content with immediate, respondent criticism. Strategist or tactician?: the question is irrelevant, since in Hulme's papers there was an outline theory of modern art and aesthetics, complete with a synopsis of recent-historical justifications.[74] This was fortuitous, but in no real sense 'given' to Read, for it was only described in barest phrases, the value of which he would not have recognized had they not corresponded with parts of his own extensive research. Nevertheless it comprised an irresistible sequence; and it also demonstrated Hulme's clear intention to have combined disparate theories within a larger system of ideas. Even in skeletal form, it made tantalizing references to psychology and to nineteenth-century English romanticism; and it hinted at the possibility that these might be parts of a consistent fabric.

A 'science of aesthetics' and an investigation of 'creative imagination' were the principal subjects of Hulme's plan: together, these constituted 'the most attractive yet the most neglected part of philosophy'. It was Hulme's aim to have initiated 'practically a new subject' – an aesthetic basis for a new criticism; and here he supported Read's admiration for the critical exactness of Ruskin. Hulme thought it quite wrong that this activity should be 'left either to the technical philosophers who knowing nothing of art have made it fit into their systems – or to the amateurs who knowing little of philosophy have used the inaccurate concepts and metaphors of a merely literary method'. To rectify these ills was the task he had set himself, for his notes anticipated a 'sudden and remarkable development of the subject', made possible by the applications of modern psychology, and based upon a legacy of ideas – 'a rich harvest of theories in Germany; this astonishing and intensely interesting literature entirely unknown in England'.[75]

Part of this harvest of theories – the works of Kant, Schelling and Hegel – had exerted considerable influence upon the English romantic poets Coleridge and Shelley and upon Ruskin. Hulme did not enlarge this casual note, but it must have excited Read's attention, offering the possibility of support for his own refusal to accept, in spite of an obvious respect for much of Hulme's theorizing, that romanticism was irrelevant to the modern sensibility. It took Read another ten years entirely to disengage his intuitive appreciation of romanticism, and to present it as a fundamental part of a theory of artistic formation:[76] if the beginnings of this effort are significant, however, it may be argued that, curiously, a small clarification was first perceived in Hulme. In his reviewing of Hegelian aesthetics now, following the tacit advice in Hulme's notes, Read would have settled upon distinctions made between three principal substances of romantic art. Because of his agnosticism it may be supposed that a religious sphere of romanticism might perhaps only have been of a general interest; and a second substance of romanticism – that inherent in the presentation of images out of proper context – may be argued to have been an element Read only found useful years later, when for a time he offered partisan explanations of surrealism.[77] But the part of Hegelian thought he would have found immediately valuable would have been that which referred to a third romantic substance, nature, or, more precisely, landscape.

According to this construction hills, mountains, woods, rivers and all the other features of natural landscape were of interest primarily because underlying *forces* could be perceived in them, producing correspondences within an observer. He might, as Worringer reiterated, contemplate his own spiritual condition reflected in his preferences for certain forms or colours or combinations of such properties. The purpose of art, as the neo-realists were to say, was to celebrate the life forces inherent in natural objects, and thus promote an empathetic response. This emotional correspondence, far from mere imitation of appearance, was considered the only factor which justified nature as the principal subject-matter of art.[78] There was an implication here, for one wishing to enlarge Hegelian arguments, that such realism was not entirely unrelated to an art of abstraction: if the recommended emphasizing of vital forces necessitated some exaggeration or distortion, however slight, of the visual appearances of nature, then it might not be perverse to approve of a non-representational art which also promoted, through its intermedium, an empathy with natural colours, rhythms and proportions. It may be suggested that when

Read sought the guidance of Worringer one of the questions he would have wished to have clarified would have concerned the apparent contradiction: a natural-empathetic response might conceivably be promoted by an art of abstraction. Abstraction, considered by Hulme to be most potent in conjunction with a classic outlook, might contain an aspect which is romantic. It might be necessary to distinguish between an objective abstraction, dealing with forms as far as possible removed from nature, and a subjective abstraction, concerned with abstracting from nature its essential formal potencies.

This latter idea had little in common with Hulme's confident assertion (in spite of what he actually promoted) that 'the necessary presupposition of abstraction is the idea of disharmony or separation between man and nature';[79] and it must have occurred to Read that a new aesthetic was likely to be much more complex than Hulme's clear-cut distinction between a classic abstraction and a romantic or empathetic realism. In fact Worringer, whose *Abstraktion und Einfühlung* had to a considerable degree inspired this simple distinction, was moving towards a more involved hypothesis in his ensuing study *Formprobleme der Gotik* (in preparation before Hulme died, though he could not have known about it because of the war). Worringer saw little historical justification for associating the concepts 'classicism' and 'abstraction': his distinction was between those arts of assured depiction of the world – the classic – and those attempting to establish permanent values in the face of a world of shifting appearances – the gothic.[80] He maintained that prevailing aesthetic values were related entirely to the classic conception of art, and he stressed that the significance of gothic abstraction could not possibly be comprehended in such terms. He implied that, in the modern world, academic art on the one hand, and empathetic realism and abstraction on the other, might best be understood in terms of dislocated systems of thought – the one by means of established aesthetics and the other by means of psychological interpretation.

Hulme himself seemed to ask for a way of making such distinction when he wrote himself this memorandum: 'Taking modern arts as known, ask this question – Is there any specific emotion which characterizes them all and found in no other activity? – a specifically aesthetic emotion, the experiencing of which constitutes beauty . . . .'[81] Read was very doubtful about such a possibility, noting that if an 'aesthetic emotion' did exist it was unfortunately peculiar to a narrow sect of people.[82] Hulme asked himself a second question, related to an 'entirely different enquiry': 'what is the nature of the state of mind characterized as creative imagination?'[83] And again Read found himself in disagreement, not about the value of the question now, but about the necessity to separate it from the former. In matters such as this he was a Crocean; and he made clear retrospectively that creative imagination and appreciation were to him inseparable. In creativity

> There are three stages: first, the mere perception of material beauty – colours, sounds, gestures, and many more complex and undefined physical reactions; second, the arrangement of such perceptions into pleasing shapes and patterns. The sense of beauty may be said to end with these two processes, but there is a third stage which comes when such an arrangement of perceptions corresponds with a previously existing state of emotion or feeling. Then we say that the emotion or feeling is given *expression*, and art is the exact attainment of this correspondence. In this sense it is true to say with Benedetto Croce that art is expression . . . . But it is always necessary to remember (which the Croceans sometimes fail to do) that expression is a final process depending on the preceding processes of sensuous perception and formal (pleasurable) arrangement.[84]

Read described – again with hindsight – the gradual shaping of these convictions. His profoundest experiences, he said, had been *aesthetic*, gained in certain moments of creative activity, and in less intense but more frequent moments of sensibility in the presence of works of art. He had been led to wonder about their vividness, and to speculate that aesthetic experience was not a superficial phenomenon, an expression of surplus energy, but that it was related to formal perception, in particular of structure. It was a short and obvious step to recognize at least an analogy, and possibly a more direct relationship, between a morphology of nature and a morphology of art. Thus he post-rationalized the sequence of perceptions which began with an uncomprehending appreciation of abstract art at Leeds. Such an analogy, he thought, would account for the formal appeal of much of western art – except the art in which he had always maintained an interest, the romantic.

At one time he was tempted to find a distinction between the classic and the romantic precisely in this difference: that one observed the formal laws inherent in the structure of nature, while the other disregarded them completely – or at least that in one formalism was of prime importance, while in the other it was incidental to some other values. Then he realized that when naturally consistent proportions, such as the golden section, were sought in works of art, more often than not the correspondences were seen to be approximate. Rather than believe that this reflected human error, an inability to match the perfections of nature in art, he was persuaded that it was very nearly wilful. He became sure

that even in its most pure and formal manifestations, classic art intuitively avoids an *exact* observation of the laws of natural morphology. It comes very near to them, and then, as if to assert the freedom of the artist's will, narrowly avoids them.

In romantic art, however, there is no such flirtation. Certain laws, of proportion and rhythm, are observed in all but the most anarchic types of expressionism; but having gone so far on the basis of such laws, the work of art then seems to take a leap into the unknown. The laws themselves are contradicted, or are entirely disregarded; and a new reality is created, requiring a sudden passage from perception to intuition, and carrying with it a heightened mode of consciousness.

The analogy for this transition was ready waiting in the new quantum theory. But to pursue this analogy, even granted that the quantum theory itself had been definitely established, would have been too delicate and difficult a task. I was content with the fact that physics had provided an escape from a situation that threatened to be wholly mechanistic. If all art could be referred to natural laws, to a system of numerical proportions, then evidently we were within reach of tests and measurements – in short, of academic rules which meant an end to all creative originality (in the Bergsonian sense) and therefore to all artistic progress.[85]

The difference, then, between the classic and the romantic, and consequently (though these terms were losing their exactness, as the two tendencies seemed to merge) between an abstract and an empathetic art, was in the degree to which the artist, deliberately or otherwise, bound himself to observe natural, structural laws. It could be said that to adopt a classic outlook would be to tend towards a strict adherence to such laws, while to adopt the romantic would be to give free rein to intuitive expression. This encapsulation, though, was too concise, for it took little account of empathetic abstraction, the romantic aspect of the classic idiom, which could be said to consist in a kind of precariousness in which natural laws were balanced by self-assertion, or, in other words, in which observations of nature were modified or rearranged. Empathetic abstraction, therefore, might probably have been explained in morphological terms, as a balancing of opposing forces, or in dialectical terms, as an interpenetration of contradictory tendencies; and so it offered minor theoretical difficulty compared with the idea of creative self-assertion, which on the one hand was now fundamental to a set of values Read wished to preserve, namely the romantic, but on the other, if it were *conscious*, would undermine the preferred theory of intuition. It has been said that Read was ill-equipped, in the early 1920s, to deal with matters of psychology; but increasingly he was drawn towards a theory of the unconscious, in which (if it may be so phrased, although he later maintained that this was entirely sensed[86]) lay the best possibility of resolving this inconsistency – equating self-assertion, if it were an *unconscious* activity, with the intuitional basis of creativity. It became clear that the aesthetic theories he had found convincing had provided a general framework for psychology, and had been pregnant with suggestions of this science before the definite elaborations of such as Freud and Jung. If it were acceptable, then, in psychological terms, to say that an artist might intuitively apprehend an external event, and at the same time intuitively apprehend his own emotional condition, before combining the two intuitions within an act of expression, such arguments would not be incompatible with beliefs already gained.

It could be held that art, in the Crocean sense, the gathering of sense impressions, involved both impressions of 'outer reality' and of 'inner self'; and that though neither of these could be absent from an authentic expression, they could be eroded to mere traces, so that according to the preponderance of one or the other a resulting work of art might at one extreme be almost entirely abstract, or at the other almost entirely empathetic, or indeed one of innumerable combinations of the two. Read could thus assert (with Kramer) that in the mind of the artist there are contradictory tendencies. In one direction he is impelled to take account of 'self', to give expression to predominant emotions, and to give form to incoherent mentality; in the other he is impelled to establish ideals of order and of beauty formed by his observations of 'nature' or 'reality'. These impulses are resolved in a process, the greater part of which is intuitional or unconscious, but which is usually completed intellectually, in conscious attention. 'You get the harmony of perfect art when the two forces achieve a balance.'[87] The struggle between classic and romantic is therefore mental: an abstract work of art results from the predomination of organization over inner forces; a work of empathy – Read did not yet have a more appropriate antithetical term – a work of this kind results from the predomination of the personal.

Read determined to be exact in his elaboration of this scheme. An early opportunity came when he reviewed Roger Fry's essay *The Artist and Psychoanalysis*; and his scathing remarks may only partly be explained by his growing sense of an obligation to skirmish with those of established reputations, for the feature of the work of which he was most critical was its vagueness.[88] He disliked Fry's use of the term 'emotion', and also, particularly, his presupposition of the inexplicable human faculty 'aesthetic emotion'. As an example of how to rid the concept of mystique, Read grasped at a 'scientific' explanation: emotional reaction (affecting poetry and, by implication, the broader matter 'art') may be caused by 'various glandular secretions' which 'physiology may yet identify and classify'. In other words, emotion is physiological and may be subject to exact analysis; and if an empathetic response is physiological so also, at the other extreme, might a mental state of attentive contemplation induced by a work of abstraction 'have its basis in some material agitation of the human cortex or glandular system'.[89] Unconvincing, perhaps, though this was, it may now be seen to have been a forcible statement of intent: art appreciation is to be considered a physiological phenomenon, art-making a psychophysical phenomenon. There is no essential difference between abstraction and its antithesis, except in the degree to which the physical or the psychological predominates. Not specifically given in his influences, this may be regarded as an original contribution:

in effect it marks a 'quantum leap' away from received, creative-evolutionary theories.

The most readily convincing part of this was the relating of physics, or rather the mathematical and geometrical languages of physics, to abstraction. Read believed, however, that psychology, 'so directly concerned with the material origins of art', would soon be accepted as offering equally valid insights into the alternative tendency;[90] and in a series of essays which represent the first tangible progress in his own direction he considered those psychological factors which bore most upon an empathetic art but which also, as Worringer had taught him, bore to some extent upon abstraction. The reviewing of Fry's paper, therefore, was not impartial criticism: it was Read's asserting a claim upon this terrain. Fry's concluding supposition, he said, was worthy of serious consideration: the response to formal beauty may get its force 'from arousing some very deep, very vague, and immensely generalized reminiscences'.[91]

Read's task would be to shift this poorly articulated idea into the light of scientific reasoning; and for this purpose he became astonishingly familiar, in a very short time, with published psychological research.[92] He realized that of the foremost theorists in this field only Jung had put forward an account of creative processes. He understood that Freud and Adler were concerned to think of art as a compensation for neurosis – a reaction, for example to certain repressed complexes; and though they had considered the analysis of works of art, they had shown little understanding, from his point of view, of art as an activity in process. Jung, however, did illuminate this activity: his theory sprang from a general principle of contrasted attitudes, introversion and extroversion, a fundamental division of the self traceable in every human act. 'Now Jung's theory', Read wrote,

> is that living reality is never the exclusive product of one or the other of these contrasted attitudes, but only of a specific vital activity which unites them, bridges the gulf between them, giving intensity to sense-perception and effective force to the idea.[93]

This added weighty argument to an abstract-empathetic scheme. By an interpenetration of opposites, it was reiterated, art gives form to reality. The main attribute of the creative mentality is an ability to make relatively shallow perceptions of the outer world, and to combine these with deep, individual associations.

Another aspect of Jung's theory, which Read found immediately absorbing, was this: the tangible forms of reality released by the artist into general consciousness were of potential *social* value, and this was related to what was termed the artist's 'fitness for life'. In other words: the more abnormal the individual, the less his fitness, the more limited would be the social value of his work (even if it were absolute for the person himself).[94] It seemed odd that Jung had not enlarged this, and considered the more-than-individual functioning of art: it would also be Read's ambition to demonstrate the dependence of a healthy social condition upon an authentic, balanced creativity. Thus he would agree with Jung that art could be said to have

> the general function of resolving into one uniform flow of life all that springs from the inner well of primordial images and instinctive feelings, and all that springs from the outer mechanism of actuality – doing this, not only for the artist himself, from whose own need the phantasy is born, but also, by suggestion and by symbol, for all who come to participate in his imaginative work.[95]

Read wished that Jung would extend this important hypothesis; but the fact that he disguised his request, as a call for the general application of psychology to criticism, may be explained in that while he was a civil servant (until he left the Victoria and Albert Museum in 1931) he felt restrained from expressing even remotely political views. Looking back, however, he was to describe how his admiration for Kropotkin's writings – long standing for *Mutual Aid*, and more recent for the uncompleted *Ethics* – was given additional justification by Jung's hinting at a theory of the social validity of art. Whereas Kropotkin could only speak vaguely of the artist's ability to 'commune with the Cosmos and inspire his fellow men',[96] Read felt certain that Jung might give an exact scientific account of such a process and its necessary preconditions. These, Read was willing to anticipate, would be anarchistic: an organic art – an evolving conception of reality, in the literal sense 'a culture' – would serve to unite a society of localized organization, by means of the artist's projecting into the community evidence of its corporate, unconscious identity.[97] This would be the collective aspect of Read's 'creative individualism', an aspect he would continuously enlarge and modify over the next thirty years, and elaborate most effectively only when he could appreciate the full range of Jung's life's work. He believed himself to be travelling towards a 'conception of the science of art, in which the work of art is regarded as an objective fact or event – as an organism evolving in time, developing styles, acquiring mannerisms; as an expression of culture in general';[98] though this, in 1929, was ambition rather than certainty. As to the individual aspect of his work, however, Read was ready to outline peremptory arguments about an essential creative antagonism. The chief characteristic of his theorizing was already formed: it was distinctly dialectical.

Chapter 3
Insight and Reason

Read's aesthetic criticism emerged from its formative stages having been affected by the large range of social, philosophical and aesthetic principles to which he had been drawn in his early reading, though having been fundamentally shaped by a relatively few decisive matters. His attraction to the writings of Bergson, Croce and, to a lesser extent, Nietzsche had apparently been vindicated by the reassuring, speculative intentions of T. E. Hulme; and the idea of a dialectically derived creativity (in the main ignored by Hulme) had been enhanced by the discovery of Worringer's thesis (a discovery Hulme had indirectly brought about). Insights given by Ginner and Kramer had offered support to dialectical interpretations, respectively, of a broad spectrum of modern English art and of the artist's individual creativity; and both had fitted the hypothesis that growth and change, manifest in natural processes, were analogous to the development of specifically modern art, that is art at the foremost point of the gradually enlarging corporate understanding. In this respect Rutter had made certain apposite assertions: there could be no art without life, no life without growth, no growth without change. An evolving art invariably would be controversial, arousing as it would the hostility of those, the vast majority of people, to whom it would be quite unknown.[1] It may have been these that prepared Read to accept an obligation to deal with a general antagonism towards his representations, and to speak of modern art as a point hardening in the fires of public criticism.[2]

In the early 1920s Read was torn between the idea of art as an enlargement upon an entirely stable body of past achievements,

53

progressing by the gradual accretion of units of emerging significance, and a similarly dynamic theory put forward by T. S. Eliot,
in which each gained increment of creative awareness was said not
only to extend but, however slightly, to change the entire preceding
order or tradition.[3] And Read was also aware that, whichever form
it took, a dynamic theory of creativity would be hard to hold in
the face of Hulme's convincing arguments about certain conditions
of art which were absolute and, necessarily, unchanging.[4] For a
while he was to see a distinction between two very different kinds
of art – the one 'organic' and the other 'universal': he was to find
himself possessed of an emotional attachment to the former and
an intellectual commitment to the latter, propounding occasionally
and in turn the supremacy of either. He objectified this dilemma
in his criticism, and took comfort from evidence, given from several
standpoints, that the two conditions were systematically related.
He gave his energies both to defining to his own satisfaction the
two conditions (which, following his influences, he took to be
polarities), and to reporting their relatedness in poetry. And in
particular (the hallmark, this, of his own approach to criticism) he
hazarded views about connections between poetic theory and the
science of psychology.

Psychologically, he said, man is a register of every object and
event which enters or has entered the field of his sensory perception.
Sensation creates images; and these, if immediately irrelevant to
the receiving sensibility, remain dormant, while those which are
relevant (that is, relevant when gained, as well as those retrieved
from past experience, suddenly made relevant in conjunction with
the new) – these are linked together in a process called reason.
Reason – the linear association of immediate apprehensions and
psychologically registered past experiences – is nothing less than
the structuring of reality.[5] Read thus considered this structuring to
be partly impulsive or fortuitous and, as it encompassed sensibility
and *thought*, intuition and *intellect*, also partly determinant. This
latter quality implied the existence of standards, and, he said,
effecting a coherence which embodied dynamic principles as well
as the static precepts of Hulme, these consisted in natural laws of
symmetry and rhythm, in an awareness of which some of the most
profound aesthetic expressions (of such as Wordsworth) had been
achieved. In this sense the aesthetic process was to Read an interpenetration of nature and mentality, giving rise to the gradual

enlargement of reality, a condition neither wholly natural nor entirely mental but synthetic of both[6]; and while the minute justification of this hypothesis became his long-term strategy, it will be seen that in its service he often made tactical changes which modified yesterday's assertions.

Read's constant, though sometimes almost imperceptible, shifting of his ground, together with his bringing together ideas intended by their originators to be distinct, were to his critics the least acceptable aspects of his work.[7] In his view, however – that of an interpreter of prevailing theories rather than a system-maker, and one who proceeded by the sensed conviction – there was nothing wrong in selective expropriation.[8] He was concerned to present his *developing* understanding; and in this (in common with Eliot's scheme) each new realization necessitated a reassessment and, occasionally, a reorganization of all preceding gains. Thus, having first fought shy of the belief expressed by Freud and Adler that artistic temperament was an alternative to neurosis, and having been attracted initially by the social inferences of Jung's arguments, Read now maintained an equal importance of these disparate elements within a composite and highly speculative arrangement of his own. According to this he could say, with Freud, that the artist possessed an unusually powerful sense of form and order, with which he could effect the disciplined elaboration of phantasy, an essential imagery which in the neurotic would remain incoherent and confused. Into contact with this prevailing sensibility would be brought the fortuitous apprehension or the fortuitously aroused memory, and the two would resolve themselves in an act of expression exhibiting universal (in Jung's view social) properties and individual associations. For the time being, therefore, Read's two essential components of creativity were on the one side a latent sense of order, and on the other a reservoir of past, and a receptivity to new, sensations. And it may perhaps be obvious why a psychological explanation of creativity in which these two were interactive[9] would have appealed to an admirer of Bergson and Croce.

Effecting another readjustment to his theory, and once more employing Freudian and Jungian arguments which were not strictly compatible, Read suggested that mentality embraced two very different kinds of experience – one individual, as he had said before, and another collective, hereditary, ingrained in the struggle for adaptation and existence. The latter had conditioned an appropriate physical structure of the human brain, which in turn had promoted further common and inevitable forms of thought. These were the roots of myths, religions and all patterns of widespread acceptance which, in the works of the present poets, were still extending.[10] Read began to amplify this vague conception, and in so doing he discovered relevancies bearing upon plastic, as well as poetic, creativity.

He observed that poetic activity, particularly when spontaneous – when the poet's innate sense of form was so strongly affected by a first fortuitous image that a swift succession of images would seem to present themselves, apparently without his conscious intervention[11] – such activity could properly be described as an evolving creative process exhibiting duration. Its manifestation would be a succession of syllabic events embodying both personal imagery and rhythmic structure; and when such structures were subjected to exact scientific analysis[12] it could be said with a reasonable certainty that every one – even that which conformed with the notion of 'regularity' – was a unique succession of differing proportions. Though unique, however, those which were more or less contemporaneous, or which were culturally similar, seemed to have sufficient in common for Read to detect general characteristics which were gradually *changing*; and this gave weight to his speculation that though universal forms were precisely that – unchanging – the artist's innate sensing of them was a continuously evolving faculty.[13] The poetic evidence of this sensing Read was prepared to call 'organisms of speech': to him these reflected the varying conditions of existence, and were 'the vocal chimings-in of man in the rhythm of life'.[14]

Universal form was constant, creative appreciation constantly changing: in 1926 Read sought to eliminate this contortion, re-emphasizing the validity of a Bergsonian analogy, and repairing as he did so an inconsistency he had seen as present in Hulme's writings. Influenced by Hulme's arguments, he had assumed that there was an absolute formal logic which human mentality, due to an inherent ineffectiveness, was badly equipped to apprehend. Now he began to suspect that in much of the world's art even the most primitive examples of such logic (for example, the golden section) were being consistently avoided, or at best were evident only by virtue of generalization. He was led to wonder whether creative differentiation might be more important than universality; and in this way he came across the scientific philosophy of Alfred North Whitehead, according to which the manifestations of nature were also said to be individuated. This offered Read his first authoritative substantiation from the realm of physics of his preferred belief in a theoretical framework which contained, for evolution and creativity alike, vast, common, original substances and unique emergent formations. He was ready to accept the face-value of concepts 'which might, without any violence, be transposed from a work on physics to one on aesthetics', such as Whitehead's assertion that the special characteristic of an evolving organism (analogously a work of art) was an exhibition of rhythm, a variety of detail in the parts contained within a greater unity.[15] Similarly, he was prepared to say of Whitehead's *Science and the Modern World*,[16] since it helped solve the seemingly intractable problems of a remorselessly mechanistic creativity, that it was perhaps the most important book published in the conjoint fields of science and philosophy since Descartes' *Discourse on Method*.[17] It accounted for the new theory of relativity, which cast doubt upon orthodox assumptions of a simultaneous, common reality; and it also accepted the quantum theory, which questioned the old belief in a continuity of time and space. Neither of these conceptions could be reconciled with the idea of a uniform, mechanistic world subject to rigid laws of nature; but they were precisely what Read required to complement a psychological explanation of creativity, which featured a leap of inspiration, and which held immediate apprehensions and past sensations to have simultaneous bearings upon reality.

Highlighting as it did this convincing similarity between a quantum-advancing formation in nature and an inconsistently progressing 'formation' in mentality, Whitehead's work was seen by Read as an enlargement of Bergson's achievements. Whitehead himself considered Bergson's bringing physiological concepts into contact with philosophy to have been one of the most fundamental contributions to modern thought;[18] though in common with Hulme and Read he felt compelled to deal with the *aesthetic* implications of a theory of organicism, which Bergson had addressed inadequately. He suggested (in a way which cast new light upon the relatedness, about which Hulme had speculated, of *Creative Evolution* and *Abstraktion und Einfühlung*) that the aesthetic activity had originated of early man's need to sense, recall and predict the vagaries of an often hostile environment. Now that a changing environment no longer threatened endurance, this inherited activity could only be effectively employed by having a proper variety of circumstances or experience to deal with; and the greatest source of such variety Whitehead found in art. He defined effective art (in terms reminiscent of Read's early, wishful resolving) as the arranging of environment so as to provide vivid but transient values;[19] and it must have seemed to Read remarkable that a single work could reinforce his several sensed convictions, gleaned from the separate fields of psychology, aesthetics and natural science.

> The doctrine thus cries aloud for a conception of organism as fundamental for nature. It also requires an understanding activity – a substantial activity – expressing itself in individual embodiments, and evolving in achievements of organism. The organism is a unit of emergent value, a real fusion of the characters of eternal objects, emerging for its own sake.[20]

Such observations as these Read could adapt quite easily to a theory of art. And here was another assertion of which Read immediately grasped the importance: for the purpose of establishing vivid values, as of modifying environment, the single organism is almost ineffective. The gains of societies of co-operating organisms are immensely greater than the sums of individual contributions; and, conversely, the individual 'mind is never so modified as when it becomes part of a pattern created in the organism of a complete society'.[21]

This led Read to the thought, which eventually would be a cornerstone of his own work in its most perfected form, that an authentic plastic or poetic creativity would be no simple linear process or matter of accretion but an uneven progression, occasionally manifesting a concrete pattern of much greater significance in its total organization than in the detail of its parts.[22] It also led him to re-examine the function of criticism in the light of this conception, and to make passing notes that the recently elaborated theory of Gestalt formation might be of relevance here. This seemed likely to provide at least a partial explanation of the direct, intuitive apprehension central to his romantic principle;[23] and it might also have been expected to reinforce the idea of art as a synthesis of intuitive, perceptual and organized, conceptual faculties.

Curiously, however, he was not prepared to follow such arguments. Instead, he addressed the theory's classical implications; and this marked the earlier of two sharp departures, first to one side and then the other, away from a central critical stance. It may be argued that Read had long been a covert classicist anyway, having consistently relied upon the notion of raw experience subjected in all its constituents to the tempering effects of intelligent thought.[24] But his work had previously been infused with the idea of romantic and classic principles as equal-opposite poles of creativity; and he now adopted, as distinct from this, a scheme in which the classical element – the principle of balance – was held to be of chief importance. Over a period of four years straddling 1930, that is to say, he favoured a description of creativity as a sequence in which formlessness became a balanced conformation. Here intuition was identified not merely as an irrational sensing but (implying a far greater degree of certainty) as an act of unconscious *knowing*; and reason was defined as a taking consciousness of this activity as it shifted from the sphere of subjectivity towards that of organized, objective synthesis.[25] Consequently, creativity could be considered a matter of co-ordinating the two modes of mentality by means of a transition from the former to the latter; and the whole of the creative process would be seen to be geared to receiving what the phenomenal world revealed to the senses – in other words, it would be considered not as characteristically seeking (for this smacked of predetermination) but as *finding*.[26]

For a brief period, therefore, Read could be witnessed putting forth not entirely consistent views. A subtly changed dialectic underlay much of what he wrote: influenced as much as anything by his own poetic experience,[27] he described a creative alternation which originated in an essential intuition, and proceeded by some kind of rationalization towards a resulting, harmonious coherence which none the less harked back to the initial formlessness. There was also a sense to him in which creativity consisted in the struggle for predomination of form over feeling; and, temporarily, there was a concomitant view (which had been expressed most forcefully by Hulme) of western European culture as a cyclic advance in which the classic was once more to the fore. The importance to Read of this last train of thought gradually diminished in the early 1930s, as he discovered surrealism, and for a time found it preferable to propose that a specifically modern art should manifest dominantly subjective properties. Now, however, he sought classic ramifications. He had least difficulty discussing modern plastic art, for he admired works of organized abstraction[28] and had no reason to doubt that the greatest advances of contemporary art had been effected by abstractionists. Neither did he doubt the sole validity of classicism in the field of an enduring literature.[29] But he had long nurtured a liking for the romanticism of Wordsworth, Coleridge and Shelley, and had acquired more recently an affection for the prose of Sterne; and while he could accept that these belonged to a previous cultural order, he nevertheless felt bound to see a *tendency* towards classicism – the beginnings of a reversion – in their accomplishments. For example, the breathless and inspirational style of Sterne, he argued, disguised the fact that his composition was deliberate and moulded by the classicizing influence of humour.[30] Only a few years later Read would use the converse of such arguments quite naturally in the service of surrealism. His present thoughts, though, were tracing other patterns; and a major study, which he now undertook, of the psychological undercurrents of Wordsworth's work[31] (a study which, it is probably true, would not have been substantially different if pursued in later life) elaborated the immediate preoccupations.

Beside his other important theme – briefly, that Wordsworth's poetic powers slowly declined as there grew in him an uncontrollable remorse which eventually stifled his sensitivity to inspiration[32] – Read arranged his own thesis that Wordsworth's theories of poetic diction, conceived during his most productive period, actually marked the beginning of a movement which had culminated, in the twentieth century, in the hard, classic idiom of imagism. Wordsworth had said – Read repeatedly referred to this – that poetry of any value had never been expressed except by one who, possessing 'more than usual organic sensibility', had found ways to shape his intuitions in thought, 'the representative of all past sensations'; and this, Read insisted, was the view of the classicist rather than the romanticist.[33] It has been suggested[34] that Read's study of Wordsworth was veiled autobiography – they were of similar stock and social type, had both suffered an early deprivation of parental care, and had both experienced the forcing effects upon creativity of extremely hazardous conditions of existence – the one in revolutionary France and the other in the Great War. While these coincidences undoubtedly would have assisted a close identification with his subject, however, there are more consistent indications that the real self-analytical features of Read's work resided in a recognition of his own convictions reflected in the theories of Wordsworth. Here could be divined a romantic-classic alternation and a dialectic co-existing within an account of creativity; and this Read seized with an evident elation.

Poetry, an acknowledgment of the beauty of the universe, takes its origin from emotional apprehension recollected in tranquil thought. Feeling and thought are resolved within a synthesis termed 'modified emotion', and under the influence of this does successful composition take place.

'Good poetry', Read now wrote,

> is never an immediate reaction to the provoking cause; . . . our
> sensations must be allowed time to sink back into the
> common fund of our experience, there to find their level and
> due proportion. That level is found for them by the mind, in
> the act of contemplation, and then in the process of
> contemplation the sensations revive, and out of the union of
> contemplating mind and the reviving sensibility, rises that
> unique mode of expression which we call poetry.[35]

The poet thus has a conception of reality which surpasses that of others. At one extreme of his mental axis he can recognize the significant among his romantic apprehensions of the world around him: at the other, he has powers to enlarge his apprehensions within the sphere of his imagination, to classify them and to make them real to others. In the process, individual experience becomes idealized, the personal becomes the universal.[36] Neither sensitivity to formless feeling, that is to say, nor the sustaining of a 'modified emotion', are in themselves sufficient to produce a work of art; but they are its necessary preconditions – of a constructive act which fabricates reality. Read had entertained this nebulous thought for some time: now he saw substantiation in Wordsworth's account of his own development, evocatively termed *The Growth of a Poet's Mind*.[37]

Wordsworth disclosed that as a child he had experienced a form of solipsism, an inability to distinguish between his own being and the existence of things external to it. He had resorted to grasping a tree or a wall in order to convince himself of its solidity and separateness; and as a consequence of this the visible world of nature had assumed for him a disjointed reality, which he had constructed for himself piece by piece, by brute sensation, until it was actual and objective.[38] Thus in Read's view an issuing poetry was evidence of mind interlocked with nature:[39] Wordsworth clearly was no idealist – he did not project into nature his own sentiments; and neither was he, in an *accepted* sense, a realist, for he was no seeker after general principles. His reality was original, if disjointed and piecemeal; and this promised an entirely more satisfactory conception of new realism than had been offered by Ginner. Though romantic in inception and classic in resolution, Wordsworth's poetry could not finally be characterized according to either tendency. By asserting the coequality of mind and nature, however, it was to Read most obviously humanist – 'the greatest exaltation of the mind of man that has ever been conceived'.[40]

For a time Read believed that such a conception of humanism was to be the culminating principle within his own theoretical system,[41] and this seemed ample justification for having persevered with a search for classic traits in an unlikely quarter. It nevertheless seems odd that the advocate of hard, precise imagery should have sought the faint traces of such hardness here. He had, of course, long sustained an admiration for Wordsworth which he had not been able adequately to explain; and he may have held his affection less and less easily while his own classicism grew, until he felt able to exorcise the popular notion of Wordsworth's romanticism. It is perhaps reasonable, however, to suppose that there were additional predisposing influences. It remains unclear exactly how great and lasting had been the effects of Read's early study of Hulme; but Hulme himself had not thought it inconsistent to maintain that Bergsonism, essentially a romantic system, carried to the fields of aesthetics and culture implications which were classic. Hulme had also recognized the singular position of Coleridge at the beginning of a modern aesthetic movement;[42] and at about the time he started work on Hulme's manuscripts Read began a lifelong association with the critical theories Coleridge had presented in his *Biographia Literaria*. He had been impressed, even in 1918, with Coleridge's contemporary recognition of classic qualities in Wordsworth's poetry (though Read was then adversely critical of these).[43] A decade later, though, when Read came to Wordsworth[44] in his discursive account of the phases of English poetry, he was prepared to applaud the view that by objectifying his sensations the poet had been organizing reality; and it is not improbable that the cause of this persuasion was in the thesis Read welcomed in 1926 – Whitehead's *Science and the Modern World*.

Whitehead, his fascination that of a scientist acknowledging the poet's ability to make observations of nature which eluded scientific analysis, had devoted considerable attention to Wordsworth. His view, it seemed to Whitehead, was of the whole of nature involved in the tonality of any particular event – he dwelt 'upon that mysterious presence of surrounding things' which unavoidably was reflected in any separate natural circumstance. He bore witness to Whitehead that it was impossible to divorce nature, as science had attempted, from its aesthetic aspects; and the most significant of these, Whitehead judged by Wordsworth's poetry, were to do with change, endurance, eternal recurrence, interfusion and organicism[45] – as fair an exposition of the natural flux and its occasional concrete patterns as Read was likely to encounter. Abstracting values from nature's fluctuations, Wordsworth had succeeded in expressing 'deep intuitions of mankind penetrating into what is universal in concrete fact';[46] and it is interesting to note that in so far as this secondary theme of Whitehead's was psychological, it featured a psychology which was collective. It is tempting to observe that Read's alternating allegiance to the classic and (embracing surrealism) to the romantic reflected corresponding counterattractions of collective and individual theories of psychology. This, however, is the only satisfactory means[47] of accounting for an otherwise aberrant statement which his current classicism itself did not explain: 'the (individual) psychological element in art is of merely subsidiary or temporary importance', he wrote. 'It is even dangerous in that it tends to blind us to the underlying plastic values.'[48] A unity of formal values held in equilibrium – this concept, adopted openly from Whitehead, constituted Read's present definition of aesthetic beauty. It is therefore a paradox, one of several in a hectic phase of Read's development, that Whitehead's scheme, to which he had been drawn because of its emphasis on individuation, briefly was held to be significant more by virtue of a perceived emphasizing of the universal.[49]

This definition was uttered shortly after surrealism began to take Read by storm; and it perhaps represented a half-hearted protest against the inevitable acceptance of new values he intuitively recognized as right. Whatever had prompted it, it was one of several observations he made in 1930 and 1931 which together gave evidence of a turmoil of bewilderment and indecision. This was also a time of tremendous liberation for Read, for he had just left the Victoria and Albert Museum for the Chair of Fine Arts at Edinburgh University, exchanging, as he said, 'an impersonal mode of existence for a very personal one'.[50]

Disoriented, he made efforts once more, as his early experience had taught him, to maintain the coequality of the romantic and the classic (though quite soon he would announce the complete irrelevance of the latter[51]). And as an early step in the reinstatement of romanticism he dealt with the recent aberration. Though a classicist might argue, he said, that an artist had no 'personality' to express, but rather an impersonal medium 'in which impressions and experience combine in peculiar and unexpected ways', he himself was now firmly of the conviction that criticism must address the artist's state of mind, and must therefore depend upon an individual psychology.[52] Read had once looked to Jung for the means of testing art's authenticity – of establishing connections between its symbolism and the root-images of a community.[53] In the absence of such help, however, and now no doubt encouraged by the different theoretical dependence of surrealism, Read directed his attention towards Freud. Freud also had a theory of symbolic origination but, limited to the sexual, it offered little indication of the criteria of *social* value such as Read had demanded. In his renewed appreciation of Freud's work, however, essentially an *individual* psychology, there were compensations.

Read saw that Freud had distinguished between the sum total of an individual's instinctive forces, which he called the id, and the coherent organization of mental processes, the conscious flow of thoughts,[54] which he called the ego. He accepted this latter concept to his own definition of 'personality'; and in contrast to this, and by means of an interpretation of another Freudian principle, the super-ego, he opposed the concept 'character', said to be a classicizing influence shaping, directing and censoring the personality.[55] He suggested nothing new in saying that the creative impulse originates in the id and proceeds to formal completion via the various organizing faculties of the ego; but he effected radical departures both from Freud's theory and his own previous beliefs when he said that the artist should endeavour to circumvent the super-ego, the ego's classic aspect, and permit his expressions to emanate as

Insight and Reason

directly as possible from the id.⁵⁶ Read's principle of the balanced
creative duality, which he had seemed to have been desperately
trying to reassert, was thus (once more temporarily) abandoned in
favour of the idea of an autonomous, unconscious force of creation.
'Reality is at every moment drawn up from the unknown' according solely to 'laws of its own origination':⁵⁷ phrases such as these
marked, in 1932, the beginning of his traversion now to the left of
impartial criticism; and though they leaned heavily upon Freudian
theory they also strained the authoritative hypothesis, in which the
issues of the id could not normally emerge uncensored.

This tendency towards synthesis – formlessness assuming proper
form unhampered by false restrictions – corresponded precisely
with Whitehead's major theme, his elaboration of the organic.
Read now placed faith in an organic art, issuing naturally from a
flux of memories, sensations and unconscious traces of experience,
maintaining that this was of the highest sphere of creativity. He
denigrated classic or, as it was now termed, 'abstract' art,⁵⁸ which
did submit to arbitrary shaping and to artifice; though he
preserved, as of habit, an antagonism in his theorizing by opposing,
as it has been said, 'personality' and 'character'. By 'personality'
he meant the free expression of psychic impulses, regulated only
(as in the sense received from Wordsworth) by an *inner* harmony,
or an *inner* perspective. By 'character' he meant an external ideal,
to which the artist's inner organization was in danger of being
sacrificed. A relegation of classic art, therefore, did not imply a
lessening importance of universals – rhythm, harmony, balance,
equilibrium: it was assumed that these would be engaged internally,
by dint of the artist's long sensational experience of the world
about him. Read did, however, now reject such qualities when they
were conventionalized and brought to bear upon creative processes
externally, as instruments of character; and it may not yet have
been clear to him that, ostensibly discussing his romantic principle,
he was really grappling with a synthesis such as his earlier dialectic
had demanded.

This synthesis, by his own standards a work of authentic creativity, had been entirely sensed. It was his critic's readiest argument
that he had been inconsistent in his use of psychological theory –
he had, for example, subjoined to Freud's 'super-ego' his own
conception 'character', and he had made no mention of those other
features prominent within a Freudian scheme, the 'libido' and the

'principle of reality'.[59] Read acknowledged an amateurism here,[60] but clearly saw nothing wrong in accepting any aspect of psychological theory relevant to his purposes, while rejecting anything which conflicted with the evidence of his own senses – that is, which might have been applied to his thoughts in the nature of a false, external influence.[61] If this less-than-respectful attitude left Read exposed to doctrinaire criticism in 1932, it is surprising that his further manipulations of Freudian psychology, three years later at the height of his enthusiasm for surrealism, went relatively unnoticed.

He had already noted that, authoritatively, the issues of the id could not normally fail to be subjected to assumed, external modifications; and he now frankly regarded this as the chief limitation of Freud's theory. He also noted that Freud, while recognizing the phenomenon, was unable to explain how material from the id might suddenly, abnormally, become present in conscious attention; and he suggested that the psychologist, without elaborating, had offered a clue to the nature of this process when he had observed that certain mystics seemed to have powers to effect upheavals in the minds of others. Accepting this casual remark, and also rearranging the principal parts of Freud's work, Read said:

> If we picture the regions of the mind as three super-imposed strata [to Freud the ego and super-ego were not so arranged, but rather confluent] . . . we can imagine in certain rare cases a phenomenon comparable to a 'fault' in geology, as a result of which in one part of the mind the layers become discontinuous, and exposed to each other at unusual levels. That is to say, the sensational awareness of the ego is brought into direct contact with the id, and from that 'seething cauldron' snatches some archetypal form, some instinctive association of words, images or sounds, which constitute the basis of the work of art. Some such hypothesis is necessary to explain that access, that lyrical intuition, which is known as inspiration and which in all ages has been the rare possession of those few individuals we recognize as artists of genius.[62]

Thus to Read, as a surrealist, the essence of art no longer consisted, as he used to maintain, in the harmony of unconscious forces and ideal form, but in an unaffected imagery won directly from the unconscious, the potency of which, he thought, might well have resided in its elusiveness. The concept 'new reality' was put aside in favour of 'superreality', a term which indicated much more positively an aim to transcend the present condition of awareness. In this event unconscious imagery would condense into symbolism, the latent significance of which would resist analysis but which, perhaps precisely on this account, would be extremely forceful.[63] Read now wondered whether such imagery, objectified in the poem or in the work of plastic art, should not merely resist but expectedly defy intellectual appreciation – in other words, he speculated that the expressions of one unconscious mind might most effectively be received by others, correspondingly unconsciously.

He believed there was sufficient evidence to be found, at least in poetry, that certain works which remained obscure to intellectual scrutiny nevertheless possessed a potency of meaning which could be sensed, and only be explained by a theory of unconscious appreciation. Some poets – the supreme example Shakespeare – had sought an absolute correspondence of language and emotion, and had naturally exceeded the limits of conventional discourse. They had been forced to invent – invent perhaps new words, new uses of words, or more frequently figures of speech which reanimated words. Read the surrealist was thus prepared to judge the poet, to the exclusion of all other qualities, even of harmonic form, on the force and originality of his metaphors. By 'metaphor' he meant not merely 'an illuminating correspondence between two objects' but (perceiving a dialectic structure even in this extreme of creativity) a synthesis of equal and remote, emotionally gained realities. The resulting new reality, or rather the superreality, defying convention – *exceeding* what had previously been conventionalized – would be bound to remain obscure to any but unconventional analysis.[64] The classic principle, now associated entirely with convention – that is, with the consolidation of the real gains of previous periods of creative effervescence – was now held to be irrelevant to the workings of a specifically modern creativity. The task of abstraction was to remain in suspension until needed to consolidate or codify the gains of the present outburst of creativity.[65] Thus recognized, as Hulme had seen them, as action and reaction rather than simultaneous opposites, romanticism and classicism were accepted as the substance of a false dialectic. The only dialectic which mattered to the present extension of human awareness was that which resolved irrationally sensed contradictions in visual or verbal metaphors.[66] In his clearest acknowledgment yet of his customary technique Read revealed that the superficial features of Hegelian logic had become for him much more convincing in the light of his newer understanding of organicism.

'This dreaded word *dialectic*', he wrote,

> . . . is actually the name of a very simple and very necessary process of thought. If we consider the natural world, we soon become aware that its most striking characteristic is not permanency, solidity or stability, but *continuous change* or development. Physicists now affirm that not merely the organic world, not merely this earth we live on, but the whole universe is undergoing a process of continuous change. Dialectics is nothing more than a logical explanation of how such a change takes place. It does not suffice to say that 'it grows', or 'it decays', 'it runs down', 'it expands'; these phrases are vague abstractions. The change must take place in a definite way. Between one phase and another of that development there must intervene an active principle . . . actually one of opposition and interaction. That is to say, to produce any new situation (i.e. any departure from an existing condition of equilibrium) there must previously exist two elements so opposed to each other and yet so related to each other that a solution or resolution is demanded; such a solution being in effect a new phase of development (temporary state of equilibrium) which preserves some of the elements of the interacting phases, eliminates others, but is qualitatively different from the previously existing state of opposition.[67]

There was claimed to be such continuous opposition and interaction between the worlds of objective fact (perceived sensationally) and subjective phantasy, which it was the business of the artist to resolve. He would do so by creating a synthesis, a work combining elements from both worlds, eliminating others, manifesting an entirely new experience. Read wished to say that surrealism was exactly this, a resolution of two unconscious modes of experience; and even as he did so he found himself beginning to return to a more balanced hypothesis, maintaining that the necessary *super-realism* was a much wider conception, embodying at one of its extremes and as one of its constituents the surrealist revolution.

Thus the superreality which was needed now to be proclaimed was one synthesizing unconsciousness and consciousness, irrationality and reason.[68] It was Read's suddenly expressed ambition to prove that such a dialectical philosophy could be the basis of an aesthetic of contemporary art;[69] and this disclosure, made in 1936, may be seen as the beginnings of just such an effort extending over some fifteen years. In this he would have to confront the fact that the other extreme of art, abstraction, was also revolutionary, in the sense that many of the most significant advances of modern art had been and were continuing to be effected by abstractionists. He realized that any comprehensive theory must account for both wings of modernism; and in 1937 he put forward the view that the two were following different routes probably towards a single goal.[70] He conceded that his previous theorizing had been ambivalent, and attributed this to contradictions inherent in his own personality which, until now, he had succeeded in balancing only rarely and never for long.[71] This was self-acknowledgment that the images of Read as classicist and as surrealist had not been convincing.

In fact there is little evidence to suggest that his devotion to their movement had entirely convinced the other surrealists either. Though accepted, that is, it may not have been positively welcomed – a view perhaps confirmed by his expulsion in 1939.[72] An intense rivalry conditioned the ways in which the abstractionists and the surrealists conducted their affairs, and it is hard to believe that Read's conversion, had it been received with an enthusiasm, would not have been propagandized more efficiently. But his contributions to the movement's major celebration in England, the *International Surrealist Exhibition* held in London in 1936, consisted in showing 'found objects', in a short speech-making,[73] and in a brief introduction to the catalogue. As editor of *Surrealism*, the publication of which coincided with the exhibition, Read acted with the co-operation of the movement's chief figures but not at their urging; and it is his lengthy Introduction to this book – much longer than the papers of other contributors – which more than anything else has distorted his involvement in surrealism. It may have seemed, to those whose efforts had been formative over more than a decade, that he had embraced the movement mainly to justify an aspect of his own theory; and there may have been a suspicion that he was using the movement to his own ends, emphasized, perhaps, by his

69

unilateral insistence upon the use of the term 'superrealism'. He carried to the London exhibition the debate about a possible tactical error of using the term 'surrealism' in English texts. He protested that the tendency was not, as the term implied, imported but, at least as far as literature was concerned, intrinsically English, a continuation upon the achievements of Shakespeare, the most obvious example, and of such as Donne and Carroll.[74] But the most damning of Read's departures from the consensus[75] was his at-first-hesitant admission of a possible surrealist compromise with, or a relatedness to, abstraction.

Recognition of his own ambivalence persuaded him that a mind without contradictory tensions would be incapable of shaking itself out of passivity and into creative development.[76] As he began to address a comprehensive theory, therefore, he wondered whether it was feasible to associate, as a consistent rule, a range of differently resolved mental tensions with corresponding stylistic tendencies in art. He looked to traditional categories of human temperament (verified by Jung) which reflected four basic types of mental activity – thinking, feeling, sensation and intuition[77] – said, depending upon their balance within an individual, to characterize him psychologically. And as he sorted a related stylistic terminology he made modifications which were to remain valid to him throughout the whole of this particular attempt at a philosophy of modern art. 'Superrealism' he now defiantly adopted to denote one revolutionary extreme of art, in which sensation and phantasy collided; and 'abstraction', at the other extreme, was recognized as being to some degree intuitional. He wrote:

> Just as we may recognize four types of personality corresponding to the four modes of mental activity, and having four distinct modes of perception, so it is possible to recognize four distinct modes of aesthetic activity expressed in works of art. This result may also be reached by an empirical classification of the historical styles of art, and the unsystematic phraseology of the history of art does in fact include four distinct styles or types. There is the style known variously as realism or naturalism, which consists in making as exact an imitation as possible of the objective facts present in an act of perception; there is the style known variously as idealism, romanticism, superrealism, fantastic or imaginative art which,

while making use of images of visual origin, constructs from these an independent reality. Thirdly, there is the style which we call expressionistic, and which is determined by the artist's desire to find a plastic correspondence for his immediate sensations, his temperamental reactions to a perception or experience. Finally, there is the style which avoids all imitative elements and invites an aesthetic response to the purely formal relationships of space, mass, colour, sound, etc. This style is sometimes called abstract, but 'constructive', 'absolute', or 'intuitional' would be more exact terms.[78]

These distinctions could be said further to possess objective and subjective aspects. 'Photographic' naturalism, Read said, for example, would result from a dominantly objective attitude, while in an impressionistic approach would reside its subjective counterpart. There would be one kind of superrealist, who desired subjectively to express his unconscious through the direct automatism of his feelings; and another, who would project his unconscious into found objects, and by this means into the external world. Objective expressionism would tend to caricature; and in subjective expressionism the artist's own sensations would constitute the material of expression. Abstraction would be objectified in functional art, and in all manner of logically derived constructions; and *its* subjective counterpart would consist in expositions of form, space, rhythm and harmony, perceived purely by sensation.[79] In this way Read achieved a disposition of current attitudes to art, accounting both for his specifically modern tendencies, superrealism and abstraction, as well as those – realism and expressionism – which would have little bearing upon the task he had set himself. He would address an antagonism within the abstract dynamic, in which a conceptual art would oppose a subjective one, resulting from the sensed perception of laws inherent in the physical structure of the universe; and he would also see an antagonism within the superrealist dynamic, in which 'expression by objective association' would oppose automatism.

He would see some similarity between the desire to create a subjective abstraction, an inner harmonizing of personal perceptions of the world, and the wish to express subjective, unconscious imagery by direct automatism. Arising out of this would come two related conceptions of specifically modern art – one individual,

71

the other collective. According to the latter he would argue that abstraction and superrealism, though ostensibly quite different, were actually linked along an axis and shared middle ground in the subjective: (later, to pursue this further, he would hold the extreme edges of this front to be dialectical opposites, and the centre to be an interpenetration, the precondition of their resolution). According to the former conception it would be said that such opposing tendencies also conditioned the work of an individual, determining the resonance of his expression. A principle of *form*, deriving from the organic world, a function of perception, and a principle of *origination*, peculiar to the mind of man, a function of imagination – these would exhaust in their counterplay all the psychic aspects of aesthetic experience.[80]

These utterances gave the first evidence of Read's regained impartiality; but they also necessitated further psychological speculation which exceeded scientific authority. This concerned the need to present the unconscious–conscious mental flow as a reciprocal arrangement, so that the new theory (far from that which had described a one-directional passage from formlessness to form) could account for a ranging back and forth across an axis. The authoritative hypothesis was of a mental process in which unconsciously received sensations were, subject to modification, projected into consciousness; but Read was ready to accept the slightest indication of a converse activity. He noted that for a more or less static view of the mental personality psychologists had substituted one thoroughly dynamic;[81] and he replaced his own idea of the mental strata with an analogy in which the various levels were fluid, and affected by dynamic, swirling forces. The interfacing of the various parts was not now due to a disrupting 'fault', but to an interpenetrating agency, the Freudian super-ego, which had its basis in the primitive undercurrents of the mind and which also projected into consciousness. On the strength of Freud's observation that 'there are people in whom the faculties of self-criticism and conscience – mental activities, that is, that rank as exceptionally high ones – are *unconscious*, and unconsciously produce effects of the greatest importance,'[82] Read was prepared to suggest that a resolution of conflicting mental forces might occur within the super-ego, and that the initiative for this might be either unconscious or conscious, formless or formed. He assumed that the ego was incapable of *controlling* the id (just as 'the bubble does not control the force or direction of the stream'); but at the same time he thought that the ego could assert an opposition to unconscious phenomena, and thus create a condition of tension demanding resolution. The conscious process of intellection, he believed, and the process of the deep unconscious, might resolve their contradictions in the relatively shallow unconscious areas of the mind.[83] This considerably modified the one-directional theory of mentality which had characterized his previous work.

It seemed further to suggest to Read that not only the formation of moral principles in the mind of an individual, but also his pursuit of a proper creativity, would involve the balanced application of extreme unconsciousness (which was in part collective or hereditary[84]) and extreme consciousness to the agency of the super-ego. In other words, the artist had to cultivate this function of his mentality in order to integrate his remotest unconscious imagery and his impulses gained by acute self-consciousness. For Jung such integration consisted in 'watching objectively the development of any fragment of phantasy',[85] which phrase succinctly described Read's necessary principle, and also emphasized the notion of a reciprocating sensibility. For the time being, though, Read was inclined to put aside questions of a possibly more-exact correspondence between the acts of moral and aesthetic judgment, for he was disposed to maintain that the linking of the two necessarily presupposed the subjugation of aesthetics to *accepted* codes of morality, an imposition upon art which was always detrimental.[86] Thus, though he had asserted in the recent past that art becomes more ethical as the result of an increasing, abstract purity because the ultimate goal of abstraction is truth, and that modern art was for this reason unpopular in that it revealed insights into a morality too exacting to be generally acceptable,[87] he was temporarily determined to keep the concepts separate. In so doing he returned to a favourite theme.

He asked:

Where, if not in a moral code, shall we find a criterion of art?
The answer is, of course, *in nature*. There, absolute and universal, is a touchstone for all human artefacts. And we must understand by nature, not any vague pantheistic spirit, but the measurements and physical behaviour of matter in any process of growth or transformation. The seed that

becomes a flowering plant, the metal that crystallizes as it cools and contracts, all such processes exhibit laws which are modes of material behaviour. There is no growth which is not accompanied by its characteristic form, and I think we are so constituted – so much in sympathy with natural processes – that we always find such forms beautiful.[88]

The artist in particular, he thought, was one gifted with conscious or 'automatic' – but in either case a most direct – perception of natural form; and all great art, even the most nihilistic, in some way transmitted a sense of scale, proportion, symmetry and balance. Once this were accepted by contemporary artists, the accumulated results of many years of experiment – the formal freedoms associated with abstraction and supperrealism – would be seen to be cohesive.[89] Arguments about natural form would therefore justify a belief that artists should reconcile extremes of their creative personalities. Read was inclined to see the personality itself as an organic, developing structure, internalizing (in rare individuals) aspects of the great cultural contradiction, combining some of them and eliminating others, and transforming them in works of art. This was central to the philosophy of modern art he was constructing. Art is not to be determined by cultural conventions (which include a code of morality): an appropriate culture will result from the creative activities of available, outstanding personalities.[90] The proper place for a moral code is among art's consequences, for

> . . . morality is essentially mutuality, the sharing of a common ideal. And the process by which we are induced to share a common ideal is none other than that indicated by Freud – the creation of an empathic relationship with our fellow citizens by means of common rituals, by means of the imitation of the same patterns – by meeting, as it were, in the common form or quality of the universally valid work of art.[91]

Such arguments as these constituted Read's major wartime theme; and it is interesting to note that, for all their reconstructive purpose, they are little different from the ones he had put at the service of surrealism, when objectives had been rather to disrupt. Now he was willing to admit, considering the social importance of art, that it was too often a partial, even perverse, expression of universal harmony, and too often an aggressive, egoistic utterance of personal phantasy. The whole conception of art would have to be enlarged and purified, he said;[92] and this (completing a cycle of argument) would mean nothing less than a synthesis of 'universal expression' and 'personal phantasy', such as was being achieved by artists he knew well.[93] He too was engaged in similar synthesis. In the mid 1930s he had been known as a man who had renounced a youthful, intellectual classicism for a liberating reinstatement of his latent romanticism. This may now be understood as a preliminary to his attention to an inclusive theory – though even here it may be seen that he made another false start. Organic form, perhaps the most important prop of his theory of cohesive styles, came to assume far greater significance than either abstraction or superrealism; and this appears to have surprised him, for he had clearly believed his construction complete.

Chapter 4

Superrealism and Abstraction

When in 1930 Read began regularly to contribute *Notes on Art* to *The Listener* he had clarified a conception of creativity (chiefly in the sphere of poetic formation) which he could apply not only to the specifically modern but also to 'contemporary' art of other ages and cultures. It was this: an art might justifiably be said to be evolutionary which enlarges the perception of reality either by means of abstraction, a creative concept-forming, or by means of empathy, an intuitive knowing. In this sense he could speak in equal terms of any art which could be said to be progressive upon its immediate context, such as (to give two entirely different examples) the geometricism of the Byzantine (which had also fascinated Hulme), and the achievements of Constable and Turner in the presence of an ambient academicism.[1] In the relatively little art criticism he had previously written he had felt most at ease discussing works which engaged his intellect – in practically his first piece, a decade earlier, for instance, he had observed that David Bomberg's way of working was constructive, scientific, distinctly developmental, and conducive of a high standard of formal beauty.[2] It seems to have been clear to him, however, as a result of his interest in the psychological undercurrents of such expression, that great contemporary art, of this as of any other time, would to some extent feature construction and its antithesis in counterpoint. Though he could see that much of the tangible development of twentieth-century art had been of the abstract – cubism and vorticism (an understanding of which he had gained initially from *The New Age*) and the work of Kandinsky (well-represented in the collection of Michael Sadler)[3] – he could detect no comparable empathetic or romantic art except in dada, which, 'only a joke',[4] he would not consider seriously as having been the left wing of a *progressive* modern art. He was ready to be receptive to the work of individuals which manifested interacting abstract and romantic or empathetic elements (thus he was keen to promote through his *Listener Notes* an appreciation of Paul Klee[5]); and he was also bound to respond to an art he could recognize as itself essentially romantic, which might counterbalance the modern tendency to abstraction within the collective art of the present. In this latter respect he recognized the importance of surrealism when, six years after its inception, it was just becoming discernible from England. His recognition, though, was qualified by the fact of his own identification, in his most classic mood, with the real gains of the abstractionists. He wrote:

Most people have heard by now of 'Surrealisme' but as the movement is not, so far as I know, represented in England, it might be worth while to define its character. In speaking of Cubism a few weeks ago, I pointed out that the principles of that revolutionary phase of art are essentially classical: it is a formal art which more and more tends in the direction of intellectualism – towards an art of number and proportion and away from the art of emotion or sentiment. Naturally the whole of the modernist movement could not follow in this direction; some people are romantic by nature and others are romantic in spite of themselves. So in opposition to Cubism we had first 'Dada' and then 'Surrealisme' . . . .

My own preferences are classical: that is to say I derive most pleasure from a work of art, whether literature or painting, in which expression is achieved with some degree of formal precision. But I could never see why, though a classicist, I should be forbidden the enjoyment of romantic art. Granted that both impulses, the romantic and the classic, exist in their own right (and the history of art is a sufficient demonstration of that), then perfection may be achieved in the expression of either, and enjoyment is the perception of any kind of perfection. A perfect representation of the workings of the unconscious mind, such as Mr. Joyce's *Ulysses*, is, therefore, in my opinion a great work of art. If I have not yet seen a 'Surrealiste' painting which convinces me in the same degree,

the fault is probably my own: I have not seen enough. The
least I can do is to admit that the *genre* is possible.[6]

Read had first approached an understanding of abstract art
indirectly, with the help of such as Kramer (whose own painting
was expressionist) and Worringer (as he was interpreted by
Hulme). His approach to surrealism was now similarly indirect,
for he was chiefly attracted by the movement's frank dependence
upon the psychoanalytical theories of Freud. So he would assert
that 'Professor Freud is the real founder of the school' and, defensively, 'you can no more dismiss Surrealisme than you can dismiss
Psychoanalysis'.[7] The psychoanalyst's view is an imbalanced
perception of art – before the great work of absolute formal values
he is comparatively dumb; and the surrealist's tendency is to parade
his own subconscious mind, whereas to become significant he must
surrender his individuality and be the mouthpiece of the collective
unconscious:[8] with these qualifications Read the classicist was
prepared to accept that psychological theory might not only explain
but actually inspire a form of modern art. He went to live in
Hampstead, close by Henry Moore, Barbara Hepworth, Ben
Nicholson and Paul Nash, whose works he came to regard as being
in the vanguard of English art; and much of his subsequent writing,
even that which preceded his commitment to such a philosophy,
conveyed his efforts to accommodate this advanced art within a
theoretical framework containing *abstraction* and *superrealism* (his
preferred term for the tendency previously described as 'empathetic', of which he came to consider surrealism to be a stylistic
manifestation). There was now the possibility of a convincing
analysis of specifically modern art; and there began a process of
categorizing what he considered to be the most advanced art practised in England (including the work of the temporary residents
Naum Gabo and Piet Mondrian) in relation to the polarities
abstraction and superrealism.

At first this was not dispassionate, for the years 1930 to 1936
saw a gradual progression from his close identification with the
abstractionists, initially to a cautious acceptance of surrealism, and
then to an unbridled enthusiasm involving his own participation
in the *International Surrealist Exhibition* held in London.[9] Read's
views during this period, therefore, should be seen in the context
of his slowly growing (and then abruptly terminating[10]) sense of

being himself a surrealist. As late as 1933 he could perceive, apart from promises of artistic 'insurrection' in surrealism,[11] that a consistent development of art was evident only in abstraction: he then proceeded as a man arguing with himself that superrealism might be correspondingly progressive. Thus in 1933, in the first edition of his book *Art Now*, there were said to be two tendencies in art which, though current, were *not* specifically modern, the symbolist and the expressionist; and two which *were* specifically modern, conforming on the one hand with 'a theory of abstract form' and on the other with 'a theory of subjective idealism'.[12] There was an attempt to demonstrate that the abstract and the subjective were somehow related; and there was the rather lame conclusion that the linking 'common element' resided in the artists' skill, in both tendencies alike, in transposing mental images into plastic forms – their abilities to express personality.[13] In 1935 Read was confident in asserting the equal prominence of abstraction and superrealism, and in noting that these two distinct types of revolutionary art were *diverging*.[14] So convinced was he of the originality and importance of this idea that he added a postscript to the second edition of *Art Now* which fundamentally changed the book's overall message about artistic progress. Whereas the main text seemed to indicate the general advance of a basically abstract modern art, continuing upon the hectic revolutionary phases of the previous thirty years, the new emphasis, by assigning to superrealism and abstraction entirely different futures respectively in 'a new mythology' and in 'pure architectonics',[15] seemed to indicate a belief in two dynamic systems.

His theory growing clearer, Read said that there were two specifically modern attitudes, both intentionally revolutionary. One, typically represented in the paintings of Mondrian and Nicholson and in the sculptures of Hepworth and Gabo, was variously called abstract, non-figurative, constructivist and geometrical, and was essentially formalist. The other was less essentially formalist and had a distinctive name, superrealism: this was represented by such painters as Max Ernst, Salvador Dali and Joan Miró, and by a sculptor, Hans Arp. 'The first movement is plastic, objective and ostensibly non-political: the second group is literary, even in paint, subjective and actively communist.'[16] Read understood the aims of the superrealists to be to discredit bourgeois and academic conceptions of art; and he concluded that their idiom had an immediate, dynamic role – it was the art of a transitional period. Abstraction, however, had a different function: its recent phases of activity over, its task was to remain inviolate until 'society will once more be ready to make use of them, the universal qualities of art – those elements which survive all change and revolutions'.[17] At the time of his most active support for the surrealists, therefore, Read was sketching a model of contemporary art containing two extreme movements, one having largely undergone a process of revolution, the other now entering a revolutionary phase. They were divergent, in the sense that the latter was seeking access to ever-deeper levels of unconsciousness; and they could be disposed *laterally*, to present a broad front of modernism, or else *linearly*, in keeping with Read's psychological ideal.

> Though at their extremes – a Mondrian against a Dali – these two movements have nothing in common, yet the space between them is occupied by an unbroken series, in the middle of which we find artists like Picasso and Henry Moore whom we cannot assign confidently to either school. Significantly these intermediate artists are among those most evidently in possession of a fertile and powerful genius.[18]

Within the short space of three years, then, Read had found it necessary to revise quite drastically the message of his 'apologia', *Art Now*; and, to be precise, the experiences which influenced a change of heart occurred in 1934. In that year it became clear to him that the predominance of classicism in painting and sculpture might be questioned as seriously as he had challenged it in litera- ture,[19] and that his defence of a psychologically founded criticism might be relevant in the realm of the plastic arts. He wrote exten- sive appraisals of Moore and Picasso as romantics; and it seemed that an alternation evident in Picasso's development had antici- pated the climatic changes affecting contemporary art as a whole.

Between 1906 and 1915, Read thought, Picasso's work had followed a logical sequence from the simplification of things seen towards a complete geometricization. There had then been a decade of consolidation, in which Picasso had sought all the ramifications of a classic approach – creating abstract structures of increasing complexity, and also, incidentally, exploring the classical themes of representational painting. And then he had begun to paint an entirely new kind of abstraction, calling for a different theory of explanation. Whereas in earlier abstractions content had been subordinate to form, in the succeeding works a representational content and a distorted, abstract form appeared to be co-equal. Two aspects of this later development were significant to Read. It reflected a concentration upon natural or vital elements, however they were reshaped − heads, particularly facial variations; and bones, chiefly those with complicated functions, such as the bones of the ear. And its manifestations could not be explained without some theory of unconscious origins of imagery. By his own acknowledgment Picasso usually painted in a state of trance; and, Read suggested, an innate talent for form and colour, thoroughly developed in relation to a classic outlook, was now all the surer for being exercised under purely instinctual conditions.[20] This divergence in modern painting (Picasso, in both his moods, had had his imitators) had been matched, too, in recent abstract sculpture. In one direction sculptors were tending to emphasize pure forms and their relationships − giving shape to conceptions as uncompromisingly abstract as any in the field of mathematics: others, in another direction, were concerned with something more than abstract qualities and also something greater than figurative representation. Moore, attempting to reflect qualities typical of living things, or at least associated with natural processes, belonged to the second type. He did not eschew complete abstraction; but the majority of his works were vital, rhythmic and essentially dynamic.[21]

It seems obvious that Read, while wishing to remain loyal to abstractionists, was searching for good reason to embrace surrealism. When he did so, therefore, it was while strenuously maintaining that a tectonic abstraction would be more positively useful in a future civilization.[22] His recent appreciation of the workings of Picasso, in which unconscious imagery issued forth relatively unaffected by an external ideal, and his view of Moore's work, convinced him that it was not inconsistent to hold on to both aspects of modern art. Picasso's work, indeed, exemplified more than any other his beliefs in a cultural alternation and in the primacy of the romantic principle in an individual's creativity; and Read might now have been expected to make much of these correspondences. It demonstrates the seriousness of his ambition to perfect a dialectical theory, however, that for many years he neglected Picasso,[23] and (after the brief flirtation with surrealism) concentrated mostly upon artists who roved between abstraction and its antithesis with unremitting frequency. And though he accepted for his temporary enthusiasm the status of an advanced condition of art, claiming surrealism to be 'the only true application of the principles of dialectical materialism' in the realms of plastic and poetic creativity,[24] this was not a synthesis of abstraction and an imaginative art such as he *would* be seeking, but the more localized synthesis of imagination and *realism*.

Marking the limit of this, his second far departure from a central critical stance, Read wrote:

> No critic of experience will return to a discussion of the terms 'romanticism' and 'classicism' with anything but extreme reluctance . . . . I only take up the discussion again (eating my own words in the process) because I think that Surrealism has settled it. So long as romanticism and classicism were considered as alternative attitudes, rival camps, professions of *faith*, an interminable struggle was in prospect, with the critics as profiteers. But what in effect Surrealism claims to do is to resolve the conflict – not, as I formerly hoped, by establishing a synthesis which I was prepared to call 'reason' or 'humanism' – but by liquidating classicism, by showing its complete irrelevance, its *anaesthetic* effect, its contradiction of the creative impulse.[25]

Then having been, within the space of six years, a partisan of both abstraction and superrealism, he immediately began to revert to a less partial stance, again to consider them as equally valid opposites (in the words of his critics he backed both horses, but his own metaphor featured his decision to ride them in harness[26]). Actually the beginnings of a normalization may be found in his reasoning which accompanied propagandist remarks about surrealism. His explanations related equally to the localized dialectic within the superrealist polarity of art, and to the greater contradiction between this and abstraction. In every age there had been artists who insisted upon the prime importance of imagination, he said, and others, opposed to this view, who would subordinate the imagination to intellectual control. The contemporary antagonism, perhaps for the first time, was an involvement of equals because an art of the imagination had been theoretically strengthened by Freud, by whose efforts the unconscious had become an admitted reality. The superreality which the artist now proclaimed was a synthesis of experience embracing the apparently irreconcilable:

> He will oppose the conscious and the unconscious, the deed and the dream, truth and fable, reason and unreason, and out of these opposites he will in the dialectical process of his artistic activity create a new synthesis.[27]

Read now set about the *cross-representation* of abstraction and superrealism in his writings, presumably in the hope of promoting a general advance of the kind Ginner had once anticipated. And in the first of such pieces – a contribution to the *International Survey of Constructive Art* of 1937, in which he pressed the claims of superrealism – he attended to a flaw which had weakened arguments that abstraction and superrealism were equal opposites. So long as the supreme example of abstraction had been considered to be that which was the purest manifestation of the intellect, abstract art had been vulnerable to numerical or mechanistic interpretation and also (putting aside the mathematician's claims to creativity) to suggestions that it might be formulated. As he began to construct an even-handed theory, then, he urgently considered the potential imbalance, and he was quick to make this adjustment: the identification required of the abstract artist, no less than of the superrealist, lies *beyond* the concept. As the superrealist could be said to believe that parallel to conscious reasoning, and *below* the conscious level of the mind, there was latent imagery which he was properly seeking to disengage for intellectual contemplation, the abstractionist could be said to be realizing latent imagery from just *outside* the range of consciousness, by a process of enlarging given concepts. 'Space', for example, he wrote, was a typical concept – one which a superrealist might in effect affirm by the negative contrasts of his 'dream perspectives', and which an abstractionist might attempt to affirm devoid of emotional encumbrances, in the most unequivocal manner. Both would be concerned, in their opposing ways, with augmenting the concept, on the one hand with subconscious, and on the other with supra-conscious, associations. It was, Read said (in his essay ostensibly supporting the constructivists) a *joint* responsibility to exceed what had previously been conventionalized.

I do not pretend that there is any one way of doing this. It

> seems to me, on the contrary, that we are at a stage of
> experimentation, trying in various ways to discover a new law
> of identification. I believe that surrealism, no less than
> abstract art, is engaged on this all-absorbing and all-important
> task.[28]

In an article on abstraction, intended mainly to be received by
the surrealists,[29] Read further elaborated the idea of an abstract
identification beyond the concept. He was primarily being defensive
against expected accusations that abstraction, a response to
external reality, would merely be concerned with the recognition
of pleasing or decorative formal relationships. He argued that
pursuing the most advanced abstractions, yes, an artist would refer
to nature, but his aim would be to gain fundamental principles of
form, approachable only by penetrating beyond conventional ideas
about 'natural appearance'. Read's claim for the abstract artist was
that his forms repeated, in their appropriate materials and on
appropriate scales, certain proportions and rhythms, inherent in
the structure of the universe, governing organic growth. Attuned
to these, he could create 'microcosms reflecting the macrocosm':
he had no need of accidental outward appearances because he
had 'access to the archetypal forms which underlie all the casual
variations presented by the natural world'.[30] In another essay,
similarly directed towards the surrealists, Read suggested that
abstractionists, having discovered such proportional and rhythmic
properties, might reassociate them exactly as musicians worked
with variations upon themes;[31] and this may be understood as his
attempt to account for an authentic abstraction which nevertheless
was not at the extreme of that particular tendency.

At this point Read's theoretical model was distinctly dynamic,
incorporating a divergence of superrealism and abstraction and
their respective revolutions. It now contained, to the left, a superrealism in which the *unconscious* and the *concept* were opposed,
creating a synthesis which was a percept; and, to the right, an
abstraction in which the *concept* opposed the *supra-conscious*,
forming its own synthetic percept. And consistent with this was
the principle, promoted in the cross-representations to partisan
audiences, of the greater resolution of opposed superreal and
abstract percepts, to achieve an advanced condition of art at the
summit of the dialectical pyramid. This arrangement dispensed

with the idea of a cyclic abstraction, contrived to permit the wholehearted participation in surrealism, and it also eliminated the unsatisfactory idea that the revolutionary phase of abstraction had been pioneered in an unspecified way. Read made a further observation which he did not immediately expound: it had little bearing upon a stylistic dialectic, but it was the faint beginning of a train of thought which would eventually supersede it:

> Just as surrealism makes use of, or rather proceeds on the assumption of, the knowledge embodied in psycho-analysis, so abstract art makes use of, or proceeds on the basis of, the abstract concepts of physics and dynamics, geometry and mathematics.[32]

A dialectically progressing superrealism conditioned by the psychological sciences; a dialectically progressing abstraction conditioned by the physical sciences; superrealism and abstraction themselves dialectically opposed: this now was the framework of Read's philosophical ambitions.

At the beginning of the 1940s Read may be imagined as having been assisted towards an unbiased critical position at the centre of his system, partly as a result of having been ejected from surrealism,[33] partly because of his reasserting sense of a balanced perspective, and also partly by his having been drawn towards an understanding of the constructivism of Naum Gabo. Read initially respected, but held back from liking, this extreme form of art (Gabo said that it took him seven years entirely to accept it[34]); but during a long and remarkable correspondence with Gabo he seems gradually to have realized that recognition of its appeal would not be inconsistent with his other preferences. Gabo's work was an excellent vehicle for study: having been nurtured in the Munich of which Worringer's *Abstraktion und Einfühlung* was a climatic factor, and having been influential in revolutionary Russia, it bore stamps of authenticity; and having undergone some twenty-five years of development it was now relatively unchanging, and as such it offered standards with which other, fluctuating and less-extreme forms of art, from various parts of the spectrum, could be compared. A close friendship developed during Gabo's three-year stay in Hampstead, after his emigration from France in 1935 and before he moved, along with such as Nicholson and Hepworth, to the then unfashionable St Ives in Cornwall. In this period Read contributed to the *International Survey of Constructive Art*, of which Gabo was co-organizer; and an outcome of this was a sympathy with some of the artist's objectives, an understanding which Gabo had despaired of ever finding in a theorist.[35] This was expressed early in what became a frequent exchange of letters, which became only slightly less regular after Gabo's further emigration, in 1946, to the USA. This correspondence offers the perhaps surprising indication (no doubt greatly welcomed by Read for its insights into creativity) that Gabo felt compelled to articulate his working processes verbally.

At first there were minor disagreements – on Gabo's part concerning what he took to be Read's persistent defending of a discredited school of art, surrealism,[36] and, on Read's reflecting a present inability, in spite of willingness, to understand precisely the supraconscious polarity of art. He recognized Gabo's work to be a crystallization of 'the purest sensibility for harmonious relationships', aspiring to 'the highest point ever reached by the aesthetic sensibility of man', and in this sense to be appropriately extending given concepts of form and space; but at the same time, perversely, he was tempted to regard it as possibly too 'egocentric' to be socially relevant.[37] Curiously, it was Barbara Hepworth, rather than Gabo, who convinced Read that this last view was erroneous, maintaining that though Gabo's constructions were devoid of imagery remotely connected with landscape, they undoubtedly were organic, expressing as they did 'the basic forms of primary construction'. She believed this to be 'the most easily understood use of images', and that its accomplished execution in Gabo's constructions was egocentric in the least possible degree.[38]

Such misunderstanding effectively repaired, there was then a sense of Gabo's requesting Read to help explain his work to the public, or rather to ensure that the public was sufficiently well-informed to be able to judge his work in fairness.[39] Gabo was aware of the regularity with which he was asked certain very elementary questions, and he was really seeking Read's advice about the appropriateness of his usual responses.

> My works are what people call 'Abstract'. You know how incorrect this is; still, it is true they have no visible association with the external aspects of the world. But this abstractedness is not the reason why I call my work 'Constructive'; and

'Abstract' is not the core of the Constructive Idea which I profess. This Idea means more to me. It involves the whole complex of human relation to life. It is a mode of thinking, acting, perceiving and living . . . Any thing or action which enhances life, propels it and adds to it something in the direction of growth, expansion and development, is Constructive.[40]

Read would have had little reason to dispute on this principle, except that, whereas he would have applied it to the whole of specifically modern art, he knew that Gabo strictly excluded from his own terms of reference the 'rival' achievements of the School of Paris and, above all, the current surrealist claims to a progressive art. When it could be overlooked, however, that to Gabo the terms 'art' and 'constructivism' were synonymous, there was promise of consistent agreement.

I believe art to be the most immediate and most effective of all means of communication between human beings [Gabo wrote]. Art as a mental action is unambiguous . . . . The way in which art perceives the world is sensuous . . . the way it acts in response to this perception is spontaneous, irrational and factual . . . and this is the way of life itself.[41]

Here was additional confirmation, if Read required it, that art was hugely intuitional; and the fact that an exponent of extreme non-figurative art was prepared to say so would have endorsed the second of Read's recent accounts of intuition – one issuing from below the levels of consciousness and giving rise to archetypal symbolism, the other gained from outside the range of present consciousness, engaging purer conceptions of form.

Gabo's most persistently recurring question, after 'Why is your art called Constructive?', was 'Where do your forms originate?'; and his normal response to this, which he put forward for Read to criticize, was not specific enough to tempt reciprocal arguments. His forms originated, Gabo said, in visual appreciation of his surroundings, both natural and man-made: he did not imitate the things he saw, however, but (disappointingly, perhaps, for Read, whose interest was precisely in this part of the process) he placed his own constructions upon them: 'The image of my perception needs an order and this order is my construction. I claim the right

to do it so because this is what we all do in our mental world
. . . .'[42]

Gabo may have thought this perfectly lucid, but it was obviously difficult for Read to enlarge upon. Instead he discussed a popular deficiency of aesthetic appreciation; and suggested that the main reason why Gabo was persistently questioned about his art was because modern man had to a large extent lost the faculty of 'immediately apprehending formal values', and was unable to perceive the answers to his questions, self-evident in works of art themselves. Read offered an explanation of this aesthetic deficiency, the subject of a current interest:[43] in western man the forebrain had undergone disproportionate development, increasing the capacity to intellectualize but detracting from the sensual functioning of man the total organism.[44] It was Gabo's integration of intuition and intellection – as he sensed the forms of his surroundings and reasoned a constructive response (though Gabo would later assert the dominant subjectivity of his entire procedure) – that Read wished to understand, for he saw here the vital property of 'the fertile imagination'.

It seemed that Read had the basis of such understanding – at least their correspondence proceeded upon this assumption – until in 1947 it was realized that in fact there was considerable dislocation of their views. This prompted Gabo to describe his motives with the greatest clarity, eventually to persuade Read he was wrong to consider them essentially objective. Read's misunderstanding came to light when, having been asked to write an introduction to the catalogue of a large retrospective exhibition of the work of Gabo and his brother Antoine Pevsner, he submitted a draft essay to the exhibition organizers, at the same time referring a copy to Gabo's attention. Gabo saw fundamental errors, the results, he later thought, of his own inadequate explanations:[45] they centred upon Read's wish to give an exact description of his constructive process, and (in the belief that the major practitioners of extreme non-figurative art shared fundamental principles) his recourse to Piet Mondrian's elaboration of his own theories, as the means of offering such exactness. Read had taken the four basic tenets of the *Realistic Manifesto* (originated by Gabo in 1920, and subsequently endorsed by Pevsner[46]) and he had extended them with arguments drawn from Mondrian's exposition of *Neo-Plasticism*.

Gabo and Pevsner had asserted that 'Volume is not the only

spatial concept', and that 'Kinetic and dynamic elements must be used to express the real nature of time: static rhythms are not sufficient';[47] and Read commented upon the close parallels which seemed to exist between these beliefs and the aims of modern physicists.

> The particular vision of reality common to the constructivism of Pevsner and Gabo and the neo-plasticism of Mondrian, is derived, not from the superficial aspects of a mechanized civilization, nor from a reduction of visual data to their 'cubic planes' or 'plastic volumes' (all these activities being merely variations of a naturalistic art), but from the structure of the physical universe as revealed by modern science. The best preparation for a true appreciation of constructive art is a study of Whitehead . . . . [But] though the intellectual vision of the artist is derived from modern physics, the creative construction which the artist then presents to the world is not scientific, but poetic. It is the poetry of space, the poetry of time, of universal harmony, of physical unity. Art – it is its main function – accepts this universal manifold which science investigates and reveals [this was consistent with the idea that superrealism was sustained by psychology] and reduces it to the concreteness of a plastic symbol.[48]

A belief in the validity of a 'new science of art' necessitated accepting new laws of composition, temporal as well as spatial, the essence of which, Read thought, had been aptly defined by Mondrian. Traditional art merely observed laws of space, as the artist had sought the static balance; but while such art might have afforded superficial resemblances of the external world, it was quite divorced from the fundamental principles of that world, which demonstrated above all the primacy not of static balance but of 'dynamic equilibrium'. Disregarding the fact that certain modern scientists, in particular the recommended Whitehead, had noted as a universal principle not 'dynamic equilibrium' (at least, not in Mondrian's sense of the term) but organic growth, that is dynamic near-equilibrium, Read offered almost as a slogan:

> Mondrian has defined this difference. A static balance
> 'maintains the individual unity of particular forms, single or
> in plurality'. A dynamic equilibrium is 'the unification of forms

89

or elements of forms through continuous opposition. The first is limitation, the second extension. [And, emphasizing the revolutionary nature of supra-conscious art] Inevitably dynamic equilibrium destroys static balance'.[49]

Gabo and Pevsner had also asserted in their manifesto: 'To communicate the reality of life, art should be based on the two fundamental elements: space and time'; and 'Art should stop being imitative and try instead to discover new forms.'[50] If the artist chose to pursue these axioms, Read said, then his activity had to be geared to the concrete representation of space and time, the basic elements of reality. Again he quoted Mondrian:

I felt that this reality can only be established through 'pure' plastics. In its essential expression, pure plastics is unconditioned by subjective feeling . . . . The appearance of natural forms changes but reality remains constant. To create pure reality plastically, it is necessary to reduce natural forms to the 'constant elements' of form, and natural colour to 'primary colour'. The aim is not to create other particular forms and colours with all their limitations, but to work toward abolishing them in the interest of a larger unity.[51]

This was the crux of Read's misapprehension: Gabo sought stimulation in the perception of an external object or event and, Read thought, his aim was to approach an ultimate reality of time and space – a matter of *constancy* – in the event divested of its accidental form and visual appearance. Gabo, however, did not believe in an *external*, absolute and constant state, but rather that reality was solely the product of mentality, *internal*, and constantly changing. His reaction to the juxtapositioning of his constructive axioms and Mondrian's, therefore, was one of indignation:

I do not share Mondrian's metaphysics at all and never did. My realism is a *Constructive* realism and the philosophy of constructive realism is based on the primary belief that there is no such thing as a pure reality . . . or that a reality can be detached from us . . . the reality of the world is constructed by us, by our senses and by our thoughts.[52]

It seems clear that this, and Gabo's further elaborations, were very important influences of Read's adjusted understanding of abstraction, its antithesis, and their collective purpose.

In a most illuminating description of his own creativity – the most informative of the long correspondence – Gabo respected Read's thought that there was a *measure* of agreement between the constructive and neo-plastic conceptions of reality; but he was insistent upon the distinction between one artist's search for an ultimate reality, and another's construction of reality unto himself. He refused to believe that the general striving for knowledge was the pursuit of a reality constant and pure; and he maintained that

> knowledge is nothing else but a construction of ours and that
> what we discover with our knowledge is not something
> outside us or a part of a constant and higher reality, in the
> absolute sense of the word, but we discover exactly that
> which we put into the place where we make the discoveries. I
> insist on this point, that the making of discoveries must be
> understood literally, namely that we *make* them . . . . We know
> only what we do, what we make, what we construe; and all
> that we make, all that we construe, are realities. I call them
> 'images', not in Plato's sense (namely, that they are only
> reflections of reality) but I hold that these images are the reality
> itself and that there is no other reality beyond it except when
> in our creative processes we change the images; then we have
> created new realities.[53]

This was not a simple, cumulative process, then: embracing as it did the winning of new, and the changing of previously defined, real experience, it had this much in common with T. S. Eliot's thought, well respected by Read, that tradition was being constantly revised.[54] Gabo's definition accommodated other activities, too, which he claimed as constructive (but which Read recognized and later maintained to be specifically superrealist) – the filling-out of once-vital, now outmoded 'symbolism' by means of an enriching imagery. Moreover, Gabo presupposed there to be, governing the whole of this spectrum of activity, a mentality collective in both its polar aspects. He said that 'human mind – sensual or thinking life – is a large entity encompassing many individuals, all participating in the process of creation.'[55] In other words, he proposed a phenomenon which offered a balanced completeness of Read's theoretical model, in spite of obvious difficulties of inclusion within a chiefly Freudian scheme. A supra-conscious aspect of collective mentality could be said to be concerned with symbolizing raw phenomena, and its unconscious aspect to be concerned with something equally fugitive – imagery associated with once-potent symbolism – testing its significance in the present context. The function of the whole of art, and of his part in it, was summarized by Gabo in these remarks:

> To me therefore the main purpose of art is to participate in the creation of concrete images for all those empty symbols which either were empty from the beginning or became empty because the old images in them had lost their efficacy;[56]

and 'I insist on my right as an artist to construct *new* images and create *new* forms and to use *new* elements for a new pictorial language.'[57]

Read's reaction to this exposition was cautiously welcoming. It was, for example, quite in keeping with Read's unique view of Wordsworth as a classicist, constructing for himself an individual, though fragmented, reality; and it was also consistent with the modern scientist's claim to be concerned more with observing discrete events than with establishing hypothetical connections. It is a measure of Read's investment in the idea of a coherent framework of natural principles, apprehended aesthetically and bearing the profoundest implications for education and society,[58] though, that he had seemed prepared to contradict earlier beliefs. He seems to have entertained the idea that the significance of advanced aesthetic form would become increasingly apparent, to widening circles of people, reasonably quickly upon its realization. Gabo's correspondence, however, was permeated with evidence refuting this; and it was clear that his insistence firstly upon an individual significance in his discoveries, as well as, paradoxically, upon a collective effort of which they were a part, challenged the accepted view of the artist as a specialist with certain highly developed faculties, and led instead to the view that everyone should be an artist. This of course was another principle Read had generally been inclined to assert. So he noted that there was a fair degree of correlation between Gabo's definition, in particular of the image, and a similar hypothesis he himself had approached and had proposed on other occasions.[59] However, he cautioned against an apparent indiscipline implicit in Gabo's remarks (which his reference to Mondrian's pursuit of absolute values had been an attempt to counter). Read wrote to Gabo:

> I still think that one has to be careful in the use one makes of the world 'reality'. I don't want to reintroduce the Platonic or the Hegelian conception of reality: I don't believe in 'absolutes' in that sense. But I do believe that our freedom to create 'reality' is dependent on the observance of certain laws or disciplines. Just as, within the infinite variety of flowers ... one can discern a few simple but essential laws – that all their forms radiate from an axis (I speak in ignorance of the scientific facts). The very use of straight lines and curves rather than broken or sagging lines shows preference for certain physical laws.[60]

Thus, following Hepworth's tacit advice, Read reconciled Gabo's art with his own customary touchstone, nature; and this marked the point at which he accepted that even this extreme abstraction was predominantly intuitive. It is difficult to be certain how Read now evaluated Mondrian's work, but he did note that by excluding as completely *as possible* intuition, immediacy and irrationality from his processes Mondrian had positioned himself at the utmost extremity of the existential axis. At this extreme, where Read previously had suspected that Gabo resided, actions were conditioned almost exclusively by deliberation, with the minutest interference of intuition. Not quite at this extreme was the work of Gabo (Read later considered it even closer to the centre), which, he now accepted, was conditioned in a 'biological freedom',[61] that is, affected by his sensed perceptions of the formal, spatial, rhythmic and temporal properties of nature. Though they were poles apart, there was one important correspondence between the constructivism of Gabo and the activity of the superrealist, considered in the light of an observation Read made in the context of surrealism: art is an entering into dialectical activity. More than mere description or reportage, it is an act of renewal. It renews vision and language, but most essentially it renews life itself by enlarging the sensibility, and arousing some inkling of the possible forms of being.[62] Read spoke of Gabo's 'virtually creating a new language, a symbolic language of concrete visual images';[63] and this sense of discovering the *new* could be said to be the equal-opposite of the superrealist's sense of re*new*ing a defunct symbolism. Moreover – Read was becoming increasingly convinced of this – both the extreme abstractionist (even Mondrian, to some degree, though apparently quite against his will) and the extreme superrealist in this way manifested 'the life process', an organic vitalism, in their works.

In 1943 Read had been content to approach this phenomenon with arguments about the *comparison* of art and nature. Discussing the question of good form in art, he had proposed that it was necessary to find criteria outside the arbitrary preferences of human beings, and that the most obviously right sources of reference were in natural organisms. The patterns that appear in nature, in the growth of crystals, vegetation, bones and flesh, take on certain shapes and proportions that not only meet functional needs but also constitute the basic formal properties of art. The physical structure of the world, and the innumerable shapes that unimpaired growth assumes, depend upon numerical harmonies that are aesthetically satisfying. The regularity of the honeycomb, the spiral configuration of the shell, the cellular structure of the bone, the pear-shape of the liquid drop – if it were possible, he had said, to find the general laws which govern these, they would provide canons of form which might be applied to works of art. Art might then be defined as mankind's effort to achieve integration with the basic forms of the universe.[64]

In fact this was a reiteration of his earlier argument, then applied to supra-conscious abstraction, the exponents of which were said to be attuned to the rhythms and proportions underlying natural appearances. So for some time Read had been grappling with this fundamental question, first considering the matter of a correspondence in turn from the standpoints of art and nature. Then he had been encouraged by his gained understanding of Gabo's work to believe that an authentic art would be *organic in its own right*; and this had been reconfirmed by Barbara Hepworth's remarking that her sculptures seemed to evolve almost autonomously, according to laws of their own development. The phrase 'the life of forms'[65] most aptly described the combined forces of which she spoke – an intrinsic vitality, originating partly in the imagination and partly in the chosen materials, which seemed not only to dictate creative development, but also to continue radiating from completed works.[66] Thus Read would say initially, with some moderation, that 'nature provides a touchstone for all creative artists',[67] and later, approaching the immoderate conclusion, 'the order or form in a work of art is not prefabricated and super-induced: in some sense it originates in the act of creation. *It is an organic event, unfolding* . . . .'[68] In the mid 1940s, therefore, Read was inclined to believe that all specifically modern art was related. Though this was a more convincing argument when applied to the activities of the centre rather than those of either extreme, it could be said that all such art was 'organic', or, in other words, that all could be located within a theoretical dialectic, in which the most vigorous forms of art might have been expected to be those at the centre, constituting equal or near-equal interpenetrations of opposites. Read's publication of this model was overtaken by his greater attention to the ensuing theory of the organic; but before he became entirely preoccupied with the latter, he did express his former views in a handful of unco-ordinated essays. Writing these, which at first were attempts to locate the various practices of those English artists he knew well, he seems to have become satisfied that his framework was not merely a device for pigeon-holing, but a working dialectic. The critical factor here was the realization that Moore, Hepworth, Nicholson and Nash could not be positioned precisely within the system (as Mondrian and, for the time being, Gabo had been) for all four tended periodically to shift their ground.

As Read gradually came to terms with this shifting, his writing bore evidence that he had found himself in something of a minefield – so much of his work being devoted to the careful defining and redefining of the term 'reality'. As it had been in the correspondence with Gabo, this was a much-used word, carrying, in the current spate of writing, several meanings, objective and metaphysical. Read had maintained that abstract artists were in some way attuned to the vital currents of nature, and that their works were apprehensions of reality penetrating beyond accidental visual appearance. And in an appreciation of Nicholson's abstraction he had suggested that, in exactly this fashion, his paintings and reliefs related to nature, although 'being moulded not by sun and soil and all the elements which determine the specific forms of natural organisms, but rather by the senses of the artist reacting to plastic material', they collectively reflected nothing but the reality experienced by Nicholson.[69] This was quite different from his understanding of Gabo; and he saw a clear distinction (in 1948, when he made a lengthy reappraisal of Nicholson's work) between Gabo's insistence upon the *creation* of a new reality, Nicholson's sense of *reflecting* an awareness of reality behind given appearances,[70] and, indeed, Mondrian's *pursuit* of an ultimate reality, which Read now was convinced had been futile.[71] If Nicholson's approach, moreover, were considered to be valid (vitally necessary, Read had suggested, in view of the needs of the present society[72]) then how might Nicholson's frequent reversion to an art of depiction be explained – his resorting to more or less faithful representation of surface appearances which, in the popular view, was more 'realistic' than his other work? In his experimentation, Read said, Nicholson quite naturally, without conscious deliberation, arrived at the extremes of natural realism and abstraction; and such contemporaneous contrasts represented, not a contradiction, nor a dichotomy, but the same sensibility reacting with a different visual 'resonance'.[73] Nicholson was never entirely content with an impressionistic response to the visible world – he seemed to require a geometrical 'mooring' even in his naturalism; and he succeeded in combining the two, in differing ratios, according to the alternating attractions of abstraction and realism.[74]

Similarly, Hepworth's work was observed to range from uncompromising abstraction to an intense and dramatic visual realism; but she was not thought to be concerned with a blending of these tendencies so much as with the strict alternative. In a letter to Read she had written: 'Working realistically replenishes one's *love* for life, humanity and the earth. Working abstractly seems to release one's personality and sharpen the perceptions ....'[75]; and Read had grasped the idea of a mutually nourishing alternation. He said (though he deliberately excluded constructivism from this argument) that abstract art was in danger of degenerating into an academicism if the artist's store of visual experience were not constantly replenished. Working from direct observation of nature, of the human form, or even of the man-made, provided just this disciplined replenishment. So whereas Read said of Nicholson that an *interpenetration* of the supra-conscious and the conceptual was a desirable achievement, he also said contemporaneously, regarding Hepworth, that an *alternation* was desirable in any artist:

It is merely a change of direction, of destination. What is constant is the desire to create a reality, a coherent world of vital images. At one extreme that 'will to form' is expressed in the creation of what might be called *free* images . . . and at the other extreme the will to form is expressed in a selective affirmation of some aspect of the organic world.[76]

Hepworth drew Read an axial diagram[77] with at one side realism, symbols of the known, figures, hands, eyes, trees, and so forth; and at the other abstraction, symbols of the unknown, including erotic, pre-natal and primitive forms, dream images and childhood imagery. She said that her work might begin at either extremity, and that a transition, if or when it occurred, far from being a matter of choice or predetermination, would happen autonomously, during the course of creative development. An initially abstract process might lead to a shape containing recognizable traces – eye-like hollows, perhaps, or hand-like forms; and drawing landscape might liberate ideas for abstract carving. Hepworth's account of such abstract working, in which she felt herself 'in the grip of an emotion . . . pursuing the unknown form to hold it',[78] and her descriptions of unconscious abstract symbolism, resembled greatly Read's conception of superrealism: they would also have reinforced arguments that the polarities of art were so related and yet so opposed that a resolution was imminent and certain. Read saw the preparations for this in individual willingness to range between the two; observing, however, that for the most part such ranging had been partial, he was suddenly filled with doubt that the opposing tensions could or indeed should be reconciled.[79] Nicholson's work was sometimes more abstract, sometimes more visually realistic; and Hepworth now made the pure abstraction, and now the naturalistic representation.

Paul Nash had also explored this territory: in other phases, however, he had participated in the superrealist dynamic, and his work had then ranged between the conceptual and the unconscious. In 1934 he had tried to found an English school of art dedicated, if not to abstraction and superrealism in themselves, at least to 'design, considered as a structural pursuit, and imagination, explored apart from literature and metaphysics'.[80] Later he had exhibited with the surrealists; and in 1939, in a letter to Read,[81] he had confessed himself perplexed at being urged, by others of the English Surrealist Group, to resign his membership because a current exhibition of his work in London contained surrealist paintings, naturalistic landscapes and ostensibly constructivist compositions. Read saw nothing wrong in such diversity: retrospectively he said of Nash's work that there was no real contradiction between art conceived as design and the unconscious 'which reveals design'.

A cubist still-life, an English landscape, a surrealist vision: these were not so many irreconcilables, but rather manners or media in which an artist could express his vision. The constant factor in Nash's ambivalence, Read observed, was a fascination for natural objects. He would collect strangely shaped stones, streaked pebbles, dried lichens, fragments of bark, pressed leaves; and these would serve for realistic representation, for imaginative juxtaposition in the still-life, and also as stimulants of phantasy, their shapes combining to form 'ideal landscapes of magical significance'.[82] He was capable of passing from one use to another of such natural objects without apparent effort, and in each phase of his creative activity he remained the same personality, manifesting the same essential qualities in his work.[83] Nash would now respect the outer world of perceptions, now attempt the structured response, and now release the irrational response; and this was a more extensive venturing than that which had engaged Nicholson and Hepworth. It perhaps indicated the existence of a front extending from abstraction to superrealism, the three English artists having traversed it or partially traversed it almost at will. Read had already perceived specifically modern art as an unbroken series, with the work of such as Moore, which he could not confidently associate with either extreme, occupying middle ground; but this was clearly inconsistent with his latest thoughts, for Moore's art was not faithful to natural appearances. However, putting aside for a while the question of how Moore's art (or, for that matter, Gabo's) related, it could be speculated with regard to Nicholson and Hepworth that

> In certain cases it seems possible for an individual to alternate between the extremes represented by this polarity – to tend in one psychological phase towards an affirmation of the world which results in a naturalistic style, and in another psychological phase towards a rejection of that world, which results in an abstract style of art.[84]

And in effect extending this argument to accommodate Nash, Read envisaged the possibility of a periodic, complete alternation between the two extremes abstraction and superrealism.[85]

The work of Henry Moore exhibited such complete alternation. In 1936 and 1937, for example, he had shown work with the surrealists and had been counted among the constructivists; but his creative process seemed far too complex to be characterized simply by the idea of a ranging sensibility. Apart from in his brief excursions to the extremities of the front, he had usually made objects which seemed to fuse the abstract and the superreal – that is, he appeared mainly to occupy the centre. But Read's axis now consisted of abstraction-naturalism-superrealism; and this obviously would not hold Moore's art as a central feature unless it could be considered a *synthetic resolution* of the equal-opposites, belonging, as such, to an advanced condition of art. Read looked to whether this might be supported in his knowledge of Moore's development. He knew that he had a great commitment to natural objects as a means of giving ideas about sculptural form: as early as 1930 Moore had generalized that the sculptor's formal under-standing would come 'from nature and the world around him, from which he learns such principles as balance, rhythm, organic growth of life, attraction and repulsion, harmony and contrast';[86] and in 1934 he had said that the principles of form and rhythm discovered in certain natural objects might properly be employed in sculptures of like materials – the forms found in pebbles, for instance, would be appropriate to stone-carving, and weathered timber would offer similar insights into wood-carving. In addition he had noted that 'trees show principles of growth and strength of joints, with easy passage of one section into the next' and, again to generalize about the principles of structuring, 'bones have marv-ellous structural strength and hard tenseness of form, subtle transi-tion of one shape into the next and great variety in section.'[87] In pursuit of these interests in the 1930s Moore had filled numerous notebooks with studies of bones, stones, shells and weathered wood; and a great many of his finished works overtly manifested organic properties.

On the subject of abstraction Moore had said in 1930 that an art devoid of representational imagery, analogous with music and architecture, could be regarded as a legitimate objective.[88] In 1934 he had enlarged this argument, suggesting that non-figurative art might offer deeper penetrations into reality than might the imitative.[89] Ten years later, having explored to some extent the possibilities of total abstraction, conversing with the International Constructivists[90] (and also having contributed to the two major international exhibitions of surrealism, in London and in New York), he demonstrated that his excursions did not imply a retreat from reality by allowing his work to enter a naturalistic phase, the products of which were the drawings he made in coal-mines and deep air-raid shelters for the War Art Commission. So within his previous development Moore's researches had ranged, as Read now observed,[91] between the abstract, the naturalistic and the superreal. Moore agreed that his interests lay – in the forms which inspired him – in intangible matters underlying visible appearances. He had said that he recognized the importance of 'universal shapes', such as rounded forms, to which he believed people responded subconsciously, by association;[92] and Read elaborated this, drawing upon psychology (though not that of Freud to which, as a surrealist, he had subscribed, but now to the theories of Jung). Read said that certain forms explored by Moore arrested the attention because they were 'biologically significant', the objects of a collective unconscious response.

> Our attention is held by the contour of a particular hill, by the shape of a rock or a tree stump or a pebble we pick up on the beach. These shapes appeal to us, not because of any superficial beauty, any sensuous texture or colour, but because they are archetypal. That is to say, they are the forms which matter assumes under the operation of physical laws.

When these forms are regular, Read said, their appeal is easily explained using terms such as 'proportion' and 'harmony'.

> But most of these shapes are more complex and irregular, and we are not consciously aware of the processes which have determined their outline or mass . . . . The beauty of a bone [or] a fungus . . . is not [immediately] obvious. But the appeal of the unknown is often stronger than the appeal of the known: it is strong because it is mysterious, because it has not been dissected and analysed. We invest such forms with our own feelings, of sympathy or of fear.[93]

Read saw that Moore frankly resorted to such forms, not to reproduce them literally, but to recombine them and distort them. At

100

one and the same time he might be concerned to reveal the 'hidden reality', to court symbolic significance, to explore the constructive nature of his material, and (even if his technique was reductive) to allow his formal concept to grow as if it were an 'organism'. For these reasons – combining as it did constructive principles, a sensed perception of nature, a respect for unconscious symbolism, and a kind of sculptural automatism – his work could be called neither abstract nor superreal. The most apt description of Moore's art was 'organic'; and for a while Read was tempted to look for sculptural distinctions between 'the organic' and 'the constructive'.[94] However, no doubt assisted by Hepworth's view that Gabo's constructivism was also in a sense organic, he did not pursue this very far. Instead he observed that the reciprocal currents in Moore's art would correlate exactly with those in the model of mentality derived largely from Freud – in which an authentic, creative resolution would occur in the shallow-unconscious, initiated both by conscious and deep-unconscious promptings. He noted that Moore frequently returned to life-drawing as a means of refreshing his inventiveness, and that he too was a compulsive collector of weather-worn objects, pebbles and bones. In his sketchbooks he allowed creative form to emerge incidentally from the data of his perceptions.

> But in later drawings an almost opposite process takes place; a given form is broken down, allowed to suggest associative forms and fantasies. If the first process may be called *crystallization*, this might be called *improvisation*. It is another aspect of the opposition between constructivism and superrealism which (Moore) is always seeking to synthetize.[95]

Read, therefore, was prepared to argue that Moore was engaging a synthetic resolution of mental and stylistic polarities, and thus to beg the question of whether he was unique in this respect, or indeed in the vanguard of a general movement. He had previously acknowledged Gabo's constructivism to be of 'the highest point ever reached by the aesthetic intuition of man'; and more recently he had endorsed Gabo's beliefs that he was materializing new, real experience, as he thought by participating in a collective mental effort, and that his (popularly abstract) art was the only art properly 'realistic'.[96] So, according to a combined understanding of Gabo and Moore, the catalyst of which had been Hepworth's vivid description of the transitional nature of her own creativity, Read now would maintain that an advancing art was the product of the artist's respecting the reciprocal tensions, while at the same time asserting his right to create reality to himself:

> Somewhere in this psychic shuttle . . . freedom intervenes – the freedom to create a new reality. Only on that assumption can we explain any form of evolutionary development in human consciousness, any kind of spiritual growth. A novelty-creating freedom exists by virtue of the intensity generated by aesthetic awareness; an evolutionary advance emerges from the act of expression.[97]

Gabo's art could not be said to have obviously flirted with abstraction and superrealism; but it was in the forefront because of its 'new realism'. And though Moore did not proclaim the 'new reality' of his work, Read recognized in it evidence of a dialectical advance.

Read continued to see certain correspondences between Moore's art and the work of Picasso, but he was disinclined to make similar claims for the latter, preferring to say that though it had once been 'revolutionary' it could not be considered 'evolutionary'.[98] Dominant characteristics displayed now for more than a decade, especially in the vast number of canvases Picasso had painted in his wartime isolation, had suggested that his work had become polarized, and quite opposed, for example, to that other non-evolutionary form of art which had preoccupied Mondrian. It has been suggested[99] that Read was overawed by Picasso's genius, and that here was the reason for his virtual neglect of him. It may be more appropriate, however, rather to suppose that Read was perplexed at what he believed he had witnessed – a transposition of revolutionary zeal and fixity of purpose. Read was in no doubt that Picasso *had* rare genius: he appreciated his delving well beneath consciousness, bringing forth images often deeply disturbing, reflecting as they did deep-seated social stress and conflict.[100] But Picasso's approach seemed now inflexible, conveying little sense of Read's reciprocal 'improvisation' – the beginning with a formal concept, reducing it and linking *back* with unconscious imagery.

As Read in effect viewed the conclusions towards which his survey of modern art had drawn him, therefore, he saw that he had distinguished between those artists who, once revolutionary, had maintained this state of mind, and others who were creating a new convention of sensibility, more in keeping with contemporary consciousness. He had omitted from his vanguard such former revolutionaries as Picasso, Braque, Leger, Chirico, Ernst, Matisse, Mondrian and others,[101] who had exacerbated the abstract-super-real contradiction (he would not call them late reactionaries, but observed that in 'the ceaseless unfolding of existence' it was reactionary to stand still[102]); and he had concerned himself more with those of the second generation, who had been willing to range between extremes as a preliminary to some sort of synthesis. It was true that Moore had ranged less frequently than others, and that Gabo had hardly deviated at all. But the special purposes of these were at the centre of Read's logic; so whereas Moore's work in particular convinced him that he might envisage 'an inclusive ambivalent attitude, a taking-into-oneself of the complete dialectical process',[103] the works of Nicholson, Hepworth and Nash gave evidence of the preconditions of resolution. The various resonances of man's apprehension of the world, he said,

> may perhaps be arranged along a polar axis, with transcendental metaphysics at one end and an intense self-awareness of physical vitality at the other end. It is along the same axis that we can place abstraction and [super]realism[104] in art. But . . . choice is not imposed on the individual artist. The axis exists *within* the individual artist, if only he can become conscious of it.[105]

At the same time he indicated a willingness to speculate that a theory of the organic might supersede his present dialectical scheme. In jotted notes he wrote that the whole scope of art would be extended if it were recognized to be, instead of an interpenetration of sensuous symbolism and intellectual idealism, the *direct expression of an organic vitalism* such as typified in certain works by Moore.[106]

Such organic vitalism engaged fundamental questions of *existence*, and here it seemed that the artist's choice was between adopting an essentially joyful or celebratory ontology, and adopting one of pessimism or dread.[107] These contradictions, as Worringer had taught, would bear upon even an advanced creativity. In other words, the temporary state of equilibrium attained by Moore and by Gabo did not imply inertia, for in some sense their works were mutually antagonistic.[108] Collectively their art was an intimate response to the vagarious natural ambience (enlarging the term 'natural' now to embrace social, economic and cultural phenomena[109]): in particular it was a most sensitive register of philosophical currents. And there was no justification in modern philosophy for regarding synthesis as stasis:

> A synthesis is merely the meeting place of two ideas, and from their conjunction arises a new idea. But each new idea is in its turn a thesis which merges into an endless dialectical chain, and the only finality is something we agree to call the Truth, which seems to recede with every step we take towards it.[110]

Chapter 5
Anarchy and Order

In his late schooldays, and in his time served at the bank, Read's political instincts had been conservative. In his distant memories he glimpsed a governess and other servants; and he retained images of his parents dressed in their finery for the annual Hunt Ball. He had become aware of reduced circumstances, and of not belonging to the class of life in which he had found himself. In late adolescence, however, he came to reject his own myth of family prestige, and began to realize that the benefits of his early life had had little to do with financial security. They had been inherent in his father's work, and above all in its location – a remote and beautiful countryside which had escaped the worst excesses of the Industrial Revolution. In this frame of mind he read the nineteenth-century social and aesthetic reformers. He joined the Leeds Arts Club, which contained a number of followers of Arthur Penty, who himself had called for restoration of the guild system as the means of abolishing exploitation of the working poor;[1] and he subscribed to *The New Age* throughout the period of Orage's most persistent promotion of guild-socialism[2] as a socialist alternative to Fabianism. Read had found this so acceptable that by 1917, in his letters home from the war, he was proposing his own version of a guild-socialist future. He differed with the Fabians, as did Orage, on the question of materialism – with their concentration upon improving wages and conditions, and increasing workers' share of goods, at the expense of those humanist or spiritual benefits, the goals of the nineteenth-century reformers. He could see no possible value in the simple transference of industry and commerce, along with ingrained capitalism, to a government's control, however

beneficent. This is not to say that he was entirely in accord with
Morris, though, for, his experience having been rural, he felt less
anxious about restoring a 'dignity of labour' to those engaged in
repetitive production. In his memory even the most severely explo-
ited had had satisfaction of working with the land, with growth
and harvest, and with animal husbandry; and even the meanest
task had been acknowledged periodically in thanksgivings, seasonal
festivities, and other forms of common celebration. So though he
was precious little better-off than the industrial poor when he lived
in Leeds (and though he had come to know something of the
sweated manufacture of clothing in that city),[3] his dominant images
of work were of hard toil cheerfully endured in the countryside,
of industrial processes perhaps centred upon the forge or smithy,
and of forms of urban employment housed in small-scale machine
sheds – in short, Read's was an imagery very similar to Kropotkin's, whose anarchist writings he had already digested.

His differences with Orage, Penty, and with 'official' guild-socialism, when eventually he came to express them, resided chiefly in
the soldier's priority to end threats of any repetition of the war he
was engaged in. He had entered the fighting readily enough, and
had been decorated twice for bravery;[4] but, in common with many
others as the reality of war became more and more horrifying, he
began to think it tolerable only because it would lead to an inevitable internationalism. The role of politics would be to assist this
transition; and in this sense true guild-socialism, with its emphasis
upon crudely local government, would be as resistant as conservatism. In his idealism Read proposed a pattern of economic group-
ings based not upon geographic divisions but upon industries and
production interests: in rural areas these probably *would* have been
localized, but the world's urban centres would have formed such
an interlocked system of economic dependence as to have made
any future international conflict impossible. He saw the existing
trade unions and industrial federations as prototype economic
groups which, with only a little more purpose, could be the regula-
tors of an international economy; and like the Marxists he could
foresee the withering of the State, though if not into non-existence,
at least to a size commensurate with its remaining responsibilities
– as 'the organ of spiritual activity' or 'the patron of a new art',
on 'the threshold of a new age'.[5]

Read's future political persuasions would range across the whole band of socialist philosophies, but always his beliefs would have roots in these early convictions: another war is unthinkable; the state has no economic purpose; and the ideal form of government is one which guarantees utmost equality while preserving individual freedoms – in particular a person's right (to a large extent ignored, Read thought, by philosophical anarchists) to detach himself from his native community-interests. This is precisely what had happened to him by accident; and it clearly both exhilarated and depressed him, as the very few 'political' thoughts he expressed in writing, while he was bound by the conventions of an apolitical civil service, make clear. These may be understood as an apologia for his having become divorced from the locality to which he properly belonged, for his having found a *role* outside the functioning of this agricultural community, and for having become an atheist, while accepting the fundamental importance of religion in the cycles of life he had left behind him. His position was summarized in a critical appreciation of Julien Benda's book *La Trahison des Clercs*,[6] in which a series of propositions were found to be so strikingly familiar that they came as self-revelations.

All real existence is the existence of an individual, either that of an isolated being or of a cohesive common-interest group. Individual existence, being essentially self-affirmation in the presence of competing entities, is necessarily aggressive. The 'clerc', or disinterested man of learning, is one who protests against a morality of aggression by honouring ideal values revealed in his contemplation of matters abstract, universal, eternal and infinite. Civilized humanity is made possible by the coexistence and synthesis of these two elements. A world observing only a lay morality, or a morality of practical necessity, would be barbarous: one which only practised a morality of ideals would cease to exist. Real existence admits the gradual civilization of communities, though these usually recover in time to avoid an over-softening of their necessary aggression.

Here was the autobiographical rural or common-interest community, and the dislocated individual, leading an ostensibly unproductive life, who, however, had the special purpose of divining principles which might be offered back for the common benefit (as Read had felt compelled to do when he had attempted to project from afar a Yorkshire Literary Movement). In this, his most classic phase, he would quite naturally – without a trace of self-conceit – distinguish between the refined aesthetic sensibility of the 'clerc' and the gratuitous, naive sentimentality of the masses; and by a combination of Hulme's and Benda's hypotheses he would see a clear division between matters human and absolute, bridgeable only by the imaginative perceptions of capable 'clercs'. At this time in his life, therefore, the goals of aesthetic contemplation were formal precision, harmony, and elegant proportion, as would befit a mind withdrawn from an 'ordinary' existence.[7] In his last years at the Victoria and Albert Museum he worked on a manuscript which was primarily a defence of the abstract artist, an individual similarly removed from ordinariness, whose researches into pure form were crucial to both the aesthetic and the commercial wellbeing of the community. This was published later under the title *Art and Industry* (1934) – that is, when once more he felt free to express views forbidden to a civil servant, but at the point at which an exclusively classic view was no longer tenable to him. This slightly perverse act was made justifiable by his introducing a distinction between abstract art, finding its purpose in industrial design or 'the means of life', and a humanist or romantic counterpart, nearer to the popular sympathies and expressing itself as 'the ends of life'.[8]

This distinction marked Read's departure from classicism and his relinquishment, too, of guild-socialism, for it was made expressly as a criticism of Arthur Penty, now advocating a clear separation of art and industry as the way of social regeneration. *His* arguments were that contemporary art accepted, and to some extent condoned, the ugliness which characterized modern industry, and that for artists entirely to throw in their lot with such sources of inspiration would result in an irrevocable loss of proper spiritual values. He wanted artists to cease participation in industry so that, deprived of a cosmetic, its full ugliness would be exposed: this would lead to its decline, to regeneration of the crafts, and to the re-emergence of forms of art which were 'leisurely and contemplative'.[9] Read was intolerant of this reactionary thinking; and when he identified what, as a matter of faith, he wished to preserve of guild-socialism, he was emphatic about revolutionary intentions. In fact for a brief period he held Marxian sympathies:[10] these were hinted at in his next book, *Art and Society*, which he wrote during the academic year 1935–6,[11] and they were spelled-out most clearly in correspondence with Wyndham Lewis (in an effort to say that failure to support communism was tacit acceptance of its antithesis, fascism). It seemed obvious that communism and fascism were about to contest for domination of Europe, and that even if Britain were not directly involved, individuals at least would be obliged to take sides. Though he recognized the repressive state capitalism that was the Russian reality,[12] Read was prepared if necessary to countenance communism, for he saw in it an essence, certainly not present in fascism, which held promises of the abolition of bourgeois capitalism and of respect for disinterested ideals.[13]

What prevented his becoming a communist was the movement's anti-aesthetic doctrine, in spite of all Marx had said to the contrary, and its antipathy towards all realities of art except the ones it had contrived.[14] Following this line of thought, the most prominent themes of *Art and Society* were that the modern artist, conscious of an ability to transform the world by his visions of a new reality, was a more consistent communist than those, so-called, who would compromise with the aesthetic and moral conventions of a last phase of capitalism, and that the greatest art of the past had belonged to communal societies.[15] Read thus looked to the anthropology of primitive, collective societies for his supporting arguments – that is, to an anthropology the status of which had been transformed by Marx. Here he found evidence of three distinct creative tendencies.[16] First, there was 'disinterested decoration' of utensils and other artefacts, communal in so far as it seemed to have been a response to a general aversion for unadorned surfaces. He identified this with Worringer's northern art, but in place of a climatic explanation he ventured a psychological one – it was a countering of '*horror vacui*'. Second, came its complete opposite, abstract simplification and reduction to pure formal symbolism, a tendency communal and collectively significant in its customary or ritualistic aspects. And he recognized, third, a more or less distorted representation of natural phenomena, an art individual and expressive, yet communal also in the sense that it always eventually *became* generally acceptable and representative.[17]

It may not be unfair to suggest that these findings were shaped, to a large extent, by what he was seeking – for some correlation between his 'authentic' forms of plastic art (disinterested abstraction; pure or geometric symbolism; distorted representation) and the common aesthetic wellbeing, and for a consistency of such principles extending to contemporary art. He now believed he had found confirmation of such endurance in another of Freud's hints at unanswered questions. Freud appeared to have been nagged by the thought that he had made too little use of what seemed to him to be true – that unconscious phenomena remained unaltered by the passage of time. Read took this to suggest that the unconscious region to which the artist, by his work, was given access was a region of timeless entities; and this explained the universal appeal of all authentic art – for what was timeless was by the same token universal[18] – and also excused Read's overlapping of Freudian and Jungian principles in the context of a collective, archetypal mental heritage. So the artist, he said (and the poet and disinterested man of letters), stood in 'psychological opposition' to the mass, drawing upon a store of common unconscious phenomena, assimilating his gains first to a very small circle, and through this indirectly to wider groups, ultimately effecting a culture. But – and this is what restrained the scale of his theory and preserved the essentially anarchistic nature of his convictions – whatever unconscious phenomena were collective were also subject to subtle, but extremely important, regional or local variations. There seemed to be good evidence in the history of ideas and beliefs to say that whenever ideologies had been transplanted they had adapted to the prevailing conditions they had encountered – those emanations of the soil and weather, climate and habitat, which were the principal formers of spiritual and aesthetic outlooks.[19] Read himself felt an affinity for abstraction through the intermedium of the northern art of his celtic and viking ancestors; but he now saw that his innate love of restless, linear and curvilinear abstraction was distinct from the taste for pure formal geometry, which he had cultivated.

He hesitated to use the term 'anarchism' to describe his ideal socio-political condition, because it conjured up images of cloaked figures with home-made bombs; but in the end he decided that there was no choice. Communism, in its Russian form, had shored up the state and its bureaucracies, while Fabian socialism was materialistic; and the new socialist urban design in Britain was largely soulless,[20] while at the other extreme guild-socialist prescriptions featured a soulful mock-medievalism, and required returns to hand production in all sections of industry. And Read could not envisage buying freedom of local action at the price of slavery to manual labour. So his political re-emergence was into anarchism, in spite of the fact that he knew he thus forfeited any general, serious acceptance of his views. And for twenty or more years, after 1935, he would be the most passionate spokesman for this cause, giving every appearance of representing an official movement, to which, however, he never belonged.[21] This would have been to subsume his individual beliefs; and in any case he was suspicious of the pseudo-proletarian attitudes adopted by many of anarchism's intellectual adherents. He enjoyed reminding himself that he belonged to yeoman stock;[22] but he was always conscious of detachment from agricultural life, and still more from the artificiality and meaninglessness of industrial existence. He hoped he spoke to ordinary people, but would not presume to speak *for* them.

His evolutionary instincts proscribed an agenda for revolution, as they did all kinds of predetermined futures; but he did occasionally give glimpses of ambitions[23] which he knew were unlikely to be realized in the forms he gave them. These included the redundancy of central government, political power effected locally, financial power withdrawn from individuals, and productive labour honoured as the prerequisite of civilized life.[24] His elementary economic fact was a man cultivating the earth,[25] an appropriate metaphor for his own life's work.

One privilege he did admit was the right of advancement by qualification or increased expertise, for this would benefit communities as well as individual social-standing. The only other was the right of detachment from immediately productive work on the part of artists and intellectuals. Perhaps because this was autobiographical it was the feature of his thought he found most difficult to justify. Such individuals were needed for their 'disinterested vision'; but there had to be safeguards against proliferations of visionaries too great to be supported by productive labour, and one of the responsibilities of art teachers, for example, would be to differentiate between an education of positive, creative capabilities in the few who would be initiators, and of taste, discrimination and sound appreciation in the many who would be consumers. These uneasy thoughts were soon displaced by 'everyman a special kind of artist'.[26]

The transition is apparent in a work Read began in 1940. He spent two years on this, an academic treatise, and another on its revision for publication under the title *Education through Art*.[27] It was one of the very few books he wrote seriatim; and as in *Form in Modern Poetry* its immediacy embodied drastic changes of heart. At its outset Read may be imagined as possessing certain longstanding beliefs – that there were distinctions in kind between the creative sensibilities of the few who were artists, 'clercs' or disinterested men of learning, and of the many who were naive and sentimental in matters of taste.[28] The purpose of a general, creative education, as he had only recently elaborated in *Art and Society*, was to help the many towards an understanding of what the few were striving for, so that authentic, creative forms might be more readily acceptable, and thus better-diffused throughout the culture. In *Art and Society* the artist was still an exceptional individual, an otherwise-neurotic who had chanced upon ways of evading this fate by expressing potentially repressed phantasy in plastic or literary form. And the masses either had neuroses of their own which could be cured by better housing, reformed industrial practices, or a more widespread distribution of well-designed goods, or else they possessed untroubled mental personalities because of their closeness to the soil and natural processes. In *Education through Art* everyone – that is, every child – is a potential neurotic who may be saved from this prospect if early, largely inborn, creative abilities are not repressed by conventional education. Everyone is thus an artist of some kind, whose special abilities, even if almost insignificant, must be encouraged as contributing to an infinite richness of collective life.

What caused this change in outlook was, in Read's own words, 'something in the nature of an apocalyptic experience'.[29] He had been collecting many hundreds of children's drawings and paintings in aid of his research,[30] and in the course of this he had come across an image drawn by a five-year-old girl, which she called 'Snake around the World and a Boat'. He was deeply moved, he said, upon immediately recognizing this circular, segmented image to be a 'mandala', an ancient symbol of psychic unity, universally found in prehistoric and primitive art and in all the principal cultures of history. The child, of course, could not attach meaning to what she had done; but Read, aware for some time of what until now had been merely an interesting hypothesis, was shocked to find phenomenal proof of Jung's archetypal imagery. He said this experience redirected the course of his life:[31] it undoubtedly encouraged him to accept the majority of Jung's teaching, to retain interest in only those elements of Freud's theories that were compatible with Jung's, and to feel justified in looking to child art for confirmation of his anarchistic beliefs. He found an astonishing consistency, in children's art, of symbols Jung had associated with an archaic heritage;[32] and this had several effects. It encouraged him to regard prehistoric art as a touchstone of authenticity, and to see modern art as a much condensed repetition of archaic patterns in transition; and it prompted an over-enthusiastic, strict comparison of child art and the 'authentic' art of relatively recent avant-gardes. (In later editions of *Education through Art* he removed several injudicious references to a child art which was 'impressionist'.[33]) Much more important, however, an association of child art and Jungian theory affected the status of art teaching, an activity considered generally to be peripheral to the fundamental business of education. It gave meaning and new purpose to the work of many thousands of art teachers: instead of merely assisting hobbyist or recreational skills, their role would be to help integrate innate creative abilities with the levels of intellection demanded in a modern world, for the sake of individual equipoise and wellbeing, and also, through this, for the health of a collective social harmony. The potential for success in such aspirations was evident in Read's observation that children, quite naturally, give forth imagery which maintains contact with the deepest levels of social experience, and with times when social cohesion was the normal order. A corollary, which armed the art teachers and explains the enormous, immediate success of his book,[34] was that the present defects of social life – injustice, immorality, harsh competition, even war – had roots in prevailing systems of education and, specifically, in an emphasis upon intellectual development *to the exclusion of all other faculties* visited on children from around the age of ten. Because of this the infant with inborn access to ancient, collective experience became a rootless ten-year-old and a centre of self-interest. What passed for liberal education was nothing more than systematic repression, the elimination of which would give rise to recovery of individual, and also more-than-individual, social health.

The social organism was thus presented as a macrocosm of mentality; and in this context Freud's model of individual mind, which was essentially diagnostic, was of much less use to Read than Jung's, which was remedial or therapeutic. An extremely revealing sequence of diagrams, each superseded by the next, in

Read's initial draft of *Education through Art*, shows quite clearly his rejection of an analysis of mind which merely located repressions in favour of ones which emphasized their elimination. But what finally converted Read from predominantly Freudian to Jungian sympathies was the principle of a dynamic unconscious. He had always sought endorsement of his own speculation in both quarters, but now became aware that the signs he had found encouraging had usually been more definite in Jung, and often barely implicit in the work of Freud. As he now began to meet Jung regularly, and to discuss his life's work with him in detail,[35] he found him favourable towards anarchistic ramifications of his theories, and discovered that practically from the outset of his career he had believed (what Read thought Freud had always disputed) that the unconscious mind possessed capacities for autonomous creativity. He wrote an outline biography of Jung,[36] largely for his own information, though it formed the basis of several future published essays;[37] and at various times he submitted it to Jung's critical appraisal. It consisted largely of interpretation – that is, it dwelt on matters of which Read needed Jung's substantiation; and in practically all respects it gained Jung's acceptance and his admiration.[38] Though Read would sporadically continue to use Freudian theory as if by habit, the newly found closeness of thought would ensure that for the remainder of his life he would be, in all major respects, a follower of Jung. These were the principal beliefs divined by Read in their conversations, and it may be seen that they were as much his own as Jung's. In fact delight in their correspondence seems to have been mutual.

Human life is lived according to some general directed aim or purpose (as well as by the principle of causality, a chief feature of Freud's hypothesis). Life is drawn onwards, and individual actions are significant for a future which cannot be foreseen, and are explicable only when the final effects of impulses-to-action become evident. In other words, life has meaning as well as explanation – a meaning never *finally* discoverable because of its continuous extension by the processes of evolution. Unconscious mental activity is the generating force: whereas conscious thought is tactical, geared to immediacy and self-interest, unconsciousness is a purposive, directed stream of phantasy, working autonomously and creatively. And it is a continuous activity, to which the dream or the work of art or the meditative moment may only offer sample access

– such samples observed in sequence providing objective analysis of the flow in question. The unconscious elaboration of phantasy follows patterns unknown to waking consciousness, but it has a normal bias towards certain specific codes which are more-than-personal, that is, racial, collective and historical. In other words, because hope in the purposive value of life is a vital necessity, the unconscious has invented, over the ages, channels or moulds of thought by which human aspirations may be shaped. And the evolutionary movement forward is assisted by resulting symbolism, often far in advance of the general sensibility and also resistant to intellectual analysis. There can be no *standard* symbols, as there are in Freudian psychology, but rather predispositions, according to which unconscious processes may arrange themselves.[39]

The most significant of these, to Read, was the predisposition towards the 'mandala', to the conception of images embodying obviously unified shapes – intricate patterns often in the form of a flower, or some other four-fold arrangement, with a distinct centre, the appearance of an unfolding, and a gathering perimeter. Especially in Eastern philosophy, though also for example in Christian iconography, these had been held to symbolize collective thought and mutual belonging. Other archetypes which gave Read shocks of recognition were the tendency to fabricate a Dark Shadow from all aspects of a personality opposed to those personified in the self; and the tendency to protest against isolation, individuation and independence by creating mother-images, earth-forms, and other symbols of dependence. All of these – a fixing upon abstract unities; a collation of personality traits specifically outside of the self; the celebration of maternity; an acknowledgment of belonging to the land – all of these projections-beyond-self, Read thought, were fundamentally anarchistic. Moreover, objectified in creative works which he knew very well indeed – the mandala in Gabo's constructions; the Dark Shadow in his own novel *The Green Child*; maternal and terrestrial forms respectively in Moore's and Hepworth's sculpture – they helped substantiate Jung's demand for a reconciliation of individuals and the group. In effect Gabo, Read, Moore and Hepworth here were 'leaders', standing apart from ordinary people, guiding the collective unconscious into normal patterns of aspiration and behaviour, and away from sinister aspects of group psychology (mass hysteria, nationalistic pride, dumb subservience to the state) to which the unnatural mode of modern life had left men prone. This was Read's unsolicited, though in the event welcomed, attempt to extend and complement Jungian thought:[40] whereas Jung had stated the necessity for reconciliation of individual and group, while merely being able to warn against diversions towards unhealthy outcomes, Read could say that a widespread, 'natural' creativity would itself ensure a natural reconciliation.

It obliged him to consider whether all forms of art were necessarily normal or natural; and a recurrent theme in his later work would be a question he had already hinted at in *Education through Art*, of whether certain prevailing forms of expression, of undoubted value to particular individuals, were of minor significance, or even of detriment, to society at large. In the present circumstances of neglect there had to be considerable regaining, perfecting and balancing of individual creative abilities – even a healing of some which had been perverted – before there could be social cohesion. So in the short term there was needed a vanguard of individuals, maintained by the community for its expertise in extending aesthetic awareness, to set necessary examples of equipoise and direction: in the longer term, however, because of a teaching revolution centred upon creative learning, in a real sense all members of the community would be creators. This explains another of Read's apparent simultaneous contradictions. He demanded a 'crusade' to revivify the arts, and encourage the most widespread participation, by patronage of central government;[41] and at the same time maintained that the only enduring culture would have piecemeal beginnings. He wrote:

> So we must begin with small things, in diverse ways, helping one another, discovering one's own peace of mind, waiting for the understanding that flashes from one peaceful mind to another. In that way the separate cells will take shape, will be joined to one another, will manifest new forms of social organization and new types of art.[42]

Both of these objectives met, and were satisfied in, his efforts to found an Institute of Contemporary Arts in London. He was by no means unaided in this,[43] but for several reasons it seems right to see it as having been his brainchild. He had been attempting to achieve something of the sort since 1918, and had almost succeeded in 1939, before the war had deprived him of backing.[44] He was chairman of the new venture's steering committee, and when this stood down in 1947 he was elected President, a position he held until he died. In the steering committee's *Outline Policy Statement* his aspirations, as well as his own phraseology, are undisguised. Its signatories proposed an Institute which would be neither retrospective (there were enough museums) nor propagandist (there were sufficient national councils) but co-operative, experimental, creative and educational, for the benefit of the community. It would be co-operative in its aim to be a focus, for mutual support, of isolated and sporadic creative enterprises. It would be experimental in its efforts to promote rarefied forms of visual, plastic and musical sensibility, ignored in the profit-seeking galleries and concert halls. It would be creative in its search for new social expression; and it would undertake research in such diverse fields as anthropology and sociology – tasks which would assume great significance as events proceeded – in a programme projected towards 'the unknown dimensions of the art of the future'.[45]

Shortly after this statement was circulated in 1947 the ICA was tentatively established as an itinerant organization, meeting in the homes of its members and holding exhibitions in cinema premises. It was established firmly in 1950 when it occupied premises of its own in Dover Street in central London, where there began an almost daily programme of lectures, debates, readings, performances and exhibitions, which was to last uninterrupted until it moved on, some twenty years after the hesitant beginnings, to a more prestigious location in the Mall. While all were agreed about the Institute's primary purpose – to nurture contemporary arts in England – to Read it also offered possibilities of an anarchistic experiment, leading in however small a way towards his envisaged social system.[46] It was to this that he devoted a considerable proportion of his energies throughout the last quarter of his lifetime; and, approached with some understanding of his work in its late and most completed form, the two major preoccupations of the ICA will be seen as having been expressly required by his theorizing. One of these respected the idea of a great unifying force in contemporary life – modern science – demanding general expression and determining the Zeitgeist:[47] the other looked to anthropology for signs of an interrelatedness of collectivist societies and properly creative cultures.

The latter was considered important enough to have one of

117

the Institute's two inaugural exhibitions[48] devoted to it. This was concerned with certain identities of value and purpose discoverable in prehistoric and ancient art, the art of primitive peoples, and in all authentic art of modern times. (There were tendencies, in some quarters, to dwell upon irrelevant arguments about a modern imitation of primitive art,[49] but Read made clear his disapproval.) It was important to him to encourage acceptance of the idea of the universality of art, and of the eternal recurrence in western art, in spite of the attentions of academies, of certain phenomena – a vitality, a challenging potency, an active, sensually satisfying, even shocking symbolism – which were naturally present in the primitive.[50] In modern art there was a movement towards such elemental phenomena, he thought, evident as a great deal of striving for what was continuously out of reach. This was accompanied by a similar stumbling and unco-ordinated movement towards mutually aiding forms of social organization. Read now needed some discussion concerning the interdependence of the two. There was little argument but that they *were* interdependent, though there was room for disagreement about priority. It was a question of whether there were certain key aesthetic factors which, on their recurrence, initiated desirable social change, or whether, conversely, there were naturally enlightened forms of social organization which, whenever they were permitted to flourish, brought changing cultural patterns as of consequence. Siegfried Giedion and Arnold Hauser, respectively, brought these arguments to the ICA.[51]

Arnold Hauser spoke about stylistic similarities between the prehistoric and the modern and, specifically, about his concept of recurring creative tendencies. He compared, on the one side, a progression from naturalism to geometric abstraction in prehistoric art and, on the other, a corresponding sequence in the modern. He began by asserting that, contrary to the thoughts of others, naturalistic styles had preceded abstraction in prehistory; and he gave an interpretation of the beginnings of art, offered in the light of what was known about the modern. The most remarkable thing about prehistoric naturalism, he argued, was not that it was older than the geometric style, but that it revealed all the typical phases of the development of its modern counterpart. It had advanced from a linear faithfulness to nature, in which individual forms were shaped rigidly and laboriously, to a more tentative style which was almost impressionistic. The accuracy of drawing had risen to levels of virtuosity appropriate to mastering fleeting movements and gestures, and increasingly daring foreshortenings and intersections; and such accomplishments, subsequently practised for their own sake, had led towards a state of culture in which artistic formulae were established.[52]

This transition was the result of a gradual change in social conditions, from those of the Old Stone Age to those of the New.[53] The social condition of the Old was parasitic, that is, men lived by searching-out the useful – flints, fruits, game – and this promoted a keenness of perception since unknown. It seemed logical to suppose that men's perceptual abilities, honed by tracking, sighting and aiming, should be correspondingly efficient when giving definition to painted images: it seemed logical, too, to suggest some identity of 'perceiving in paint' and 'perceiving in actuality'. The circumstances of New Stone Age man, however, were more settled, agrarian, planned: because his efforts of husbandry were vulnerable to climatic and other factors he could not control, he developed animistic beliefs, and for him the world became divided into reality and superreality. These social distinctions constituted the main reasons why the paleolithic artist reproduced things true to life and reality, whereas the neolithic artist opposed ordinary reality with a stylized and idealized super-world. This, according to Hauser, was the onset of rationalization, 'the replacement of concrete pictures and forms by signs and symbols, abstractions and abbreviations, general types and conventional tokens'.[54] The work of art ceased to reflect direct experience, becoming instead the conveyor of an idea; and its pictorial content was reduced to pictographic shorthand. This condition enjoyed a stability which lasted over four thousand years, in relation to which all later geometric and classic movements seemed mere episodes. Creative stability was nurtured by an equally stable sociological condition, the result of homogeneous economy and social co-operation, which contrasted sharply with an individualism evident in preceding hunter societies and in succeeding, highly competitive eras. This gave rise to the argument that the transitional forms between naturalism and geometric superrealism had corresponded, and would correspond, with the intermediary stages between exploitative, or opportunist, and planned, productive economies.[55]

These were Hauser's arguments, and in a sense they were conventional wisdom at the ICA. They had obvious drawbacks, modelling as they did the art of thousands of years upon that of a mere century, comparing simple cultures with others of relatively infinite complexity, and assuming that modern creative advances were the result of enlightened social beliefs (rather than achievements). But they were in the air at the ICA even before Hauser gave them his authority: they were acceptable to many of the membership and, with some reservations, to Read himself, in so far as they linked certain forms of refined creativity with highly civilized modes of social organization. They were based upon a flawed understanding of prehistoric art, however, according to the alternative theory.

Siegfried Giedion interpreted the evidence of prehistoric art differently, no doubt partly because his own photographs of cave paintings, technically superior to existing documentation, had revealed details of handling and imagery previously unseen.[56] Giedion could not accept that a progression from naturalism to abstraction had been a consequence of a change from exploitative to productive economies in prehistory (or the projection of this argument upon a future society). He was concerned to say 'The need for abstraction is one of the constituent elements of the human spirit in every aspect of its expression'; and 'Like the symbol, abstraction came into being with the beginnings of art.'[57] Paleolithic animal paintings had actually been abstractions – ideals or standard types – the residues of countless sightings of different animals rather than the portraits of specific ones. In this they were characteristically similar to the works of certain pioneers of modern abstraction, which had concentrated the absolute essentials of object-types (bottles, glasses, pipes, musical instruments, and so forth) instead of reflecting individual or accidental aspects. True abstraction had returned to human consciousness, Giedion said, as soon as artists had tried to come to closer grips with reality than naturalistic representation permitted. This concentration of essentials had been connected with a new conception of space.[58]

Prehistoric art, then, had begun as abstraction, and had pursued developing phases of abstraction, attaining the particular condition known as abstract symbolism: a similar progression had occurred in modern art, beginning at the 'rebirth' around 1910. Both had started with a simplification of imagery, and a concentration upon essentials, in non-perspective, or almost non-perspective space. From this had derived a second kind of abstraction – the prehistoric having been echoed by twentieth-century constructivism – using forms which displayed no tangible evidence of 'starting point'. The work of Mondrian, beginning with naturalistic representation of seascapes and tree-forms and progressing towards pure formal expression, was a microcosm of such normal development. A third type had intermingled the 'objective' and the 'constructive', creating mixtures of transformed objects and abstract symbols such as now were evident in the works of Leger or Kandinsky. A most advanced abstraction, however, had attempted to superimpose or to interrelate simultaneously several different images, such as in the overlaying of many animals in the cave paintings at Lascaux, or in their modern counterparts – say Boccioni's *Unique Forms of Continuity in Space*, or in Duchamp's *Nudes Descending Stairs*. These works exemplified the assimilation of new experience, effected by fusing disparate, often contradictory, phenomena within the hybrid form.[59]

This most advanced abstraction, in which the highest achievements of the prehistoric and the modern artist met, suggested to Giedion that the determinants of authentic art were eternal, or more precisely recurrent, due to a periodic intensification of the need to reconcile certain opposed aspects of reality, which he called 'constancy' and 'change'. Constant was the human organism, in itself virtually fixed in a physical pattern, but subjected to an environment of restless change, and therefore engaged in a ceaseless effort to maintain equilibrium. Changing adjustments of an inner to an outer reality thus constituted the texture of history; and only rarely had humanity succeeded in achieving equipoise, manifested in moments of classic serenity.[60] Contemporary art was to be understood as a counteraction of aesthetic decline, and a regaining of cultural, and therefore social, stability. This dialectic, of course, was very similar to Read's, and it is obvious why he would have encouraged its dissemination at the ICA: along with Hauser's views, it emphasized a fundamental relatedness of society and art. So far as Read's own work was concerned, it may be seen that he drew strength from Giedion, and only quarrelled with his idea of an intrinsically *abstract* continuum, while also leaning to some slighter extent upon Hauser, reversing his argument and suggesting that some future, attainable, anarchistic society would result from an extension of aesthetic sensibility, most probably responding to a scientific – a creative scientific – Zeitgeist. In this way Read matched his convictions against others, though Giedion's hypoth-

121

esis seems to have afforded more than simple correlation, for there are traces of his thought in Read's immediate writings.

It seemed obvious, now, that human consciousness had arisen not merely from the perception of time, space, shape, number and other concepts as discrete phenomena, but from certain *significant arrangements* of these permitting comparisons and judgments.[61] In this sense the overlapping images at Lascaux (and those modern examples of Giedion's constancy and change combined) could be said to have served enlargement of experience, not only in their mastery of imagery, but also by encouraging 'unconscious but increasingly conscious' comparison of disparate perceptions.[62] The significant elements here would have been the image itself (specifically, at Lascaux, an accurate eidetic reproduction), the nature of an unconsciously emergent pattern of overlaid or proximate images, and *the use made of the pattern*, by which a new knowledge of the whole would have been qualitatively greater than an accumulated understanding of individual aspects. This would have involved not only the subsuming of discrete observations within the pattern or larger form, but also an ability, confined to rare individuals, to *stretch the pattern*,[63] which concept gave a new insight into 'aesthetic progress'. So whereas Read had consistently stressed the unchanging nature of an essential creativity (and the need, in deviant times, to swim against a tide of false art towards this essential authenticity), he now turned his attention to aspects of aesthetic activity which *had* changed and *were* changing – namely, its consequences. *Art and Society*, written just before his announced ambition to a dialectic theory, admitted of a creativity with polar tensions, the one or the other occasionally dominant, but relating to a single reality.[64] Interim writings followed upon sensed convictions about what a fusion of these opposites would promote – initially an advanced condition of art (a conclusion overtaken and unpublished) and then, more definitely, an advancement of human consciousness. And so in a sequence of lectures, published bearing the title *Icon and Idea* in 1955,[65] he engaged new definitions: art is pattern selection, combining discrete perceptions the more diametrically opposed the better; and great art is pattern extension, the creation of new synthetic percepts. *Art and Society*, then, had been a survey of the recognition, at certain times in history, of significant forms or patterns: *Icon and Idea* was more concerned with the uses that had been made of these patterns. Images had always preceded ideas in human consciousness.[66]

Paleolithic art had been an automatic projection of nature's patterns, a reflex response to the good Gestalt. Its resulting 'idea' resided in a growing capacity to retain the perceptual image – the founding of an intelligence specifically human. And certain images had had priority in this development – those to do with primary instincts of food-getting, procreation and survival (in other words, Jung's archetypes.)[67] The animal, on which man was entirely dependent, entered human consciousness in the prehistoric period. Or more precisely certain mammals did: birds and fish were easier to catch than game, requiring lesser mental concentration to outwit them, and so were less likely to become ingrained, as heritable 'engrams', in the collective mind. Memory-retention invited comparison, rearrangement, composition and design, the characteristics of neolithic art. Images here were assembled, ranged, reversed and moved into position wilfully: they were not retained in all their vital actuality, as the paleolithic had been, but were transformed. Such synthetic activity represented a development of consciousness, initiating predispositions towards planning, co-ordination and order which became reflected in a culture and in society.[68] A new reality emerged from the patient fixation of what was relevant in human experience; and it was communicable only in virtue of its aesthetic form.[69]

Recorded history could be interpreted as a sparse succession of such moments which had included (in so far as Read's view of them will submit to drastic summary) the brief time in the fifth century BC when, an empathetic appreciation of nature having become stylized and geometricized, a science of harmonic relations had emerged, as yet without detachment from its origins in sensuous experience. These moments had included, too, the relative instant in the twelfth century when that finite and most logical of forms, the Gothic cathedral, had focused man's infinite and transcendental aspirations.[70] But each consciousness-enhancing moment had given way to corruption of consciousness – when harmonics had become an unrelated phenomenon, embodying beauty, it is true, but devoid of contact with vitality; and when artists had accepted as a duty the illustration of religious dogma they had not first apprehended as sensation or feeling. Symbols so divorced from sensibility seemed always to have degenerated into mannered manipulation. And of course the greatest corruption of all had occurred when men had been persuaded by an illusion of imperishable reality, positive, substantial, measurable, and representable by practical methods which could be acquired in academies of art.[71] Near the present time, Cézanne had struggled to achieve a pure state of consciousness in the presence of nature, though his gains had been almost discarded by the cubists before, recognizing this, they had abandoned analytic for synthetic procedures. And subsequently such as Mondrian, by evolutionary stages, and Gabo, by immediate percipience, had established pointers towards the total reconstruction of a twentieth-century aesthetic, a culture and an environment.[72]

Read's only reservation, in this latter respect, was terminological. In spite of the long, beneficial correspondence with Gabo, it seems, he was still wary of the term 'constructive'. It was exclusive, he thought, whereas he believed that all immediately significant patterns, including the 'organic' forms of an Arp or a Moore, were in the same sense constructive. It also held impersonal connotations; and these could be avoided, with no loss of meaning and a considerable increase in clarity, by substituting the term 'creative'. It was the *creative* image, he said, that he saw burgeoning in the work of particular contemporary artists; and the reality taking shape was 'not the inhuman world of the machine but the passionate world of the imagination'.[73] Read exorcised his difficulty concerning the term 'constructive' in two passages written in quick succession; and it is important to see them both in case the second appears, falsely, to be a rejection of the constructivist tendency. *Icon and Idea* carried the simple exchange of adjectives as one of its main conclusions; *Anarchy and Order*,[74] published immediately following, completed a circle of argument by engaging social ramifications. Construction is the skilful manipulation of given elements, he wrote here: creation is the extension of consciousness itself, gradually annexing what was never before perceived. Consciousness is a social, collective phenomenon, generating within itself sensitive points which are the minds of individuals. Individuals relay to the community their creative acts of perception; 'and there is a gradual, a very gradual, change of consciousness in the whole body'.[75]

This encapsulated Read's consistent difference with all brands of socialism, including some interpretations of anarchism: he advocated, paradoxically, an equality providing for creative elitism, the safeguard of vitality. In the guise of equality the Fabians had seemed willing to suffer a sterile cultural uniformity, and the communists had required a complete corruption of individual consciousness before the most banal of academic prescriptions. The preservation of imaginative freedom, however, was a fundamental constituent of Read's anarchism – vital because consciousness is initially an individual advance. *Education through Art* had been an attempt to help recreate conditions favouring the development of lucid consciousness in individuals – not only in those exceptional individuals whose efforts would be required at the growthpoint of a culture, but to some degree in everyone, so that such lucidity might be most effectively diffused, penetrating and transforming all walks of life.[76]

Chapter 6
Formlessness and Form

A unique currency of ideas came into existence during the first few years of the Institute of Contemporary Arts: the terms 'process' and 'development', applied to the making of works of art, acquired precise and important meaning, and many of the most prominent painters and sculptors there were keen to say that their works were 'organic'.[1] They did not mean by this that they were artists of nature; and they were not conscious of extending any deeply rooted, ethnic tradition. This concept, for some, simply helped rationalize a way of working in which images or forms would seem to emerge, and to gain their ultimate characteristics, with little specific pre-intention on the part of the artist, during the course of creative activity. And for others it signified that their works, considered as chronological successions, constituted 'time-lapse' recordings of their evolving creative awarenesses.

Both meanings were associated with Read, who had given them recent, extensive definition (in *Education through Art*). They had stemmed from his desire to see in art an expression of the scientific Zeitgeist, and to find respectable common principles – a theory of organic formation – in physical science, a science of mind, and an explanation of creativity. He had suggested, as an initiative, that whatever maintained consistency of direction and purpose in the physical world of mass, space and time, seemed to be active in mentality too. Below consciousness, just as beneath the surface of palpable reality, there appeared to be some principle of integration, organizing rudimentary images and fragmentary elements into tangible forms.[2] Following Whitehead's example, he had been happy to see some common, co-extensive principle here – though

126

even with such authority he had argued hesitantly, even defensively. Nevertheless, his incoming correspondence, from around 1944, demonstrated an increasing willingness on the part of scientists to contribute discrete observations to his outline thoughts; and if occasionally this was to embarrass him,[3] for the most part his hazarded argument not only survived criticism but from time to time was endorsed by singularly respected opinion.[4]

One authority Read acknowledged most consistently (though without persuading any positive reciprocation) was D'Arcy Wentworth Thompson, whose standard biological text *On Growth and Form*[5] came to assume an orthodox importance at the ICA. Thompson appears to have been worried by the reception of this great work outside the field of the life sciences;[6] and indeed, though Read recommended its urbanity and charm to the general reader,[7] it must have been substantially opaque to those non-scientists who tackled it. In spite of this, its influence was profound, and it is interesting to speculate on the passages which gave those illuminations of artistic creativity for which it became renowned.

Thompson's general thesis, pursued in numerous studies of the growth of all manner of living things, was that natural form was the product of growth and that this, stated simply, was conditioned by protoplasms responding to internal energies and external force-fields to produce *unique conformations*. In a very few simple organisms the results of growth could be predicted; but in organisms possessing several 'growth points' (organisms, for example, composed of flesh, liquids, bone, cartilage and other tissues, which exercised varying rates of growth), though generalities might be anticipated, the particular results of growth were always individuated, complex and unpredictable. In all cases healthy growth was manifested in equilibration, unhealthy growth in aberrations which contributed to imbalance. There had been obvious temptations to seek analogous connection between such arguments and those relating to the growth and development of artistic imagery. It was astonishing to Read, and to others, to see an extensive consistency, as for instance between this initial premise of Thompson's and corresponding ideas here framed in parentheses:

The form, then, of any portion of matter (of a work of art)
. . . and the changes of form which are apparent in its
movements and in its growth (in its development) may in all

cases alike be described as due to the action of force. In short, the form of an object is a '*diagram of forces*', in this sense, at least, that from it we can judge of or deduce the forces that are acting or have acted upon it: in this strict and particular sense, it is a diagram – in the case of a solid (in the case of a finished work of art) of the forces which *have been* impressed upon it when its conformation was produced . . . in the case of a liquid (in the case of a work in progress) . . . of the forces which *are for the moment* acting on it to restrain or balance its own inherent mobility.[8]

Acceptance of this hypothesis as being relevant to art, along with the two corollaries – that the work of art may be conceived as a diagram of forces, and that in the formation of the work these forces are inherently mobile – carried certain implications. One made irrelevant the traditional practice of rehearsal or preparation, in sketches and cartoons, prior to the execution of an accomplished final work. Another suggested that the themes, experiments, extemporizations embodied in each work constituted a record of the artist's creative development. In addition, if a work of art were said to be a unique conformation of such matters held in equilibrium – if, that is, a property of an authentic work were its condition of exhibiting a good Gestalt[9] – then it was instructive to look to nature for the principle of achieving variety in the parts of a unified totality. And there was an appropriate insight in Thompson's discussion of variety within apparent symmetry, which he found to be effected in nature by means of a peculiar give-and-take.

> Symmetry is highly characteristic of organic forms [he had written], and is rarely absent in living things – save in such few cases as Amoeba, where the rest and equilibrium on which symmetry depends are likewise lacking. And if we ask what physical equilibrium has to do with formal symmetry and structural regularity, the reason is not far to seek, nor can it be better put than in these words . . . . In every symmetrical system every deformation that tends to destroy the symmetry is complemented by an equal and opposite deformation that tends to restore it. In each deformation, *positive and negative work is done.*[10]

'Positive and negative work', effecting creative expression, was an important concept at the ICA in the early 1950s: so too was the principle of a balance of growth. At least, this is what appears in the evidence of what was going on there; for on the one hand certain artists were concerned with specifically painterly problems – making images by progressive accretion of marks, allowing movement, enlargement, reduction, even erasure in the process, and acting with as little premeditation as possible[11] – while others were exploring the relevance of stage-by-stage construction, proceeding by trial and error and inventing an assemblage technology to suit their needs.[12] Now these two activities, a spontaneous abstract expressionism and a meticulous constructivism, seem unrelated if not fundamentally opposed; and yet they possessed one common essential principle which in effect unified them. They were process-dominant. Creative direction was not determined by standards, or pre-set goals, or prescribed compositional criteria: instead, direction was divined in the work as it progressed. At each minute stage the work was 'read', and 'suggestions' were elicited from it about succeeding development. In place of academic strategies there were simple tactics – for example, to balance growth and reduction, or to follow the course of an idea across dimensional boundaries, from point to line, line to plane, and plane to freestanding construction in space.[13] It is not wholly true that end-results were completely ignored, but more accurate to say they were allowed to take care of themselves. The *means* became a focus of attention: indeed, it became a virtue to be as explicit as possible about *process*, and to regard ends as almost incidental by-products.

According to such values, artists would (to make use of Thompson's words) 'look upon the form of an organism as a function of growth, or a direct consequence of growth whose rate varies in its different directions.' Resulting works of art (again to use Thompson's words) would typically be 'events in space-time' rather than mere 'configurations in space'.[14] In Read's view they would also be the immediate facts of developing consciousness – not the evidence of development already gained, but the vital embodiment of the development itself.[15] Artistic form would be an emerging or unfolding event, consisting of aspects of universal reality interpenetrated with individual mentality. And the chief problem of this individual would be to free the mind of any reliance upon pre-existing art: the spontaneously emergent *form*, that is to say, had sharply to be distinguished from such superinduced *shape*, for it would be *deformed* if it were forced into the ready-made container. The artist would abstract from the realm of formlessness a temporarily appropriate form, the significance of which, as he worked, would gradually be revealed to him. This was Read's confident assertion; and it accommodated a neat relationship of consciousness and unconsciousness, the physical and the psychological.

Curiously, these polarities became objectified in simultaneous though independent, critical exchanges with two men who had found support in Read's writings, each in a different extreme. One, the psychologist Anton Ehrenzweig, was particularly interested in a principle of formlessness he had identified as having been paramount in Read's aesthetics from as early as the 1930s. The other, Lancelot Law Whyte, a physicist, was working on a unitary theory of art and science, centring on a common tendency towards Gestalt formation, and of course he had seen in Read's work an essential principle of materializing form. Read's encounter with the theories of Ehrenzweig and Whyte was exactly contemporary with his view of modern English art as an unbroken series embracing superrealism and abstraction – a view considerably strengthened, it may be supposed, by the recognition of a similar phenomenon in the image of modern science which they provided.

Ehrenzweig was an Austrian who had settled in England in 1938. He was most unorthodox in his work,[16] interested as he was in the sensibility and motivation of particular kinds of individual – highly creative artists and musicians. He was thus isolated from other schools of psychological theory (which only slightly touched upon his interests), and in fact he had derived most aid and comfort from Read's amateur delvings into Freud and Jung. He had been impressed by Read's announced ambition to a dialectic theory of art, recognizing this as something to which he was capable of contributing;[17] and he had worked alone on this for a number of years before nerving himself for an approach and a comparison of notes. He saw implicit in all Read's work a *de facto* acceptance of formlessness as the primary creative state, and recognized a recurrent need to understand what happens to this as it emerges into consciousness. Ehrenzweig's belief – and his suggestion to Read – was that it becomes differentiated, and that all ordinary perception would consist in minute intervals of formless confusion followed by greater periods of Gestalt-supported certainty. In the extraordinary perceptual state of the creative artist, though, this rapid oscillation would become a slower-moving cycle; and Ehrenzweig's findings had persuaded him that, in order to be genuinely creative, this individual had to try to dwell on an undifferentiated receptivity. This required the suppression of reflex perception – a suppression evident in the automatism of the surrealists and pregnant in the theories of Bergson. It demanded Gestalt-free apprehension as the essence of creativity, and in consequence suggested that appreciation of an achieved, or fully realized, work of art would be incomplete to this extent – that an essential apprehension, now organized and made acceptable, would be lost to it. What would be accessible would be a new phenomenon, an emergent Gestalt, unique to each apprehending sensibility though contributing, with the countless appreciations in other minds, to a steadily forming, corporate sense of style.[18]

Ehrenzweig thus differed with Read to this slight degree. Read's artist recognized the significance of his or her perceptions in the immediacy of creative working. To Ehrenzweig, however, such 'recognition' – the transformation of undifferentiated apprehensions into conventional perceptions – resided not in the making of an image or form but in its reception by an unproductive public, and this by a psychological continuity spanning generations. The emergence of accepted form from chaos seemed to him to be gradual, each generation engaging the task without having to repeat inherited achievements. He considered it impossible to appreciate, for example, an original, style-free chaos of prehistoric, or of Greek, or of Gothic art; though he thought it feasible to suspect that such forms of overtly stylized art were the ones most likely to have been initiated by great emotional upheavals – that is if style, as he maintained, were subsumed emotion. Once a Gestalt perception were superimposed upon undifferentiated form, this would initiate a process of acceptance by the community, leading to gradually more-certain, conventional recognition; and the crystallizing concept would be forever passed on.[19]

Now this brought several consequences to a Readian view of modern creativity, the most obvious of which was the suggestion that an art of pure form – an art as restrained as, say, Nicholson's or Mondrian's – was in fact not the product of dominantly intellectual activity, but instead a camouflage for the sort of highly emotional apprehension more usually associated with the mysterious formal compositions of a surrealist such as Ernst or de Chirico. This would be to suggest an identity of superrealism and abstraction, or at least a relationship closer than even Read had yet attempted. On the other hand, it would rob him of belief in the artist as selector, interpreter and organizer – in short, as the conservator of perceptual values.[20] It would also question the idea of everyone potentially a *productive* artist; though in spite of Ehrenzweig's admitted ill-disposition towards Jungian theory, it would strengthen Read's faith in the archetype. If children in their 'mind pictures' produced primordial symbols, it was because these were the echoes of emotions powerful enough still to possess hereditable significance, and sufficiently intense to have survived in typified form. Ehrenzweig accepted that arguments such as these, featuring inborn, conventionalized emotion and inherited Gestalt perception, contradicted current physiological thinking.[21] Read, however, was in touch with scientific opinion which accepted something very similar to 'inborn memory' as a shaper of emergent organic form in nature; and with Lancelot Law Whyte he was planning a collaborative publication[22] which would have argued the case for an evolving, collective consciousness, transcending both time and individuality, and possessing such features in its physiological aspect as Ehrenzweig's theory demanded.

Read had first met Whyte at the suggestion of Josef Paul Hodin,[23] an art historian, who was the ICA's librarian and co-ordinator of its recent-historical research.[24] Whyte was a physicist who had been conducting a one-man campaign, from as early as the 1920s, for recognition of a single discipline embracing subjects as apparently diverse as physics and psychology, biology and art.[25] Read of course, for his part, had long respected the Goethean arguments that organic form could be said to be present 'not only in the crystal and the bone, in the leaf and the cloud, but also in the painting and the poem'; that there were no essential differences between these manifestations of form; that the form discoverable in nature was the same as the form revealed by art; that there was one creative process, formation and transformation.[26] And Hodin, recognizing that their convictions were complementary, had introduced Whyte to Read's writings, leading to their meeting, to a speculative collaboration, and to Whyte's enthusiastic participation in the ICA. What they possessed in common at the outset was thoroughgoing knowledge of the scientific philosophy of Alfred North Whitehead (in fact they both seem to have reached back to Goethe through this intermedium); and they reappraised Whitehead's arguments, expecting to enlarge upon them in the work resulting from their joint venture.

Whitehead's contention had been that the world of science had always remained perfectly satisfied with its peculiar, standardized concepts, but that these, in the twentieth century, were now too narrow for the concrete facts which were before it for analysis. This was said to be true in physics, and even more urgent in the biological sciences; and in order to understand the difficulties approached by modern scientific thought, Whitehead suggested, there should be 'some conception of a wider field of abstraction, a more concrete analysis, which shall stand nearer to the complete concreteness of . . . intuitive experience'.[27] Significantly to Read, Whitehead saw examples of 'a more concrete analysis' in the romantic reaction of the poets Coleridge, Shelley and, particularly, Wordsworth, whose consistent theme he took to have been that the important facts of nature elude scientific method. His poetry seemed to be haunted by a mysterious, enveloping, interactive Nature, a phenomenon which rang true, but one with which the scientist, who dealt with individual aspects (and, Read would have said, the traditional artist, who was concerned to reflect particular instances of nature) was incapable of coming to terms. Wordsworth, Whitehead had written, could grasp the whole of nature in the tonality of the particular instance: he could express to the height of genius the concrete facts of human apprehension – facts which were distorted in the scientific analysis.[28] This had supported the following conception, which was exactly relevant to those practising an 'organic' art.

Nature for Whitehead consisted in moving patterns of growth and development, the movement of which was essential to their being. These patterns could be analysed into *events* – stages of development consisting, at any moment, of the interaction of organic growth, the mentality of those observing, and all other impinging phenomena. Any further analysis of the event, however, for example into the condition of isolatable parts, would be destructive, for their significance would severely lessen if they were detached from what were systems of mutual enhancement. Such analysis would disintegrate the structure of the pattern; and

Whitehead held that the essence of an organism was the changing pattern of its total structure extending in space and time. Thus to Whitehead reality was a structure of evolving structures; and the particular instance of reality was structural process embodied in the subdivision called the event.

An event was said to have contemporaries – that is, it mirrored within itself 'the modes of its contemporaries as a display of immediate achievement'. It had a past: it reflected 'the modes of its predecessors, as memories fused into its own content'. And it also had a future: it was permeated by 'such aspects as the future throws back onto the present' or 'as the present has determined concerning the future'. Thus the event was not an isolated stage of development but the fusion of aspects of a temporal activity: 'the concept of the order of nature', Whitehead had written, 'is bound up with the concept of nature as the locus of organisms in process of development'.[29] In other words, for him the activities of the organism formed the substance of the organism: substance and activity were the same. His process of nature was not merely cyclic or rhythmic change: it was creative advance. The totality was evolving by a process of constantly producing new forms in every part of itself. It may not be surprising that such ideas were considered illuminating in the realm of contemporary art.

Support was given to these propositions. Organic development in a work of art is at least analogous to, and probably identical with, organic development in nature. The essence of art is in its processes rather than its products; and such artistic events as *are* thrown up are significant merely in that they reflect past, present and future aspects of the dominant process. A theory of organic art thus required (to paraphrase Whitehead in parentheses)

> a conception of organism as fundamental for nature (for art and for the ambient culture.) It also requires an underlying activity (creativity), a substantial activity – expressing itself in individual embodiments, and evolving in achievements of organism. The organism is a unit of emergent value .... On the materialistic theory there is material ... which endures. On the organic theory, the only endurances are structures of activity, and the structures are evolved. Enduring things are thus the outcome of a temporal process ....[30]

An implication of this for Whyte was that science should adopt

134

the conception of process, and review the sum of empirically gained knowledge in its light. A consequence for Read was that he would begin to address the subject of a process-dominant aesthetic. Their co-operation produced a blending of these views – a shared acceptance of the fundamental importance of pattern-extension in mind and matter; and agreement on a principle of elegant balance in 'atoms, organisms and healthy societies'.[31] But this was not a full complement of ideas so far as Read was concerned, because it did not embrace the vital 'human creativity'. There was no disagreement here: it was simply outside Whyte's field of attention. So far as he was concerned, art respected the same principles as nature, and threw an interesting sidelight upon them, while remaining essentially peripheral.[32] To Read it was the source of everything else, increasing an intelligence towards nature, in an absence of which nature might as well not exist – *would not* exist. Whyte also saw in Whitehead a predominant movement onwards, a process of gradual simplification and perfection which effectively abandoned previous states of achievement. But in the same place Read found a mixture of Bergson and Jung, as well as Whitehead, and a sense of process extending also backwards, enabling inherited traces of long-past achievements occasionally to surface and to confront the new.[33]

Their combined efforts, then, resulted not in a treatise but in protracted debate – Read for his part accepting most of the other's arguments, but failing to persuade him of the generative significance of art. Their exchange was channelled into a symposium entitled *Aspects of Form*, held at the ICA in 1951, which presented a large variety of aesthetic and scientific accounts of formative processes.[34] Perhaps surprisingly, some specifically aesthetic contributions tended to support Whyte's arguments,[35] while Read no doubt was happy to draw strength from science. For example, the following themes, selected from the published proceedings of the symposium, would have combined to create an imagery quite familiar to him.

As the physicist's contemplation passed from larger objects towards atoms and their minute nuclei, it was argued, elementary ideas of 'visual shape' gave way first to 'occupation of space' and then to states of seemingly chaotic movement which never died down.[36] Astronomy witnessed similar phenomena – occupation of space, continuous movement, and chaos (in the tendency, to which certain bodies of the solar system seemed prone, towards erratic deviation from predicted courses.)[37] Through microscope and telescope came evidence of flux, precarious balance on the verge of instability, and – of greatest significance – unpredictability. In other words, Creation exhibited formation and deformation, contraction and expansion, contrast and adaptation – properties characteristically similar to those endowed in works of art.[38] Or rather, in works of art considered as psychological experience, for in their physical properties alone most paintings (simple accretions of matter) and most works of sculpture (the results of sequent, rather than simultaneously competing, forces) exhibited no such striving and yielding. On the other hand, considered *as* psychological experience, works of art were organic formations of the highest degree,[39] transcripts of processes assumed to exist in corresponding brain fields, and analogues of nature in their identity of origin and descent. Coupled with allusions to Whitehead's belief in an evolutionary fusion of memory and novelty,[40] a considerable proportion of the discussion (as perhaps this small sample may have indicated) could be taken to support Read's partiality.

When he summarized the proceedings, however, he went further than a consensus had strictly allowed:

> The increasing significance given to *form* or *pattern* in various
> branches of science has suggested the possibility of a certain
> parallelism, if not identity, in the structures of natural
> phenomena and of authentic works of art . . . . The revelation
> that perception itself is essentially a pattern-selecting and
> pattern-making function (a Gestalt formation); that pattern
> is inherent in the physical structure or in the functioning of
> the nervous system; that matter itself analyses into coherent
> patterns or arrangements of molecules; and the gradual
> realization that all these patterns are effective and
> ontologically significant by virtue of an organization of their
> parts which can only be characterized as *aesthetic* – all this
> development has brought works of art and natural phenomena
> onto an identical plane of enquiry. Aesthetics is no longer an
> isolated science of beauty; science can no longer neglect
> aesthetic factors.[41]

Though he had stretched the pattern of agreement to incorporate an aesthetic principle, this was not Read at his most outspoken.

What he had really meant was that human creativity and natural evolution were to occupy a single plane of enquiry; and in fact he had attempted to say that science could no longer 'escape' aesthetic 'evaluation'.[42] He felt obliged to defend these convictions; and when next he spoke in public he stressed what he believed to be the proper priority. This was in a lecture entitled *Art and the Evolution of Man*[43] at the Conway Hall in London, presented very shortly after the ICA symposium; and, as Whyte shared the same platform, in effect it was an extension of their debate. Actually Whyte's views had moved towards Read's, but not far enough to have made much difference. He now accepted works of art to be images of matters of special importance, isolated from the evolutionary process and made available for close consideration.[44] To Read this hardly amounted to concession, for works of art were not 'images of . . .', but the matters of special importance in themselves. It was as if, when challenged, he resorted naturally to poetic affirmation, for what he had clearly intended to be a lucid argument about an identity of modern aesthetic and scientific philosophy became instead a none-too-calm reiteration of one of Bergson's inspired conceptions.

A broad current of consciousness appeared to have penetrated matter (went Bergson's hypothesis), inhabiting it and moulding it to its chief purpose of enlargement and extension. It had shaped a vast array of organisms, providing it with varying degrees of potential for expansion. In some, consciousness had retarded: in others – in the so-called 'inorganic realm' – it had become dormant. But in the human organism it had developed to a degree which had made it unique – that is, capable of reflecting intensively upon (without being essentially different from) the consciousness evolving in organisms outside itself.[45] Consciousness-reflecting-outwards (as human intellection) had adapted the latent geometry of this particular organism to the function of understanding the geometry in others: intellect and matter had assumed comparable form.

It was this comparability that Whyte had concentrated upon, giving it less fanciful description as a unitary principle of pattern-formation embracing diverse kinds of human understanding. But it was at the heart of Read's argument that this principle was not comprehensive (and therefore not really unitary) because it neglected, to a large extent, the counterpart of intellection –

intuition, consciousness-reflecting-inwards, or non-discursive apprehension. Read regarded this as the spark and sustaining energy of human creativity: to Whyte it created nothing more than analogies. What made it difficult for Read to argue with this was his admission that every proficient work of art, even the most disruptive and rebellious, seemed to exhibit formal organization and respect for the good Gestalt. There was no genuinely formless art; and his predicament was similar to that in the early 1930s, when he had been 'waiting' for surrealism to become evident here in order to complement classicism. All he could do was to comment upon a looseness in Whyte's reasoning – his faith in an 'unknown law' governing the development and transformation of patterns. Non-discursive intelligence, Read suggested, was the unknown and mysterious aspect of Whyte's hypothesis, responsible for enhancing the patterns which intellection identified; and human creativity, expressly fitted for pattern-extension and the origination of new entities, could not be deemed analogous of anything else.

> The point I am trying to make [Read said], the whole point of my hypothesis, is that the work of art is not an analogy – it is the essential act of transformation; not merely the *pattern* of mental evolution, but the vital process itself.[46]

There was a shade of desperation in this resorting to Bergsonism, a philosophy Read had once put aside because of its naivety; but this was an indication of his disappointment at merely being able to persuade a liberal scientist, such as Whyte, so far towards his viewpoint but no further. In spite of this, their agreement was considerable; and it could be expressed as a series of convictions which seem to have had general acceptance at the ICA.[47] Biological organization and mental activity (even 'creativity' to those who agreed with Read) are processes of closely similar, or even identical, character. The formative principle has been neglected in both; but this has been to overlook the obvious, for at the centre of each is an inherent self-ordering tendency, by means of which partial or incomplete forms are extended or perfected.[48] This is most apparent in the data revealed by modern studies of the human brain, an organism in which physiology and psychology have assumed identical form.[49]

As it has been said, certain painters and sculptors who were members of the ICA were shaping their works in accordance with the comparable concept – their 'structure' and 'content' was assuming identical form. Read celebrated this in a series of lectures to the Institute;[50] and the ideal he consistently put forward for others to relate to was the oeuvre of Naum Gabo. Gabo's constructions of polished metal, glass and plastics, strings, wires and enveloped space were particularly important to Read now, because they were definitive Gestalt formations of a double nature. Unlike most other works of art they were *both* physical and psychological Gestalten, composed as they were of numerous structural and perceptual forces held in tensioned equilibrium. Moreover, their strictly formal, almost austere appearance belied their probable origins (following Ehrenzweig's observation[51]) in great emotional incoherence. Read had once speculated that Gabo's work occupied the highest point attained by man's creative intuition: now, in spite of its having no evident 'organic' appearance (unlike, say, the archetypal forms of Henry Moore), a theory of organicism persuaded Read he had communicable proof. This was easily received, for the most part, by those who were party to the ICA's unique ethos; but there was one notable occasion when it failed entirely to convince.

This was in 1953 when Read was one of an international jury of ten, invited to adjudicate in a competition for the design of a *Monument to the Unknown Political Prisoner*,[52] held under the auspices of the ICA. Read argued in favour of Gabo's submission, as the likely major prizewinner, on the grounds that it was a symbolic encapsulation of hope and passive idealism – emotional content which could be conveyed in no other way without descending to expressionistic crudity. But his views were defeated because of a dominant symmetry in the construction, which fellow jurists could not accept as either 'intuitive' or 'organic'. They would have been persuaded by a more obvious display of emotion; and this provoked the realization (which to Gabo was all too familiar, but which appears to have shaken Read) that individuals outside his special circle of criticism, while otherwise enlightened, could fail to see distinction between an image-in-itself and an image as reflection of external phenomena.[53] Many of the ICA's early promotions had been retrospective, aimed at informing its members about occurrences in twentieth-century art which had gone largely unreported in England. Now, however, it appeared that the Institute's mainly young membership was more alive to a contemporary aesthetic than were eminent critics from abroad. This vindicated Read's efforts to found an English centre of modernism, as it did too his investment in the idea that a new native art would emerge from some combination of the constructive achievements of Gabo (the honorary Englishman) and the organicism of such as Moore. A new generation seemed to have accepted the need for undifferentiating sensibility – that individuality would reside in *this* rather than in any overlaying, spurious personal 'style'. Painters and sculptors alike were approaching 'formlessness' as closely as possible, by rejecting preconception, post-elaboration, and indeed any stifling of simple informality.

Read was not demonstrative in his support for the new tendency – he knew that overt campaigning by an older guard would have been counter-productive. Instead, his prompting was individual, tentative and piecemeal, and only outspoken when he came across what he saw as wilful sacrificing of hard-won values.[54] In his prepared lectures to the ICA (becoming fewer now that his home and family were in north Yorkshire) he concentrated upon establishing a pedigree for what was going on, which in the realm of sculpture extended definitely over thirty years and harked back as far as the linear Gothic. Immediate progenitors were the English achievements of the 1930s and 1940s; and distant relatives were Picasso's wire sculptures and Vladimir Tatlin's monumental projects, each of which consisted of dynamic volumes bounded merely by lines.[55] Referring to the latter two prototypes, Read would suggest that an art of minimal form had been a steady twentieth-century 'goal'. The furthest projection of this had been Gabo's work, appearing as if executed in light itself. His constructions conveyed little awareness of material substance, but rather of 'space defined by line and given significant form'. His were poetic images; but they also had a more than sympathetic relationship with modern science, in that they were fundamentally concerned with inner structure and organization of the material world.[56]

A tendency to minimal construction, comprising linear forces, stresses and tensions held in equilibrium was one polarity evident in the work Read was now becoming familiar with. Its counterpart had had a history of quite different origins and purpose. The impact of light upon intentionally *solid* sculptures, it had been realized, had created *highlight*, the most serviceable means of interfering with static visual tension or appearance. The effect of high-light was as if a hole had been eaten into mass by the action of acid; and certain English artists had grasped the potential afforded by form which, instead of reflecting light from protuberant bosses, would admit it through holes punched into mass as if at points of impact. Moore had been the master of this device, creating spaces and objects interfused. And some of his works had even been virtually linear, though his 'line' had always retained a vital variability of section.[57]

The next, irresistible step was in process of being taken. Works were being created – typified in the linear sculptures of Reg Butler – which defined space without occupying it, and which held back from the differentiation of form and space. They fused the archetypal memories of a Henry Moore and the scientific insight of a Naum Gabo. And the result was something sympathetically close to D'Arcy Thompson's 'dynamic equilibrium' – his flux of formation and deformation – for it was most obvious that the new works exhibited *near*-equilibrium, as aspects of form arrested for close attention from within processes of change and development. Emotional content here was greatest when mass was understated – when formal integrity and distinctness were secondary to a lively, linear 'facture'. The slight sense of imbalance this created, the result of an immense number of forces held in changing equilibrium, was to Read evidence of both vitality and unsettled psychological experience. His first resort, in an attempt to explain this to himself, was to suppose that the younger generation was responding to an existential crisis caused by the atomic threat to world peace. He noted that similar phenomena were apparent in English painting, and, later, that they had been the subject of spontaneous effusion throughout the western world.

He himself expected to be largely insensitive to whatever was affecting the sensibility of a 'waste land' generation: he was aware, though, of a slightly changing aesthetic preference, or rather of an extension of the range of his appreciation. In 1952 he had confessed himself unable to respond adequately to painting or sculpture which appeared not to have placed high premium on formal organization.[58] Two years later, however, having witnessed the emergence of a dynamic, linear sculpture and the beginnings of something comparable in painting, and having surprised himself, perhaps, by his liking for them, he was able to report objectively on the changing tone of his appreciation. The nature of form in art remained obscure, he said, but a great deal of light had been shed on it by Gestalt psychologists. There was form in perception; and imagination was 'formed' even as it originated and revealed itself in art. But he was uneasily aware, in himself as poet, of 'a vague penumbra of feeling, seeking form rather than finding it'. He had always accepted that this would be carried along by form, to be equally present in an ensuing work of art. Now he was inclined to believe that it could be present to the exclusion of organized form, within the totally Gestalt-free work.[59]

In the latest sculptural developments, *physical* Gestalten were manifesting unsettled psychological experience; and in contemporary painting there appeared to be scant respect for form (apart from that demanded by the conventional, rectangular boundary). In the work of such as Patrick Heron and Alan Davie in Britain, the tachistes in France, and the action painters in America, images were being created – 'various forms of the formless' – which, while for the most part abstract, differed with the successors of cubism by intentionally deforming the data received in ordinary perception, rather than refining them. Onlookers were invited to inspect an amorphous streaking or veining (Read's first impression had been of a similarity to the marbling which had decorated the endpapers of nineteenth-century books[60]); and they were expected to make contact, by sensation, with whatever compulsion the artist had enacted, or traced out like 'a graph of uncertainty'. Such images were formless – not in the sense of being indistinct or out of focus, but in their symbolic representation of a chaos reigning on the other side of consciousness. By comparison to their *genuine* automatism, that of surrealist works now seemed mannered, or overlaid with conventional interpretation, like the effort involved in remembering a dream. The new painting was instinctive, reflex, and completely devoid of intellection: its practitioners delivered themselves not so much to the unconscious force of the imagination, as to 'something as irresponsible as an angry gesture'.[61]

Read once more looked to antecedents, seeking to be satisfied of this painting's status as an evolutionary stage in the growth of modern consciousness (rather than as 'failure of nerve', a condition he thought had afflicted modern poetry[62]). His youthful enjoyment of Kandinsky's *Improvisations* came to the surface; and he connected the considerable emotional content, which the new painting most obviously possessed, with the great compulsive force or moment of 'internal necessity' which had sustained Kandinsky's most powerful imagery. Kandinsky's later work had consisted in a gradual discarding of the unconscious, spontaneous, non-material feeling, and in the revelation of well-organized form beneath it or within. It was that which he had thus discarded, and which had had compelling presence in the work Read had known as a young man, that now featured so prominently in the painting which, in Britain at least, had no generic name. Certain Americans had claimed descent from the surrealists, and Read could accept this as one side of the new work's parentage. What had been bred out of the strain, however, was most significant – surrealism's use of a realist vocabulary, which by its too-specific references to the familiar had prevented a consistent emergence of 'unknown' feeling. In connection with this, certain of Kandinsky's explanations, which had seemed vague when he had uttered them, now made sense. He had spoken of a 'symphony of forms' arising from a 'chaotic hubbub of cosmic elements in the music of the spheres'. The latest picture of the universe offered by science was of an infinite explosion of matter, a state of continuous creation and destruction, within which had been found nuclei of form and structure and, within these still, an infinite recession of perfect form. The contemporary artist was finding forms similar to those which had permeated Kandinsky's *Improvisations*; though now, in the 1950s, there was considerable reassurance in science for an enterprise Kandinsky had pioneered unaided. This enterprise consisted in penetrating an unconscious, Gestalt-free matrix of forms (as Ehrenzweig had called it) by intuition and contemplation, and allowing aspects of it to materialize without their becoming attached to images already known. They would acquire form only in the moment of expression; and their only artificial constraints would be imposed by the physical properties of coagulating paint.[63]

With a rare absence of chauvinism, Read acknowledged that the artist whose work best exhibited a Gestalt-free matrix was an American, Sam Francis.[64] He had been encouraged by discovering, in conversation, that Francis considered his creative awareness to be directed, not inwards towards the self, but outwards 'towards a source from which proceeds the primary substances of light and colour'. Thus channelling the formless properties of his unconscious outwards, allowing them to be caught in the light and transfixed, without, so to say, using more or less conscious thoughts to snatch them to the surface, Francis seemed to ensure the most faithful materialization of an unconscious flux in all vitality. 'It is the Cloud of Unknowing itself that he depicts', Read ventured, 'and he seeks for no mysteries behind it: he is content with the colour and the turmoil of a primordial substance.'[65] Artists of this compulsion would manipulate paint until significant forms emerged upon their canvases; and the ideal to which they would aspire would be a process of crystallization, taking place without conscious intervention, creating shape simple or complex and appealing to the sensibility for reasons unknown. The result would be a synthesis entirely Readian – some configuration or Gestalt formation possessing distinctive individuality, the harmony and proportion of its totality at odds with a superreality or non-aesthetic vitality in its fluid details.[66]

As to the means which made this possible – this was very close to Kandinsky's slowly formed inner feeling, worked over and tested by non-directed purpose.[67] It was something Jung had noticed, and had attributed to creative elaboration within the unconscious mind. Consciousness was its anathema, forever correcting or negating; and Jung's advice had been to cultivate, by meditation, ways of watching objectively the development of fragments of phantasy. Read, for his part, needed no persuading about a formative principle at work in the unconscious, the purpose of which was to create, unaided, objects with apprehensible form and colour answering to unconscious needs.

> The artist begins with a background that is mysterious, unformed . . . . Then he begins to elaborate, to delineate, never resorting to logical or verbal processes, but nevertheless proceeding by purposive steps – one stroke or spot determining the shape and place of the next stroke or spot; until finally he is left with an image whose origins or significance he cannot explain (and does not desire to explain) and yet which constitutes for him something valid, something *true*, something deeply necessary, a vital presence . . . . The image in question may possess all . . . possibilities of interpretation all the time, and be most potent when we do not attempt to reduce it to any one of them.[68]

It obviously occurred to Read, after his initial enthusiasm for what appeared to be an authentic formless art, that to promote it as a culmination of modern painting would be to advocate a stasis, a termination of aesthetic development which would have been contrary to all he had stood for in the past. In fact its scale and energy, in its American form, appear to have taken him by surprise, to which his delighted response was a spontaneous reaction. And though he never withdrew his welcoming of it he nevertheless made implied reservations, here and there in certain qualifying statements, sufficient to indicate how horrified he would have been had painters generally made a headlong rush down this particular avenue. It was not as simple in its execution as it appeared, he protested:[69] it required some prior apprenticeship to form (as evident in, say, Kandinsky's pictographic abstraction), the gradual simplification of which would lead to formlessness legitimately. And it was to be regarded as an extreme edge of a painter's range of sensibility, to be visited occasionally though not, perhaps, to be dwelt upon.

Read's appreciation of an extreme abstract expressionism, then, was at first sensational but ultimately 'scientific', in the sense that it completed his picture of modern art, and actualized an aspect of it which had been a merely theoretical possibility. In its American form – in a Sam Francis or a Mark Tobey – it determined certain limits beyond which he thought it not feasible to proceed, in the directions of large scale, vacuity, and obsession with the purely personal. He was now inclined to see its British form – a Patrick Heron, an Alan Davie or a William Scott – as representing movement back from 'the edge of nothingness', some slight traversion in the direction of a more concrete, a more-than-individual, and therefore a social symbolism. This was more to his *consistent* liking of course – an art essentially humanist in its more readily apprehensible scale, in its devotion to aesthetic enquiry and development,[70] and in its recomplication of pictorial form.

It is quite possible to argue that Read's reception of American abstract expressionism reveals him in very poor light – as an opportunist, and as one inconsistent enough to disregard longstanding values for the sake of identifying with a new cause. But this would be unjust, for his own arguments anticipated it and seemed to have been confirmed by it. After a brief moment of intoxication, he placed it soberly within his customary framework of co-ordinates – at the 'personal' extreme of an axis ranging across to the

145

'impersonal', and at the base of a vertical scale plumbing the unconscious. He thought that if only it were possible to measure the depth of an artist's *descent* into the unconscious, some standard might be derived for discriminating between different types of non-pictorial art. One type might not reach beyond the shallow depth of reflex gesture, or of automatic response to emotional stimulus. Another might go deeper, to the realm of forms possessing social, archetypal significance. And, deeper still, another might tap an immense, amorphous energy, potentially capable of assuming diverse forms.[71]

So his temperamentally English art continued to occupy the centre of his scheme of things – always in some sense 'humanist' (defined as a fusion of 'personal' and 'impersonal' values), and engaging primordial substances of archetypal significance. To a generation which had matured in the 1930s, such archetypes had had rather gentle characteristics – maternal, terrestrial, mutually aiding. The archetypes of a younger generation, however, were shot through with violence, anxiety, and something akin to primitive superstition. The tensed animal, the stranger flexed for flight, and the watcher, for example, were principal presences in Lynn Chadwick's work, to which Read ascribed the suitably synthetic epithet 'a geometry of fear'.[72] This was part of an emergent vital, animistic sculpture, wrought from iron rod and strip steel, a true descendant of the northern Gothic, beside which there was an equally vital painting, making virtue of displaying traces of a passionate energy which had traversed it.

Typical of the older generation's values, Moore's art was a fusion of humanism and the organic, Hepworth's a fusion of humanism and universal harmony. Reg Butler, of the younger generation, interfused humanism and expressionism; and the work of his contemporaries featured a 'humanism of the absurd' – universal in its evocation of archetypal myths and legends, but the antithesis of a universal classicism.[73] And occupying space between the two generations was the painting of Victor Pasmore, patiently fulfilling Read's ambitions towards a synthesis of the constructive and the numinous.

Pasmore had been a very successful impressionist, combining an English atmospheric facture and a strong sense of area division. Around 1950, however, he had made an astounding, abrupt departure into austere construction, making large numbers of assemblages, often uniformly painted, badly made, and deliberately 'without finish'. His work had ceased to be significant to him except as evidence thrown up by methodical search or, as he said, 'laboratory research'. He had confined himself to positioning a few simple elements – points, straight lines, regular curves, geometric areas – exploring many minute variations in order to gain incremental experience. Conventions had been ignored – even the one which requires a picture plane to be flat and usually rectangular. He had tried projections from it forward, by degrees, as far as he had dared, and also backward. An obvious step had been to make it transparent, revealing dimensions before it and behind in complex relationship. And the transparent membrane, which had made this possible, had reintroduced lyricism into what were otherwise plain constructions, reflecting every nuance of change in their surroundings, creating confusions of real and reflected images, and providing very sensitive registers of ambient conditions.[74]

Read had observed all of this with some detachment, commenting occasionally on its revolutionary significance for English art,[75] but offering a reasoned interpretation only when the painter had seemed to pause for consolidation. Now Read noted that while Pasmore had sometimes refined purer plastic concepts than even Mondrian, he had never relinquished the sensuous basis of perception. The interaction, or collision, of the *determined* dimensions of his work, with the *unpredictable*, fleeting effects of shadow and reflection, was to be seen as an interplay of classic and romantic tendencies, rationality and the irrational.[76] Complex, unanticipated effects had resulted from a simple, self-propelling process. Their 'unfolding' or 'emerging' had provided an example of how, in principle, a creative sensibility might expand 'organically', that is to say 'aimlessly', having no further goal beyond each temporary objective.

Pasmore's achievement was a link in the chain of Read's appreciation of a changing English art. The pioneering gains of Moore and Gabo had been substantially *social*, reminding of (in a north-country sense, 'minding-on') anarchistic archetypes of the past and egalitarian prototypes for the future. As representative of a middle generation, Pasmore had isolated the aesthetic from the rest of his inheritance, and had concentrated upon mirroring the modes of contemporary achievement, left and right. And those of a younger generation seemed, on the contrary, to have seized upon social aspects of the selfsame legacy, though the essential concept, for them, appeared to have radically changed. It was more immediate than visionary, pessimistic rather than optimistic. Its relative formlessness, or informality, was not an indication of inferior aesthetic judgment (as Read may have once suspected) but of anxiety, or *angst*, in the face of an uncertain future.

Chapter 7
Reconciliation

Read's career spanned exactly fifty years, from his demobilization at the end of the Great War until his death in 1968. Judged by his eventual achievements, he had written comparatively little by 1933 when he was forty; yet by the close of his life he had published a work on aesthetics or criticism for every one of his active years, as well as having had a contributor's hand in many more. It is true that most of his books were collections of essays; but he did not republish, in this way, everything he had written, for his yearly average of essays was a little over twenty. He was afflicted with a gradually intensifying illness in his last years; and he saw the end of his life approaching quite clearly even when still some way off. And in the time which he guessed to be left to him he made determined efforts to order his achievements into reasoned coherence. In so doing, he came to realize that for all their apparent diversity they were principally concerned with the truth of a few simple ideas. This is quite evident in his milestone publications. *Icon and Idea* (1955) re-emphasized an argument first elaborated (as a result of provocation) in the Conway Hall lecture *Art and the Evolution of Man*: image has always preceded idea in the development of human consciousness. This was followed by *The Forms of Things Unknown* (1960), Read's mature, assembled thoughts on the social and biological necessity of creativity. Much of this thinking was conducted aloud in the presence of learned audiences – in particular, of the Eranos Tagung, an annual, Jung-inspired gathering on the shores of Lake Maggiore. The favourable reception he gained for his ideas on such occasions, together with his evident satisfaction at their eventual fitting-into-place,

149

convinced him that this was his *magnum opus*, and a proper culmination of his life of criticism. In this sense his further major works were anti-climactic: *The Origins of Form in Art* (1965) gave further evidence of his 'constant search for a social, indeed, a biological principle in art';[1] and *Art and Alienation* (1967) reasserted that 'the aesthetic activity is a formative process with direct effect both on individual psychology and on social organization'.[2] He also compiled a further collection of essays on the subject of education through art,[3] and another, revisiting his early, still-shaping thought.[4] He completed a full-scale biography of his old friend, Henry Moore,[5] recognizing a consistent equivalence of Moore's plastic, and his own theoretical creations. And, conveying a sense that his serious purposes were at last accomplished, he wrote an astonishingly relaxed and joyous celebration of the life and work of Hans Arp,[6] which superficially seemed to mark a late departure from the favourite subjects of his criticism. Whereas this work indicated that Read was still prepared to be led into new areas by his intuition, the four books on organic formation were perhaps his most systematic works, though they gave evidence not merely of the ordering of his thoughts but of their continuing evolution. One of the most significant features of these books is the insight they offer into a lengthy 'conversation' with Jung, in which Read attempted to overcome Jung's reluctance to see value in contemporary art. Not surprisingly, then, Jung was influential throughout the whole of this venture: important at the outset, though, was a new influence, Susanne Langer.

Reviewing the second edition of Langer's book *Philosophy in a New Key*,[7] Read confessed that though he had received a copy in 1942, when it had first been published, and had even noted that it had been dedicated to Alfred North Whitehead, he had no more than glanced at its contents, and it had remained on his bookshelf, unread, until 1949. He could not say why he had then been compelled to take it up. Perhaps he had unconsciously absorbed a phrase or two, the significance of which had gradually dawned on him. Perhaps he had come across references to Langer in his general reading.

> In any case [he said] I began to read the book . . . and gradually
> realized that it was something I had been waiting for for
> many years – one of those synoptic works which, by bringing

together separate areas of knowledge, suddenly reveal the
pattern of reality, and give a new meaning to all one's
piecemeal explorations.[8]

The confluence in question was recognized in the term 'symbolic
transformation', which at once signified the concern for an *organic*
art and the belief that its results were of *symbolic* importance. At
first sight it is hard to accept that Read had not appreciated the
enhanced value of these concepts so combined. It is recalled,
however, that before 1949 he had been preoccupied with a dialectic
of styles; and it may not be improbable that Langer provided
additional good reason for his change of direction around 1950.
Beforehand it had been enough, to him, for artists to engage in
recognition and formation: afterwards the artist's crucial activity
was not pattern-perception so much as pattern-extension, or
transformation. If, as Read now suspected, extended patterns,
embodied in works of art, symbolized correspondingly extended
or heightened states of awareness,[9] he could say in concert with
Langer's view that a developing symbolism was philosophy's new
key, that it was also the key of aesthetics.

Or rather, deriving support from Langer's remarks, he could say
that two parallel conceptions of symbolism together were characteristic of art. He was drawn to her observation that one such
conception could be seen to lead to logic and a theory of rational
knowledge, inspiring an evolution of science and a quest for
certainty; while another could be observed taking an opposite
direction – to emotion, religion, phantasy and everything *but*
knowledge. Her common denominator was also convincing: 'the
human response, as a constructive, not a passive thing'.[10] Symbolization was the purpose of constructive activity on both sides
alike; and Langer made clear her belief, Read said in *Art and the
Evolution of Man*, that this might only be possible by virtue of
aesthetic effort. This encouraged him to persist in the view (after
his first attempt to express it had been held in check by Whyte)
that all the means of enlarging human experience, including
science, were essentially aesthetic. And a corollary of this, which
Read also found to be endorsed by Langer, was that though scientists and artists tended to express their respective forms of experience by different means – one discursively or sequentially, the other
non-discursively or simultaneously – both were equally rational.

He recognized the summary argument: 'Rationality is the essence of mind, and symbolic transformation its elementary process. It is a fundamental error, therefore, to recognize it only in the phenomenon of systematic, explicit reasoning.'[11]

The whole of Langer's work Read considered to culminate in this: the work of art is to be received as a vivid presentation of itself. It is not to be regarded as a stimulus to spurious feeling, but rather as the symbolic form of a specific, extended or heightened experience. Such finely articulated symbols might not be translated into other modes of expression; and (supporting, perhaps, his reluctance to discuss individual works of art) the pretence to interpret them discursively is vain.[12]

Read was intrigued that, apparently unaware of Jung's psychology – knowing nothing of his unconscious, autonomous creativity, his forms of social importance, his Archetypes – Langer had offered an explanation of creative mental evolution which placed many of his beliefs in a clear perspective.[13] 'A mind that works primarily with meanings', she had written, 'must have organs that supply it primarily with forms.'[14] In the course of human mental development form was abstracted from chaos; and pattern was segregated from the confused sensory field, imprinted on the cortex, and gradually 'developed' by means of successive, related experiences until it acquired meaning. Form then became detachable as symbol, an extended pattern which could be used to fix further meaning. This was comparable with Jung's suggestion that intense or frequently recurring experiences left hereditable imprints on unconsciousness. Both Langer and Jung would have agreed that the structure of the human brain was now receptive to certain patterns which, precisely because of this receptivity, had come to be described as 'beautiful' or 'aesthetic'.[15] It could be suggested that such patterns of awareness were continuing to be developed or extended by means of symbols forming at the forefront of experience, taking their place before a vast progression formed in the past. Because of a decreasing relevance, in relation to the present 'growth point' of experience, the aesthetic appeal of such symbols would diminish by degrees as they moved into history.

Approaching this from a different direction, Read asked himself why certain non-discursive symbols conveyed aesthetic sensations, while others did not. It seemed to him that symbols devoid of aesthetic appeal must have lost it, for in the first place they would

have gained aesthetic distinction only because of their attrac-
tiveness of form.[16] Deserting his usual practice, he explored this
argument in relation to a specific work of art. Though in the
past he had praised Picasso's painting *Guernica* as an image of
'apocalyptic vision',[17] now he was inclined to say that it was
impressive in spite of its burden of outmoded symbolism. Picasso
quite clearly had deployed formerly vital symbols which had
become clichés – the bull, the horse, the woman with dead child,
the light-bearer, the sacrifice – and the development of the painting,
well-documented in sketches and photographs, could be interpreted
as a gradual, but only partial, replacement of these with the artist's
more-immediate symbolism expressed in distortions and exaggera-
tions. Read thus maintained that there was a stage in the evolution
of symbols at which they became clichés, and that these formerly
vital conceptions could be accommodated only with the greatest
difficulty in an authentic work of art. Creation was spontaneous,
and valid symbols were those which rose with immediacy from the
depths of the unconscious. What redeemed *Guernica* was that
which was effective in any great work which made use of religious,
traditional or mythological imagery: every line, every form, every
colour had been dominated by the artist's secondary-aesthetic
sensibility expressed as 'handling', 'facture' or 'handwriting'.[18]

The development of this particular painting, unusual in Picasso's
oeuvre, represented the artist's wilful resorting to outmoded
symbolism, and his attempt, so to say, to disguise this fact;[19] and
it could be contrasted with a typical work of Moore's (or, for that
matter, a more-typical work by Picasso), in which there would
have been no such attempt to orchestrate specific emotions. Read
admired Moore's confidence in accepting 'as a gift from the unconscious forms of whose significance he is not, at the creative
moment, precisely aware'. His forms appeared to have life of their
own, and he merely to assist in their fruition as created symbols.
Their archetypal significance would thus be discovered, not super-
induced. This was the first of several now-relevant paradoxes: the
forms of art are only significant in so far as they are archetypal,
and in that sense predetermined, and only vital in so far as they
are transformed by the artist's sensibility without conscious
premeditation, and in that sense free.[20] Art transforms archetypal
patterns into extended symbols for which, until the moment of

realization, appropriate concepts do not exist: 'in the artist's mind a peculiar consciousness of the world is in process of development.'[21]

This paradox both fascinated and alarmed Read; and he gave it a great deal of thought during the early 1950s, consulting all Jung's major references to the archetypes, and as many of his more remote allusions as he could get translated. This highlighted the related paradox: archetypes are indispensable as social condensers, but are ineffective if deliberately deployed. A school of thought appeared to be gathering credence, without Jung's evident objection, which held archetypes to be specific Gestalten or definitive configurations. If this were so they could be made academic, and their conscious contrivance would become a matter of usual practice; and this would promote sterility in artists of lesser stature than Picasso, that is, possessing nothing like his ability to breathe life into hack-neyed forms. So Read was genuinely worried by apparently author-itative references to the archetype as a figure, the *formulated* result of countless typical, ancestral experiences, 'the psychic residue of numberless experiences of the same type'.[22] He had believed – he thought with good authority – in archetypes as deep, unconscious predispositions (but nothing more than predispositions) towards certain modes of expression or symbolization; and this is why he had been confident to criticize Picasso for obscuring natural archetypal expression (his facture and his distortion of form) by his liberal, too-literal references to symbolic 'types'. Jung's writings were scoured, as well as those of his closest associates;[23] and the consensus which emerged, despite Jung's prevailing vagueness on the subject, was in fact quite close to Read's own interpretation. Archetypes were not 'closely circumscribed, static figures' after all, but unconscious, inherited tendencies to certain modes of manifes-tation, determined 'only in principle, never concretely'. They would inhabit and invigorate – *inform* – the shapes and colours of spon-taneous expression, but they would not submit to preconceived depiction.

So the general tenor of Jungian thought and its interpretation bore out Read's own belief; but it offered little indication as to why archetypal significance would be apparent in the art of some individuals, but not in that of others. This was something Read felt he himself could enlarge upon; and he proceeded from the view that though authentic symbolization was patently a natural activity, it was actually being practised by a minute number of people. Even within the phalanx of the avant-garde the creation of potent archetypal imagery was a relatively rare event. This was because the finding of symbols to represent previously unknown states of awareness required tremendous effort, and those who would do this would have to live on their nerves. Many individuals would not attain the fitness required for so arduous a task. Some would break under the strain. Others would fall back and abandon the effort; and a number, either having lost or never having possessed the necessary zeal, would augment an unfavourable climate for authentic creativity by their recriminations.[24] A large proportion, no doubt forced by real needs to procure a living, would settle for pleasing imagery. (Jung had observed that the most pleasing, and therefore most easily communicated, images seemed to emanate from superficial levels of unconsciousness.) The very few who would fish deeper, and who *would* net authentic symbols, would have to cope with a general resistance to the dissemination of their strange discoveries. Jung's ambivalence on the question of creative, archetypal manifestation would be explained by his suspicion of the aesthetic, if he thus equated it substantially with the pleasing: in this case Read would have to distinguish between a proper, and a pseudo-aesthetic, creativity. Of course, the thought had to be entertained that Jung may have been right, and an aesthetic attitude ineffectual in the present age, since though Read was convinced of the presence of a valid aesthetic in the works of certain artists, it was clear that Jung, whom he would have expected to have been receptive, had not perceived it. Ineffectualness, such as did exist, could be explained by artists' scepticism in view of the popular acclaim for facile works of art, and a popular scepticism in the face of authentic works which could not immediately be comprehended.[25] But there was nothing here to invalidate image-making as Read understood it.

It was true that art, at various times, had become introspective, even destructive – the course of twentieth-century art, in particular, could be seen as a cyclic advance, a downward swing to nihilism and a subsequent return to symbolic effectiveness.[26] Read was convinced that a small number of artists, including Klee, Kandinsky, Mondrian, Gabo, Moore *and* Picasso,[27] had shaped the foundations of a cultural regeneration. There was no proof of this, but a growing recognition, now that the world was becoming accustomed to their earlier works (as the 'extremism' of these gradually diminished) that their forms had corresponded intimately with the Zeitgeist. This had consisted in a widely diffused sentiment, a sense of bewilderment and anxiety, which had registered on the faces of politics and economics, science and metaphysics, and on all other barometers of spiritual atmosphere. These artists, acutely sensitive to such collective intimations, could not help but find symbols representing the prevalent state of human consciousness. But however sympathetic their *present* reception, such images were actually of slightly outmoded, rather than immediate, significance; and contemporary works by the survivors of this number continued to be received with great hostility. Thus Read would resign himself to the idea that a vital, immediate interaction of the mass and its creative avant-garde would be much more antagonistic than his anarchistic values (inherited from guild-socialism) had accounted for. All that could be hoped for was a lessening of this antagonism's capacity for corrosion. Such corrosion affecting the people's general, receptive sensibility was manifested as a prejudice against artists' glimpses of the future, or more precisely as a desire to have artists anticipate acceptable change. And it was a corrosion of the artist's creativity (this was Jung's explicit rejoinder) which led to false or misleading symbolism, arising not only from an arbitrary pre-selection of images, but also – this had destroyed Jung's faith in modern art – from a wilful distortion of forms otherwise properly conceived. Who in art, Jung asked, was like

> the awe inspiring guest, who knocks at our door portentously? Fear precedes him, showing that ultimate values already flow towards him. Our hitherto believed values decay accordingly, and our only certainty is that the new world will be something different from what we were used to.[28]

His own answer was that it was Picasso[29] – or rather that it *almost* was, because whenever his authentic processes had seemed about to create integral shape he had ceased to trust them. Instead, he would 'hollow forms out and hack them up', arranging 'a field of ever so attractive-looking and alluring shards'. The great problem of the time was an ignorance of what was happening to the world: there were no perceptible values. And those very few individuals – typical of whom, Picasso – possessing the strength to illuminate this by materializing their unconscious knowing, were instead expressing a fragmented vision, a vision mutilated by their wilful personalities. Thus Jung did not exactly concur with Read, who had said that certain artists *were* putting forth images of a nature expressly demanded by Jung's philosophy; but he was greatly pleased by Read's interpretation of this essential requirement.[30]

This was said in an exchange of correspondence in 1960, but it may be assumed to have represented arguments against which Read had pitted his contributions to Eranos over the preceding four years. He was no doubt happy that Jung would validate his interpretation; but there was an explicit demand in all his Eranos presentations that an element of personal, formal distortion was not to be seen as an impediment, but as a vital necessity, to consciousness-extending works of art. It was not enough, for Read, for works of art to materialize singular, ancient presences in the same guise over and over again (such harking to tradition was to *comment* on a present crisis of consciousness, without attempting to do anything about it[31]): constant meaning had to emerge and re-emerge in changing form. In this context (except when he was deliberately displaying mythological erudition) Picasso's attitude was exactly right. Though his work was too aformal for Jung's liking, in fact he was submitting fragments of a highly formal phantasy (such as Jung had required) to a ceaseless mixing and matching in a search for new archetypal significance.

What seems clear from all of this is that Read and Jung were hampered by a slight terminological difference concerning the word 'archetype', or rather that Read wished Jung to extend his use of the term to embrace Read's own special meaning. To Jung, it was synonymous with 'myth'; and his analysis was predominantly traditional, requiring an obvious appearance of historic forces in the present. To Read, this was valid only in periods of great stability, when constant patterns would stand some chance of remaining acceptable.[32] But it would not be surprising if in times of volatility such patterns should become confused; and in requiring some familiar stability here Jung was behaving no differently from a public wishing to anticipate change expectedly. Instead of looking for literal archetypes, he was to accept the value of images which appealed by virtue of inexplicable sentience. It did no harm to Jung's theory, and possibly enhanced it, to suggest that these were archetypal too. The painter, like the poet, was merely conscious of the mystery of being; and the blind emotion with which he confronted such mystery created desires, not to 'designate and signify', but to affirm unanalysed excitement.[33]

Perhaps there was a difference of aesthetic preference too. This would have been less obvious in relation to contemporary sculpture, for there would have been little disagreement about the coherence, integrity and archetypal significance of, say, a Moore or a Gabo. But it would have been most pronounced in relation to painting, at a time when Read was praising the virtues of 'handwriting' and 'facture' (as the great strength of a Picasso and the total content of a Francis or a Tobey), that is, the 'looseness' and 'imprecision' Jung abhorred. To Jung this was obscuration by the personality: to Read it was an attempt to penetrate obscurity, as he said in a statement which also made clear that, in this respect, he saw no distinction between Picasso's late work and abstract expressionism. Behind the 'Cloud of Unknowing' is an unchanging reality; but 'the clouds are continually moving, swirling round and distorting the image . . . and what is "new" is each distorted image that an artist seizes and records. Our knowledge of reality is the sum of all these distorted images.'[34]

Read was anxious to point out that his arguments did not *depend* upon acceptance of an ultimate reality, imperfectly glimpsed, and that in some respects they would be strengthened by its rejection:

> Let us rather agree,[35] that 'since there is no complete truth, our movement toward it is itself the only form in which truth can achieve completion in existence, here and now. In its very process the boundless acquisition of truth experiences that completion which it never reaches as a goal'. This emphasis on Process is in agreement with the conclusion of Bergson and Whitehead, and it is indeed in conformity with Jung's own earlier notion of integration as a process of conscious development, a ceaseless activity involving the symbols of integration. Creativity is of the essence of the process, and every great civilization, seen in historical retrospect, seems to centre on a characteristic symbol of processive integration . . . perhaps the greatest ever conceived by man [is] the reconciliation of nature and spirit. . . .[36]

Had such symbols of reconciliation been created in the modern epoch? Read, of course, maintained that they had; and now he was inclined to see a distinction, as to purpose, between the great, pioneering, early modern works and those being shaped at mid-century. There had been balanced, geometrical, mandala-like images, images inviting withdrawal from the chaotic distractions of everyday perception, images the prime purpose of which had been to induce selfless meditation; and there had been others (increasingly, as time had passed) which had put selfless meditation, so induced, to good effect. These latter images had been produced by arbitrary methods, desiredly without the intervention of conscious will. Though they had been criticized as regressive – as evidence of an inability to give forth form – they were proof of the success of earlier form-giving experiments, and their logical successors.[37] A work executed around 1917 by Mondrian, for example, would have represented an unprecedented freedom of creative mind, detached at last from its historic dependence upon the world of appearances. And a slightly later, surrealist, painting – the complete antithesis of a Mondrian – would have been inconceivable had not creative independence first been symbolized in non-representational form. Moreover, the whole of Mondrian's development had led from pictorial depiction of landscapes and seascapes towards a pure plastic art embodying dynamic movement in equilibrium; and in some sense, now in the 1950s, the whole of this 'becoming' was acknowledged in every contemporary, authentic work of art.[38] So it may be assumed Read considered the vitality of a Heron or a Butler to be indebted to the prior, poised equilibration of a Gabo, and the late work of Picasso to be an entirely logical outcome of his youthful persistence with 'revolutionary' form. The point was, however, that the real creative revolution had hardly begun, and that the assured dignity of early abstraction had quite properly given rise to subsequent frenetic exploration, instead of the other way around. This may explain the fact that Read had never been able to account satisfactorily for the 'improvisations' of Kandinsky, which had provided his first experience of modern art, and which surely ought to have figured more prominently in his writings. Unsettled, dynamic – they had existed before their time: only now[39] was it possible fully to appreciate their urgency, expressed as spontaneous permutation of form and informality.

To Read this epitomized human creativity; and it may be that all along, unknowingly, he had been trying to rationalize his formative, vivid, appreciatory experiences. Kandinsky's 'improvisations' (but not his earlier pictographic expressionist works, nor his later, more cerebral compositions) encapsulated the most fundamental sensory paradox, which had originated at the dawning of human consciousness. There had been two equally valid and mutually antagonistic outcomes of prehistoric circumstances, one placing high premium on form, the other on informality; and this had been the cause of the at-once most vexing and most enriching aspect of the human experience. Read rehearsed these customary arguments, as if surprised by a newly perceived simplicity. Consciousness is formal, he said – not so much form-giving as form-receiving: experience is understood in so far as it is presented to consciousness as form. Consciousness is a symbolizing activity: nothing is found in it that does not offer meaning and reference beyond itself. There was form in the universe before there was human consciousness of it; and, after this initial fact, man must gradually have acquired a conditioned response to those physical properties of symmetry and harmonic proportion which were obvious in his own body, the forms of animals and plants, the rhythm of day and night. Since form was prior to human experience, it may be assumed that a consciousness of form was received from the natural environment of man, and then spontaneously matched in his images and arte-facts. But it was the form that was matched (for example, in those paleolithic animal paintings Siegfried Giedion had studied), not the appearance, and the form was symbolic.[40]

This, then, was Read's train of thought concerning the origins of a formal aesthetic: first there was environmental form, then there was consciousness of it, the gradual result of man's ability to codify sensations. When he considered the origins of an informal aesthetic, however, he found an equally-convincing priority. Primitive man registered his surroundings, because they were yet outside his comprehension, as pre-existing formlessness or chaos. While one aspect of man's mentality had structured an understanding essentially formal, another aspect had remained fascinated by the informal. Ignoring possible ramifications of such arguments – that a formal aesthetic would be the means of coming to terms with a reality preordained, while an informal aesthetic would depend upon the idea that reality was a construct of creative mind – he asked:

. . . why do we exclude the possibility that chaos and dark

nothingness were from the beginning the source of emotions of an aesthetic kind? In other words, must we logically associate art [only] with an emergent consciousness of form? Might there not have been, from the beginning of human consciousness, such a thing as an awareness of the aesthetic significance of informal objects?[41]

Read was drawn by what seemed to be true – that in paleolithic cave paintings, while the matched forms themselves were executed with great precision and clarity, there was invariably informality of their grouping, and of the placing of 'realistic' forms in relation to non-figurative signs presumably intelligible only to initiates. This intermixing of pictorial and non-pictorial elements was not so germane at present, however, as the informality of their arrangement, for according to Giedion it had been this intuitive arrangement, and particularly the superimposition, which had given rise to the activity of *comparison*, the chief means of extending awareness. Read was thus certain that the origins of aesthetic form and informality were coeval, supporting his longstanding belief that a balanced creativity should accommodate both, perhaps as an intuitive, informal mixing and matching of formal perceptions, or at any rate because out of their fundamental discord would emerge new symbolism and new meaning.[42]

At this point Read accepted the fortuitous endorsement of his views. He had received a review copy of a book about the avant-garde of early modern art by an American critic, Roger Shattuck.[43] He was indifferent to much of it, but full of admiration for certain of the author's conclusions, and in particular for the assertion: 'The twentieth century has addressed itself to arts of juxtaposition as opposed to earlier arts of transition.'[44] Shattuck had distinguished between an historically recurring classic art concerned with formal unities, and an alternating romantic art, which had not challenged the basis of such unities but merely expanded them with subjectivity. Before this century the two alike had been discursive or transitional, a concept illustrated by the long-accustomed use of 'linear perspective, relating every object to every other object along imaginary lines'. The assertion which had caught Read's eye was thus extended. The initial phases of modern art, especially cubism, inherited a formal aesthetic based upon certain unities of form, and an informal aesthetic which had enlarged these unities by means of subjective feeling. The modern sensibility, however, did not proceed with the habitual expansion of unities (or even with their reduction to essential form) so much as with a violent dislocation of them in order to test the possibility of new coherence. A work of art began to co-ordinate as equally valid a variety of times, places and states of consciousness. This process, because it sought to hold all such elements in meaningful relationship, relinquished both classic unity and the vagueness which characterizes romanticism.[45] '*Juxtaposition* is the key-word of this new sensibility: setting one thing beside another without connective.'[46]

In order to understand this turning away from beauty and vitality,[47] and the ensuing disfiguration which actually gave rise to gains of great sublimity, Read resorted once more to the idea of the creative evolution of man as macrocosm of individual creativity. Individual aesthetic satisfaction could be defined as, in some sense, 'the perception of a reconstructed whole,' or a conception of chaos overcome;[48] and so too might aesthetic history. If this were appropriate, the pioneers of modern art could be seen to have been instrumental in a dissolution of aesthetic experience and the beginnings of a reconstruction.[49] Now this *had* been an initiative of great sublimity – many of the century's images of reconstruction, or reconciliation, were as awe-inspiring as any in history; but it had also contained the germ of a malignancy capable of assuming threatening proportions. A certain faction of modern sensibility had remained fascinated with disintegrated form.

This was the negative, destructive side of a phenomenon which, in its positive aspect, was manifested as informality. While informality was essentially good, however – perhaps the most desirable addition to modern art's repertoire – disintegration was just about as harmful as could be, leading, unchecked, to relaxation of consciousness and to civilization's decline. Informality, while irregular, was not necessarily chaotic, and the sentience evoked by abstract expressionism was proof of its significance. Disintegration, though, in all its modes – incoherence, insensitivity, brutality, privacy – was essentially disruptive of all significant relationships. It was purposeless, valueless and meaningless. The final criterion of authentic creativity appeared to have boiled down to the artist's 'style', his power to elicit some identification, on the part of others, with meaning, value and purpose as uniquely apprehended by his self. Putting aside those formal elements of a work of art which would constitute its relative beauty, then, Read would say

> ... those elements that make it organic are by contrast flexible and tentative, advancing by trial and error, achieving effectiveness by individual effort. This power in an individual to achieve the effectiveness of any organic activity we call *style*, and it is as essential to art's integrity as is form. Form becomes organic by virtue of an individual's ability to refine form until it has vitality. This is always a personal achievement – that is to say, there is nothing concrete or measurable about the quality thus achieved: it is a presence . . . . There is always in a work of art this intangible, indefinable element to which it owes its vitality, its magical power to enhance life, and an artist's possession of this transforming power is his style.[50]

The modern movement had been an immense effort to restore to art its vital function, to make art once more an organic mode of perception, communicating traces of unique sensibility. It had 'redeemed vision from its merely reproductive task, the obsession of the degenerate Renaissance tradition' and had 'dared to be creative'. But this great enterprise was in danger of betrayal, Read felt, by a permissive art of the 1950s and 1960s, an art, moreover, which had resulted from corrupted understanding of all that he had willed into the substance of the ICA. The fascination for modern science had, in some quarters, been corrupted into love of science-fiction: the Jungian preoccupation with a specifically new mythology had been reduced to enthusiasm for allegory, found as epic and phantasy commercialized in the cinema and in consumer advertising. To have taken the typical imagery of such 'popular culture' (Read considered this itself misleading since, largely associated with advertising, it was exploitative) and to have adopted it to the work of art with some respect for 'facture' and sensitive feeling for colour and composition, Read would have found barely acceptable – though he was doubtful whether such remnants of aesthetic conscience were really enough to redeem commercialized images from final incoherence. He could not tolerate, however, and felt impelled to condemn, the casual re-presentation of arbitrary forms, a mindless repetition of the clichés of an imposed pictorial regime, an impersonal execution and a lack of style.[51] He opposed arguments that an art which did not possess his special

163

sense of style was nevertheless not necessarily unexpressive; and one of his last theoretical excursions was an attempt to demonstrate the paramountcy of unique, individual, expressive style.

He was quite clear about where, in his own experience, this had been lacking: surrealism, in relation to subsequent art, seemed academic. Though he had supported surrealism, and would have done so again had its circumstances returned, he now accepted that it had been inadequate, in view of its revolutionary intentions, because it had placed no value upon evoking sentient feeling for brushstroke, gesture, or indeed any individual 'nervous' communication.[52] This was the only way to effect any change in perception: all others (in particular, surrealism's reliance upon academic realism) depended on widely accepted values which were, by definition, conventional. By the same token his one-time attempt to found a dialectic theory was an embarrassment, for the dual reason of its having been nurtured in an enthusiasm for Hegelian theory inspired by 'revolutionary' surrealism.[53] Surrealism had enlarged art's field of explicit reference, and its followers had been aware of a sense of uniqueness expressed as unconventional behaviour. But this had not been carried to painting and sculpture. Surrealist art had merely been explicit about what had usually been disguised, and it had not given rise to uniqueness in the sense of unprecedented aesthetic perception. Its technique had been prescribed and its focus (on dream imagery – that is, intimations recollectable only in conventional or literal form) misdirected. Uniqueness was ultimately reducible to the occasion on which beauty and vitality were brought together by an individual managing to avoid such impositions. This *event* would be unique, the manner not the matter.[54]

Merely to reveal phantasy, then, referring only to a world of private complexes, was not enough to create a work of art. Neither, at the opposite extreme, was to 'look beyond abstraction, towards metaphysical nothingness', rendering back no more than a sense of vacuity, a more-than-individual complex. Art would have no history but for the individual artist's efforts to invent significant form – a form (whether or not the artist was aware of it) seeking to integrate mind and concrete reality. A chief characteristic of mind, Read maintained, is to be constantly describing itself; the purpose of creativity to present to mind evidence of existence beyond itself. Style is where these meet and interfuse – a concentration of personal emotion projected into the impersonal, an expression inevitable and organic to an individual mode of experience, and the creation of a centre from which might irradiate style in its general or secondary capacity, that centre being 'a small, incontestable discovery and possession of one individual'.[55]

This was the acid test; and Read was sure that it explained the importance of historic personalities such as Giotto, Michelangelo and Poussin,[56] and also that it demonstrated the comparable, contemporary significance of such as Gabo, Moore and (Read seemed only lately to have become aware of this) of Hans Arp. The works of these three were held to be equally potent manifestations of style; though it was remarkable, and proof of art's infinite variety, that in spite of this there were pronounced dissimilarities at the growthpoints of experience. Works by Gabo, Moore and Arp exhibited differences of manner if not of matter; and it may be observed (marking the full cycle of Read's thought and his vindication of primary influences) that any stylistic dissimilarities were reminiscent of his earliest predispositions – to the natural, to the social (now subtly realigned with the humanist[57]) and to the metaphysical influences of his self-education. What obviously interested Read in the work of Arp, for example, was that it was explicitly natural and transformative. Forms suggested by certain natural phenomena were somehow reduced to essentials, and these, in the course of subsequent elaboration, were allowed to assume other, apparently accidental, associations. Forms originally suggested by birds or by shells might be transformed into suggestions of fruits or of clouds: this practice seemed to have been based on a belief that all natural forms were modifications of a few basic types. In this way Arp could be said to have identified the impersonal, understood as certain essences of nature, and to have engaged it with aspects of his unique personality – gentleness, grace and humour.[58]

While Arp had taken elements of the external world as points of departure, Gabo, in contrast, had 'dared to conceive the independent existence of a work of art, deprived of all naturalistic content or inspiration, existing solely as an image of impersonal forces'.[59] He too had begun with deeply unconsciously realized truths – in his case relating to space and time – but while Arp had been concerned with the ways of growth, perceived in physical mutations of natural phenomena, Gabo had attempted to emphasize aspects of reality possessing no material existence. Comparing these two attitudes, Read recollected D'Arcy Thompson's influence upon his own thinking. Gabo's work, he thought, had begun with natural form, and had arrived at a distillation of the life force within it.

> From a wider philosophical view . . . the two procedures are reciprocal. 'In an organism, great or small, it is not merely the nature of the *motions* of the living substance which we must interpret in terms of force (according to kinetics), but also the *conformation* of the organism itself, whose permanence or equilibrium is explained by the interaction or balance of forces, as described in statics.' This sentence from D'Arcy Thompson's great work clearly distinguishes the different aims of Gabo and Arp.[60]

And it also removed the last traces of an apparent contradiction which obviously had worried Read. He had believed Gabo's work to be synthetic in spite of the fact that it had offered no superficial evidence of having accommodated the vital, or the organic: now, though, it could be argued that it had been concerned with spatial and temporal order,[61] or the immutable context of such vitality, and that in this it *was* organic.

If Arp's work had been predominantly 'natural' and Gabo's 'metaphysical', the term which most readily characterized Moore's art was 'humanist'. His work had persistently referred to two principal archetypes – the mother and child and the reclining female form – emerging from his fascination with other matters, such as bones, stones and tree-forms. He had been most conscious of having addressed *vitality* (thirty years earlier he had made a distinction between beauty and vitality, probably as a result, Read thought, of his having brought to Moore's attention Hulme's notes on Worringer);[62] and now his work could be seen as an interpenetration of what was most vital in human archetypal memory – those 'forms of things unknown' he was empowered to project into consciousness[63] – and what was most vital in his studied perceptions of the vast range of natural forms he collected for analysis. Bringing together vital archetypal recollections and equally vital organic perceptions, forming a synthesis of the two, constituted, according to Read's recent definition, creation of the 'reconciling image'. And the shaping of such symbols of social cohesion[64] was the greatest service to humanism. 'My desire is to redefine humanism in the terms of a sensuous apprehension of being',[65] Read had lately written. Whereas once he would have emphasized Moore's apprehension of organic nature as the essential feature of his work, and considered its archetypal significance to reside specifically in this, he now was more inclined to say that the most potent symbols of a humanist art would find nature in the human form and fix humanity in nature. The reclining women were archetypal: interfused with nature, however, they assumed the appearance of landscape, and in this they gave access to those even more primary archetypes called 'earth symbols'. Thus Read's thirty-year commentary on Moore's art concluded with his own image of reconciliation. Longstanding, intuitive appreciation was reconciled with more recent, reasoned arguments about formation and transformation: Moore's images were symbols of processive integration, vital to psychic wholeness and the social wellbeing.[66]

Recent references to Bergson, Whitehead, D'Arcy Thompson and Worringer were typical of a late phase of Read's thought which was full of reminiscences and noddings towards influences, including some of his earliest. This was another kind of reconciliation, a closing of the ring, and a welding of late thoughts and early initiatives to form a perfect cycle of events.

The most agreeable time of his life had been sandwiched between his Edinburgh appointment, after which he had gone to live in Hampstead, and the looming fact of a Second World War, which persuaded him to move his family into the country. While he had been searching for a house in Hampstead Henry Moore had lent him his, and thirty years later Read could remember vividly Moore's works which had been in progress then, and their positions around the studio. Temperamentally he had much in common with Moore, and everything he subsequently wrote about his sculpture was founded in totally accurate recollections of the appearance, texture and feel of a past progression of representative works. In a very real sense Moore made objects Read would have made if his skills had been plastic instead of literary; and Read spoke to those who could not listen to Moore's art unaided. This was partly due to the fact that, as close neighbours, they were in almost daily contact throughout the 1930s, but perhaps chiefly because they had a common mental landscape (though Moore seems not to have pined for his Yorkshire quite so much as Read did). Read had found his own house a stone's throw from Moore's and almost next door to Barbara Hepworth and Ben Nicholson; and with Paul Nash in the vicinity, and such as Naum Gabo, Walter Gropius, László Moholy-Nagy and Piet Mondrian arriving at intervals, a community of friendliness, criticism and mutual support was created in Hampstead, the closest Read ever expected to approach anarchism in his lifetime.[67]

  This had been a time of ferment, giving rise not only to seminal works such as *Art Now, Art and Industry, Art and Society* and *Poetry and Anarchism*, but also to his most original creation, *The Green Child*. It was simply a new life, quite eclipsing the one before his move to Edinburgh, which had had a much more restrained, or rather reserved, creative aspect, sustained as this had been by weekly contact with T. S. Eliot. Eliot had taken Read seriously when his lack of a 'proper' education for an aspiring man of letters would have been all too apparent. He had done so, Read presumed, out of respect for his having published T. E. Hulme's philosophy, to which Eliot was devoted.[68] Whatever the reason, it initiated friendship, regular contact, intense argument (they were opposed on many grounds – religious, political, aesthetic[69]); and Read's rapid acclimatization to the world of criticism was due in no small part to his having been tested in the fires of debate with Eliot. Read was aware of having been cultivated by Eliot. (Eliot encouraged him to contribute to *The Criterion*, and, as a director of Faber and Gwyer, commissioned the book which established him as critic, *Reason and Romanticism*.) But there was never any sense of Read's being patronized, and this was probably due to the first footing of their relationship when Read's had been the role of commissioning editor, offering Eliot space in *Art and Letters*.

  There is no doubt that Eliot encouraged Read's 'reason', and considered his 'romanticism', and his interests in psychology, to be largely irrelevant and transitory. Read's awkward classicism in the 1920s may have been due to Eliot's pulling; and it seems significant that even in late life Read could not discuss Wordsworth (in the context of his memories of Eliot) without reviving arguments about a perceived classicism. Wordsworth, in classic fashion, Read said, had tried to impose unity on sense impressions in an attempt to create images of wholeness. This too had been Eliot's objective: he had had great respect for tradition, and had possessed a sense of extending it and shaping it coherently. But Read had increasingly

168

come to admire Eliot's work for parts he recognized as eclectic, fragmented and distorted – that is, for a poetic vision the counterpart of Picasso's or Klee's, and peculiar to romanticism. Eliot then, believing himself, in their lifelong correspondence, to be helping Read retain some vestige of his classicism, actually reinforced convictions about the disjointed nature of experience and an essential, romantic outlook on the world and its events.[70] Though the frequency of Read's references to Eliot in his aesthetic writings may have been sufficiently implicit, he does not seem to have openly discussed Eliot's involuntary example (perhaps for fear of hurting his feelings) until the time came to defend Eliot from those who found fault in an inconsistent classicism.[71]

At this time too Read revealed that Richard Aldington had done his best to redeem him from his overtly intellectual stance of the 1920s, for which Aldington had felt substantially responsible. Aldington never disowned imagism – indeed he strenuously maintained that he[72] (and neither Ezra Pound nor T. E. Hulme) had invented it; but he regarded it as having been a necessary clearing the decks of a tired and over-elaborate romanticism, before a much more spontaneous and immediate art of feeling could take its place.[73] He had begged Read to devote himself to poetry, not to dissipate his energies in criticism; and he had mourned Read's having been tempted into academic life, then celebrated his quick return to a freelance existence. Aldington rallied to him at this most difficult time (one other who did so, unexpectedly, was Roger Fry, recommending Read as his successor at *The Burlington Magazine*); and it seems clear that Aldington by now considered Read won away from the course which Eliot had steered for him. It is ironic that in his brief academic career, which Aldington so bitterly regretted, Read had proceeded to structure his teaching around Worringer's distinction between abstraction and empathy, emphasizing the latter as a peculiarly northern characteristic. There is nothing to suggest that Read ever discussed Worringer with Aldington; and, if he had, Aldington would probably have associated him with Hulme (whom he disliked[74]) and with an essentially pessimistic view of the worth of human existence. But Read – though he remembered many discussions with Eliot and others on the necessity of having a tragic sense of life, and though the influence of such as Nietzsche and Hulme had persuaded him that this was desirable *intellectually* – never was comfortably a

pessimist; and the empathy he prescribed was a joyous identification *with*, rather than a sense of inadequacy before, the world of
nature.

This positive feeling for nature, of course, was always to a large
degree an identification with the life which by rights he should
have led, had his family not been turned off the land when he was
ten. In late life he was given to wondering about alternative
patterns which might have unfolded if this decisive occurrence,
and the longing it created, had not intervened. He never seriously
considered a 'return' to farming, because he could never have
afforded an enterprise large enough to have guaranteed his family
freedom from enslavement to the soil. But he realized that it had
been agrarian instincts that had encouraged his guild-socialism at
the expense, perhaps, of a political future in the Labour Party, and
that it had also been these that had led him to Anarchism instead
of the much more fashionable Marxism, always seeming to him a
philosophy for an industrial proletariat.[75] Read was convinced that,
in this way, the whole of his life was lived by his first ten years –
that the moulding of childhood sensibility in a natural environment, amongst a family and a wider community not given to the
suppression of feeling, formed instincts which guided him at every
point of his life as if he had no choice.

He had always retained a firm grasp on childhood memories,
initially for the security they had provided in an orphanage. It
never occurred to him that other people would relinquish naive
experiences, permit them to evaporate, or struggle to avoid their
influence on adult perception, until he witnessed Eliot's immediate,
acute poetic sensibility diminishing (as Read saw it), pressurized
by reason and convention.[76] Long after it had become obvious to
him that dislocation with naive experience was the norm, he wrote
of his *alter ego*, Eugene Strickland,[77] who *had* allowed his innocent
vision to fade, had put poetry aside, and had risen high in the
hierarchy of public administration, without gaining any real
appreciation of the meaning of his life. Read was appalled at the
thought that this might have happened to him, and happy at
his 'choice' of remaining alive to remote and elusive childhood
sensations, and of projecting these into public consciousness as
archetypes of uninhibited feeling.[78] According to this standard, his
success will be judged by his most spontaneous works – *Form in
Modern Poetry*, *The Green Child*, *The Innocent Eye*, *Art and the*

Evolution of Man; and readers who are convinced by these, and by the very many passages of immediate apprehension in other works, will share his own discomfort at the thought of his too-contrived attempt to construct a theory of art in the 1930s.

But how will his earliest *critical* experiences be judged? He made so little mention of an indebtedness to T. E. Hulme that one must either have escaped him or embarrassed him so deeply as to have been unmentionable. He was so scrupulous in his acknowledgment of influences, however – indeed, this was considered a vice by those who knew him well – that only the strongest wish to distance himself from Hulme's intellectually polished system of ideas would have prevented an admission of reliance upon the *Speculations*. Will his readers be entitled to judge him harshly for this? There is no doubt that initially he depended heavily upon Hulme, and that a fair proportion of his work may be regarded as realization of Hulme's initiatives. But there are two good reasons why there was nothing disreputable in this. One, slightly the weaker, is that Hulme appears to have been so disorganized in his literary affairs as to have made any coherent, popular exposition of his theory, on his own account, unlikely: if he had survived the war he would in any case have required a mediator between himself and a potential public. And the much stronger reason resides in the fact that Read preserved his innate romanticism while editing Hulme's manuscripts, in spite of the great disruptive force they must have occasioned, and eventually managed to temper, or complement, Hulme's thought by means of his own.

Read's critical attitudes were quite well-formed when he encountered Hulme. He had already read extensively, following his liking for romantic poetry and his predispositions to certain natural and social theories; and his immersion in Hulme's work may be seen as a first attempt to widen his horizons, by coming to terms with matters for the most part unrelated to his own inclinations. Hulme had admired Kropotkin, but there was little relating to revolutionary socialism in the *Speculations*. There was little reference to nature either, though there was of course the natural analogue, a fundamental principle of the admired Bergsonian theory. Hulme was decidedly anti-romantic; and in order to sustain his own romanticism while appreciating Hulme's classicism, Read obviously would have had to compartmentalize the two. He was assisted in this by Hulme's interpretation of Worringer (one Read was to reiterate repeatedly throughout his lifetime) which offered at first the possibility of constructing two separate aesthetics; and in view of Hulme's strongly argued convictions, Read may have felt compelled to give an equally articulate account of romanticism, the most appropriate means of which resided in the new developments in psychology.[79] While Hulme's distinction between the classic and the romantic was one of greater and lesser value, however, Read preserved faith in romanticism while simultaneously respecting Hulme's classicism, and this seems to have been the faint beginnings of a dialectic theory. And a general tendency, already present to some extent in Read's self-education, would have been reinforced by Hulme's clearly stated intention to interrelate often quite disparate theories in the service of a greater argument. In this respect Read followed the tacit advice of Hulme, and superimposed Croce's *Aesthetic* upon Bergson's *Creative Evolution*; and he also, quite openly, began to accept psychological arguments from whichever quarter suited him best, disregarding the fact that their sources or contexts were often incompatible.

There were other aspects of Read's later theorizing, too, which had precedents in Hulme. For example, there was this cycle of events. Hulme, 'desperate to escape the nightmare of a mechanistic conception of reality',[80] discovered the means in Bergson's theory, which opposed a continuous, mechanistic evolution with a creative evolution, that is, a system which incorporated discontinuities comparable with the inspirational leaps of mentality. This was to prepare Read (who also spoke of an escape from mechanistic nightmare) for his eager acceptance of the quantum theory, which in turn permitted his arrangement of exactly symmetrical halves of a dialectic – the one conditioned by quantum-advancing physics, the other dependent upon an inspirational leap from perception to intuition. Later arguments that the physical and the psychological were resolved in the organic (understood to have been supported by Whitehead and D'Arcy Thompson, and to be evident in the sculpture of Henry Moore) may have assisted Read's return to fuller appreciation of Bergson. He had thought himself to have outgrown Bergson's influence, but later confessed to a continuing devotion. And in the late ordering of his own theory Read recognized that Bergson's synthesis of material reality and unconscious mentality demanded acknowledgment of 'the inspiration I continue to receive from the only metaphysics that is based on biological science',[81] and of his consistent reliance upon Bergson's definitions of 'consciousness' and 'intuition'. If, then, at quite late stages of his theorizing – at the outlining of a theory of organic formation, and at the point of adopting the idea of symbolic transformation – Read was a Bergsonian, he was still empowered by the licence given him by Hulme. And there were other precedents of Read's later work (if 'precedental' is not inapt description for the merest traces of ideas) in Hulme's *Plan for a Book on Modern Theories of Art*.[82]

The foremost part of Hulme's programme would have been the initiation of 'practically a new subject', an aesthetic philosophy more exact than prevailing critical conventions, and founded upon psychology. Hulme clearly had in mind a Bergsonian substantiation; but, by the time this speculation was published, others, chiefly Freud and Jung, had achieved significant scientific advances, and an eminent art theorist, Roger Fry, had made a considered assessment of their relevance to art criticism. The uncharacteristic manner of Read's treatment of Fry may be understood as reflecting the young man's determination, following Hulme's example, to claim this special area to himself. As he did so he was fixed upon an ideal – a vindication of the romantic principle – which was quite outside Hulme's own intentions, but which, paradoxically, was actually given impetus in his outline theory.

What is art? Is there any specific emotion characterizing modern art? What is the nature of creative imagination? Hulme would have channelled these questions of his towards an explanation of the modern art of his preference – imagist poetry, Epstein's sculpture, Bomberg's painting, and an imagined future art, the civilized equivalent of the primitive. Read's work followed personal preferences in a remarkably similar way – preferences for a precise poetic diction (essential to accurate communication of feeling), for the sculpture of Moore, the painting of Nicholson and Nash (though his *first* art criticism had been an appraisal of Bomberg's work), and an avant-garde art which embodied the eternal presence of prehistoric principles. Read, like Hulme, was obviously not concerned to establish an impartial method: his concern was to express personal convictions with as much resonance as possible. Present in his late work were several very serviceable answers to Hulme's primary questions.

Art is supra-conscious, engaging universal principles of beauty.

173

Read often said that such art was of measurable effectiveness, but he was vague in his extension of this argument, speaking of tried and tested conceptions such as the Golden Section, or settling for the idea that proportions and harmonies perceived in such art would be well-received to the degree that they coincided with those found in nature. Art is unconscious expression. The chief weakness of this explanation, to some, was in its shifting of attention from art to mentality, that is, to Read's psychological construction and away from the aesthetic fact. Art is an organic event unfolding: it is the creation of form and the fixing of reality. This, resolving the two previous, equal-opposite assertions, provided the means of linking art to other formative processes, for example physiology. But its weakness, if it had one, might possibly have been in this – it was not so much a conception of art as of formation. There was a vast number of form-giving activities (witness the little-explored argument that science was equally creative), the majority of which quite clearly were not art. This conception could not be sustained while maintaining belief in a vanguard of artists, themselves equipped with the only authentic creativity. It underwrote, however, the idea of a desired, general creativity serving the cultural diffusion. Art is symbolic transformation: an authentic artist is one who has powers to symbolize archetypal feelings and intuitions in previously unseen form. Art is the sensuous apprehension of being, an indispensable focus of a new humanism.

It is now most apparent that while certain facets of Read's thought were constant (the natural and the social values) his aesthetic arguments continuously shifted their ground. This movement was intuitional and discontinuous. A systematic theorist would have taken pains to articulate fine gradations between a dialectic of styles and one of organic formation, and to explain a further transition to 'symbolic transformation'. Read left such pedantry to others: his thought was a quantum-advancing creativity. Even so, it was paradoxical. It manifestly was evolving; but, conditioned as it was by longed-for nature and hoped-for anarchism, in a sense it was also constant reaffirmation. His ideas responded to a peculiar give-and-take: they grew and diminished, and were continuously readjusted, in keeping with D'Arcy Thompson's observation that in an organic phenomenon 'every deformation that tends to destroy the symmetry is complemented by an equal and opposite deformation that tends to restore it'.

He took occasional self-contradictions in his stride, as only to be expected in an approach which placed high premium on spontaneity. He may not be considered to have made an original construction, so much as to have left embodied in his day-to-day writings an image of organically developing thought. All that he would perhaps have wished for would have been credit for trying to reclaim art from the fringes of human experience, for attempting to realize Ruskin's wish to make criticism more genuinely appreciatory, and for endeavouring to create works of art, as works of words, which rang of truth. His last words on Henry Moore[83] might have been about himself:

I would like to emphasize once again the unprogrammatic, the almost naive, nature of the process. Critics may interpret his achievement against the background of their knowledge of the history of art, of the science of art, of human psychology and social history; but the artist himself is not a scientist, a psychologist or an historian. He is a maker of images . . . and he is impelled to make [them] by his sense of the forms that are vital to the life of mankind.

Notes and References

Many of the following references relate to unique materials in the *Sir Herbert Read Archive* at the McPherson Library, University of Victoria B. C. A typical reference here would be '48/102 Vict' (i.e. Lot 48, Item 102), although occasionally additional numbers, for example as in '10/3/16 Vict' (i.e. Lot 10, Item 3, Part 16), would indicate a part, subsection or page(s) of an unusually large item.

Chapter 1 Innocence and experience

1 See Read's autobiographies *The Innocent Eye*, Faber, London 1933; *Annals of Innocence and Experience*, Faber, London 1940; and *The Contrary Experience*, Faber, London 1963. See also the catalogue of the exhibition *A Tribute to Herbert Read*, Bradford Art Galleries and Museums, 1975.
2 cf. *Annals*, pp. 17–62 (early childhood); pp. 67–72 (formal education); and pp. 126–31 (the 'conversion' to socialism).
3 ibid., p. 188.
4 Read: 'Why I was inspired by Nietzsche', *The Listener*, vol. XXXVII 13 Feb 1947, pp. 295–6.
5 Read: 'The Philosophy of Anarchism' (1940); repub. in Read: *Anarchy and Order*, Faber, London 1954, p. 41.
6 ibid.
7 See Read: 'Definitions Towards a Modern Theory of Poetry', *Art and Letters*, vol. 1, no. 3, Jan 1918, pp. 73–8.
8 See Read: *In Retreat*, Woolf, London 1925.
9 'Definitions' (n. 7), p. 78.
10 Read had extensive correspondences with Nash and Aldington. See Lot 48/99 (Nash) and Lot 48/2 (Aldington), Read Archive, University of Victoria B. C.
11 Lewis was to have provided illustrations to a book (of poetry?) Read proposed to publish: see corres. Lewis to Read dated 17.12.18 (48/82

Vict). In 1934 Lewis suspected Read of being the author of a damaging, unsigned article in *TLS* (Lewis to Read 3.12.34). This was unfounded, and he apologized (7.12.34); but this was the start of the deterioration of their friendship which led to Lewis's vitriolic attack on Read, published in Lewis: *The Demon of Progress in the Arts*, Methuen, London 1954, Chap. XV.

12 The 'Readers and Writers' column, weekly throughout the second half of 1921.

13 See corres. A. R. Orage to Read, esp. dated 1.7.21 and 21.5.21 (48/102 Vict).

14 He wanted to work for a year with Ouspensky in Paris, and asked Read to edit the paper in his absence: Orage to Read 10 Aug 1922. In fact it was not until 1931 that he returned to England.

15 Notably S. Matthewman: cf. corres. Read to Matthewman dated 8 May 1922 (62/80 Vict), and also Read to W. R. Childe dated 27.4.22 (62/4 Vict).

16 cf. corres. W. R. Childe to Read, esp 30.4.19 and 20.10.20 (48/16 Vict) and Read to Childe 27.4.22 (62/4 Vict).

17 See Read: *Wordsworth*, Cape, London 1930, pp. 107, 110.

18 See Eliot's holographed notes dated 23.8.22, on Read's synopsis interleaved with Eliot's corres. (48/32 Vict).

19 ibid. (Read's synopsis).

20 Noted by Hulme (p. 5) in his commonplace book – the so-called 'Notebook on Notebooks' – which was the only Hulme document Read retained (coll. Benedict Read).

21 Read: 'The Early Influence of Bertrand Russell', *The Cult of Sincerity*, Faber, London 1968, p. 143.

22 Read: 'T.S.E.: a Memoir', ibid. (n. 21), p. 107.

23 See Read's review of Russell's 'Analysis of Mind' in *The New Age*, vol. XXIV, no. 18, 1 Sep 1921, pp. 211–12.

24 See corres. Read to H. W. Hausermann dated 6.8.37 (61/86 Vict).

25 See corres. Read to G. Lowes Dickinson dated 4.6.23 (48/27 Vict).

26 See corres. Read to I. A. Richards dated 18.4.25 (49/22 Vict).

27 ibid. (n. 17), p. 159.

28 See corres. R. Aldington to Read dated 3.9.24 and 23.12.24 (48/2 Vict).

29 Read criticized it for tending away from 'compression, intensity, essential significance': see Aldington to Read 23.12.24.

30 See adversely critical report 7pp by publisher's referee (unsigned, undated) clearly discussing a preliminary version of this essay. (61/29 Vict): Read's provisional outline is attached.

31 ibid., p. 1.

32 See below, Chapter 3, n. 58.

33 See corres. to I. A. Richards (n. 26).

34 Read: *Surrealism*, Faber, London 1936, pp. 43–4.

35 Read: 'Surrealism: the Dialectic of Art', *Left Review*, vol. 2, no. 10, July 1936 (supplement facing p. 508), pp. ii–iii.

36 Read: Foreword to catalogue of the exhibition *Realism and Surrealism*, Guildhall, Gloucester May–Jun 1938; p. 1 (unnumbered).
37 See corres. Read to G. Pailthorpe dated 30.4.39 (61/52 Vict).
38 Read: *Art Now* (2nd edit), Faber, London 1936, p. 146.
39 See corres. R. Fry to Read (nd) (48/43 Vict).
40 Repeatedly made clear in corres with T. S. Eliot (repres. Faber) throughout 1947–9 (48/32 and 49/6 Vict).
41 It is tempting to believe that Read first speculated about a broad front of modern art, then about an ability to range across it, later about the possibility of synthesizing extreme aspects of the front, and, later still, about a further dialectic opposition featuring advanced, though essentially different, forms of art. Though he published such thoughts in this order, culminating, for example, in *The Philosophy of Modern Art*, Faber, London 1952, pp. 93–5 and 237 (Gabo's advanced condition of art) and p. 207 (Moore's counterpart: see also Chapter 4 below, n. 106), it is not certain that his theorizing was in this way chronological. Much of it was already evident in his corres. with Jean Helion: see Helion to Read dated 2.1.36 (48/59 Vict).
42 As is made evident by the fact that he published his efforts to construct a dialectic of styles (in *Philosophy of Modern Art*) after it had been superseded by later concerns.
43 With Frank Rutter, who had been his mentor in matters of art criticism at Leeds. Their initial objective was to publish a successful quarterly review, *Art and Letters*. See Read: *Cult of Sincerity*, pp. 97–9.
44 See discussion of the first issues of *Art and Letters* in corres. from W. R. Childe dated 304.19 (48/16 Vict).
45 See Read: 'Proposals for a Scottish Philanthropist', typescript 7 pp (37/55 Vict).
46 See corres. M. E. Sadler (who was consulted on financial matters) to Read dated 3.3.39: 'To secure for public possession some of the finest examples of modern painting and sculpture ... would be a national service.' He provided rough estimates of capital and maintenance costs (48/122 Vict).
47 cf. corres. Read to J. Alford dated 9.8.57 and enclosure (Alford's defence of Read to J. S. Keel): (49/1 Vict).
48 See Chapter 5 below, pp. 117–21.
49 Read, Fordham and Adler (eds): *The Collected Works of C. G. Jung*, Routledge, London 1953. He was capable of this translation himself, but was quick to recognize R. F. C. Hull's exceptional expertise as both translator and interpreter of Jung.
50 Read: Preface to L. L. Whyte (ed.): *Aspects of Form*, Lund Humphries, London 1951, pp. v–vi.
51 See corres. N. Gabo to Read dated 4.1.53 (48/44 Vict).
52 According to his son, Benedict, Read considered *The Forms of Things Unknown*, Faber, London 1960 to be his most accomplished work.
53 See Stephen Spender's criticism of Read in Spender: *The Struggle of the Modern*, Hamilton, London 1963, pp. 177–85.
54 Alford to Keel (n. 47).

55 See corres. B. Dobree to Read dated 15.5.50; (48/28 Vict).
56 See Allen Tate's Foreword to Tate (ed.): *Herbert Read: Selected Writings: Poetry and Criticism*, Faber, London 1963, pp. 7–14.
57 (48/141 Vict).
58 ibid. (n. 56), pp. 8–9.
59 See Read: *Coleridge as Critic*, Faber, London 1949.
60 See F. Berry: *Herbert Read*, Longmans Green, London 1953 (Rev. Edn. 1961).
61 ibid., p. 13.
62 See G. Woodcock: *Herbert Read: the Stream and the Source*, Faber, London 1972, pp. 70–4.
63 In a lengthy corres. with Louis Adeane, who was writing a monograph entitled *To the Crystal City*, about this particular book of Read's (61/3 Vict).
64 See corres. C. G. Jung to Read dated 17.10.48 (48/72 Vict).
65 ibid (n. 62), p. 70.
66 See, for example, R. Melville's criticism in H. Treece (ed.): *Herbert Read: an Introduction to his work by Various Hands*, Faber, London 1944, pp. 81–90.
67 Read: *The Green Child*, Heinemann, London 1935 (1945 edit Grey Walls Press, p. 130).

Chapter 2 **Empathy and abstraction**

1 Read: 'Extracts from a Diary', in *The Contrary Experience*, Faber, London 1973, pp. 70–146.
2 See *Leeds Arts Club* programme dated 10 Dec 1909, p. 4 (Leeds City Reference Lib.).
3 See W. Martin: *The New Age Under Orage*, Manchester U. P. 1967, pp. 21–2.
4 See P. Mairet: *A. R. Orage*, Dent, London 1936, pp. 12 et seq.
5 This information supplied, and other matters relating to the Leeds Arts Club confirmed, by Tom Heron in a letter to the author dated 28 Feb. [1980].
6 Which had engaged the attention of Roger Fry and Clive Bell, and which Bell would subsequently describe in his book *Art*, Chatto & Windus, London 1914, Chap. One.
7 Mairet, p. 25.
8 *Contrary Exp.* p. 257.
9 M. Sadlier: *Michael Ernest Sadler: a Memoir*, Constable, London 1949, pp. 237–40.
10 M. Sadler: *Premonitions of the War in Modern Art* (lecture), Leeds 26 Oct 1915, p. 2 (Brotherton Lib., Leeds University).
11 M. Sadler diary entries 3.10.13 and 10.12.13. (Bodleian Lib.)
12 Report on Sadler's lecture *What is the Secret of Art?* dated 27.7.21, in which he recalled Bell's publication of the theory of 'Significant Form' (1914). (Brotherton Lib.)
13 ibid., n. 9.

14 F. Rutter: *Since I was Twenty-Five*, Constable, London 1927, p. 194.
15 Read: Diary entry 17.7.16. (*Contrary Exp.* p. 72).
16 See *The New Age*, vol. XIV, 1914, pp. 625, 689, 753, 814–15, 821.
17 A. R. Orage: *Friedrich Nietzsche: The Dionysian Spirit of the Age*, Foulis, London 1906.
18 See Bergson's testimonial to Hulme in Read (ed.): *Speculations by T. E. Hulme*, Kegan Paul, Trench, Trubner & Co., London 1924, p. x.
19 ibid. pp. 203 et seq.
20 T. E. Hulme: 'A Preface Note and Neo-Realism', *The New Age*, vol. XIV, no. 15, 12 Feb 1914, p. 467.
21 T. E. Hulme: 'Modern Art I', *The New Age*, vol. XIV, no. 11, 15 Jan 1914, p. 341.
22 T. E. Hulme: 'Modern Art II', *The New Age*, vol. XIV, no. 21, 26 Mar 1914, pp. 661–2.
23 op. cit., n. 16, p. 753.
24 For an account of Rutter's interpretation see F. Rutter: 'Nine Propositions', *Art and Letters*, vol. II, no. 1, Winter 1918–19, p. 52.
25 Sadler's housekeeper was a family friend of Read's, and he thus had frequent access to the collection 'through the back door'. See R. Parrington Jackson: 'Herbert Read: the Yorkshire Background', *A Tribute to Herbert Read*, Bradford Art Galleries and Museums 1975, p. 68.
26 Read: *The Philosophy of Modern Art*, Faber, London 1952, p. 259.
27 M. E. Sadler: Diary 18.10.1913, recording a paper given that day to W.E.A. delegates at Leeds University (Bodleian Lib.). 'Ruskin believed in the clan. Loyalty to a brave leader seemed to him to be one of the greatest things in human life. To organize society in such a way as to bring great leaders to the fore and to impel men to follow them, through self-suffering and self-sacrifice to death was the message . . . he gave to the world.'
28 ibid.
29 Read: Diary entry 2.10.1916. (*Contrary Exp.*, pp. 77–8).
30 Read: *Annals of Innocence and Experience*, Faber, London 1940, p. 191 (Bergson) and p. 86 (Nietzsche).
31 Martin (n. 3), Chap. XII.
32 See R. Cork: *Vorticism and Abstract Art in the First Machine Age*, Fraser, London 1976; vol. I, pp. 186–7.
33 C. Ginner: 'Neo-Realism', *The New Age*, vol. XIV, no. 9, 1 Jan 1914, pp. 271–2.
34 op. cit., n. 20, pp. 467–9.
35 C. Ginner: 'Modern Painting and Teaching', *Art and Letters*, vol. 1, no. 1, 1917, pp. 19–24.
36 Diary entry 17.6.1917 (*Contrary Exp.*, p. 99).
37 Diary entry 27.8.1916 (*Contrary Exp.*, pp. 76–7).
38 Annals (n. 30), p. 191.
39 Diary entry 15.4.18 (*Contrary Exp.*, pp. 121–6).
40 Letter Kramer to Read dated 10.3.18., pp. 12–13 (48/76 Vict).

41 Read: notes of a speech given in honour of Kramer at the Leeds Art Gallery, Sept 1960 (47/1 Vict).
42 op. cit., n. 40.
43 Letter Read to Kramer dated 6.4.18 (47/3 Vict).
44 Memorandum in Read's handwriting verso p. 2 of the letter from Kramer (n. 40).
45 op. cit., n. 43.
46 Read: 'Definitions towards a Modern Theory of Poetry', *Art and Letters*, vol. 1, no. 3, 1918, pp. 73–4.
47 op. cit., n. 25, pp. 67–8.
48 Annals (n. 30), pp. 191–2.
49 A. N. Whitehead: *Concept of Nature*, Cambridge U.P. 1921.
50 Read: 'Readers and Writers', *The New Age*, vol. XXIX, no. 16, 18 Aug 1921, pp. 187–8.
51 Read: 'R & W', *The New Age*, vol. XXIX, no. 15, 11 Aug 1921, pp. 176–7.
52 ibid.
53 ibid.
54 Read: 'R & W', *The New Age*, vol. XXIX, no. 18, 1 Sept 1921, pp. 211–12. See also Read: 'R & W', *The New Age*, vol. XXIX, no. 21, 22 Sept 1921, p. 249.
55 ibid. (*New Age*, XXIX, no. 18). He thus rejected the theory of 'Significant Form' as it had been expressed by C. Bell, though not necessarily as expressed by F. Rutter: see n. 6.
56 Pascal quoted by Read in 'R & W', *The New Age*, vol. XXIX, no. 20, 15 Sept 1921, pp. 235–6.
57 Read had written: '. . . for all his greatness Whitman was not a perfect poet. But that aspect does not need stress – as romantic boundlessness and pantheistic deliquescence it is obvious enough – and there are aspects of control, of positiveness, of concentration, that outweigh the multiplicity of the included sensations.' ('R & W', *The New Age*, vol. XXIX, no. 17, 25 Aug 1921, pp. 200–1). Orage took 'the liberty of saying that the discussion Romanticism v. Classicism is just a little on the scholastic side.' Letter to Read dated 22.8.21 (48/102 Vict). See also Martin (n. 3) p. 54.
58 Benedict Read: Cat. Note 32 (op. cit., n. 25, p. 19). See also Orage–Read corres., particularly Orage to Read dated 17.5.21 (invitation to edit the MSS): 'I have them all, but have not even opened them, owing to preoccupation' (48/102 Vict).
59 op. cit., n. 18.
60 ibid., p. xv.
61 See A. R. Jones: *The Life and Opinions of Thomas Ernest Hulme*, Gollancz, London 1960, pp. 190 et seq.
62 Read allowed his excitement for the latter to persuade him to publish it first: see *The New Age*, vol. XXX 1922, pp. 148–9, 167–8, 193–4, 207–8, and (Bergson's Theory of Art), pp. 287–8, 301–2, 310–12.
63 ibid. n. 62 (part 2): see also *Speculations*, pp. 143–69.
64 ibid. n. 62 (part 1): see also *Speculations*, pp. 217–45.

65 Read: *The True Voice of Feeling*, Faber, London 1953, p. 109.
66 *Speculations*, p. 222.
67 ibid., pp. 28–30.
68 ibid., pp. 78–81.
69 W. Worringer: *Abstraktion und Einfühlung*, Munich 1908, translated by M. Bullock as *Abstraction and Empathy*, Routledge & Kegan Paul, London 1963.
70 And abridged in *The New Age* a few weeks later: see n. 20.
71 W. Worringer: *Formprobleme der Gotik*, 1912, translated by Read as *Form in Gothic*, Tiranti, London 1927.
72 Read: Dedication of *The Philosophy of Modern Art* (n. 26). See Worringer to Read corres., particularly 14.3.25 (a discussion of Hulme's meeting with Worringer); and 14.6.27 (a discussion of *Form in Gothic*) (48/161 Vict). See also Read to Worringer dated 18.12.63: 'Your work remains with me and I scarcely write a book in which I do not draw upon it for support and inspiration' (48/161/verso p. 33 Vict).
73 See (i) *Speculations* pp. 81–5; (ii) Read: *English Stained Glass*, Putnam, London 1926, pp. 4 et seq.; (iii) Read: Introduction to *Form in Gothic*, and (iv) *Philosophy of Modern Art*, pp. 217–19.
74 *Speculations*, pp. 261–4.
75 ibid., p. 262.
76 See Chap. 3, pp. 63 et seq.
77 See Chap. 4, pp. 81 et seq.
78 cf. T. M. Knox (trans.): *Hegel's Aesthetics*, Oxford 1975, pp. 831–2. The edition Read used was probably that of H. G. Hotho, 1842.
79 *Speculations*, p. 87.
80 *Form in Gothic*, p. 31.
81 *Speculations*, p. 262.
82 A sideswipe at Fry and Bell, in the course of reviewing B. Russell's *Analysis of Mind* in *The New Age*, vol. XXIX, no. 18 (see n. 54).
83 ibid., n. 81.
84 Read: 'The Meaning of Art'; *The Listener*, vol. II, Supplement no. 1, 25 Sept 1929, p. ii (my italics).
85 *Annals*, p. 204.
86 ibid., pp. 192–3.
87 Read: 'Psychoanalysis and the Critic'; *The Criterion*, vol. III, 1924–5 (pp. 214–30), p. 221.
88 Read: review of Fry: *The Artist and Psychoanalysis* (Hogarth Press, London 1924), *The Criterion*, vol. III, 1924–5, pp. 471–2.
89 Read: 'The Nature of Metaphysical Poetry', *The Criterion*, vol. I, 1922–3 (pp. 246–66), p. 249.
90 op. cit., n. 87, pp. 214–15.
91 op. cit., n. 88, p. 472.
92 He may have been prepared by the numerous papers on psychology which appeared in *The New Age*: see Martin (n. 3), pp. 139 et seq.
93 op. cit., n. 87, p. 219.
94 ibid., p. 220.

95 ibid., pp. 219–20.
96 See Read (ed.): *Kropotkin: Selections from his Writings*, Freedom Press, London 1942, p. 129.
97 cf. G. Woodcock: *Herbert Read: the Stream and the Source*, Faber, London 1972, pp. 231 et seq.; and Read: *The Politics of the Unpolitical*, Routledge, London 1942, p. 155.
98 Read: 'Aesthetics and the Science of Art', *Times Lit. Supp.*, 18 Apr 1929, p. xxi.

Chapter 3 **Insight and reason**

1 See Chap. 2, n. 24.
2 See Read (ed.): *Unit One: the Modern Movement in English Architecture, Painting and Sculpture*, Cassell, London 1934, p. 12.
3 Read: 'Art Tradition and the Visual Arts' (holographed notes), Spiral Notebook 3 (10/3/16 Vict).
4 ibid.
5 Read: 'A Note on Imagination', *The Tyro*, no. 2, 1922, pp. 44–5.
6 See Read: 'Metaphysical Poetry' (Chap. 2, n. 89), repub. in Read: *Reason and Romanticism*, Faber, London 1926, pp. 46–58.
7 For example, see the criticism offered by H. W. Hausermann in H. Treece (ed.): *Herbert Read: an Introduction to his Work by Various Hands*, Faber, London 1944, pp. 52–80.
8 Read: 'Psychoanalysis and the Critic' (Chap. 2, n. 87), p. 218., repub. *Reason and Romanticism*, Chap. V.
9 ibid., pp. 220–5.
10 ibid., pp. 229–30.
11 ibid., p. 222.
12 Read: 'The Future of Poetry', *Times Lit. Supp.* 1925, repub. *Reason and Romanticism*, Chap. IV, p. 75. The means of such exact analysis was a device called the kymograph, which could 'measure exactly the duration of every syllable in speech (and) therefore reveal the exact quantity of spoken verse'.
13 ibid., pp. 78–9.
14 ibid., p. 80.
15 *Annals* (Chap. 2, n. 30), p. 203.
16 A. N. Whitehead: *Science and the Modern World*, Cambridge U. P. 1926.
17 See Read's review of Whitehead (n. 16), *The Criterion*, vol. IV, 1926, p. 581.
18 Whitehead (n. 16), pp. 183 et seq.
19 Read's review (n. 17), p. 586.
20 ibid., p. 583.
21 ibid., p. 586.
22 ibid., p. 582.
23 *Reason and Romanticism*, p. 25.
24 See R. P. Blackmur: 'Notes on the Criticism of Herbert Read', *Larus*, vol. 1, nos 5–7, June 1928, p. 46.

25 See Read: 'Notes on the Originality of Thought', *The Criterion*, vol. 6, no. 4, 1927 (pp. 363–9), p. 368.
26 *Reason and Romanticism*, pp. 62–3.
27 Read: *Form in Modern Poetry*, Sheed & Ward, London 1932, pp. 1–5.
28 See Read: 'Beyond Realism', *The Listener*, vol. III, 1930, p. 679.
29 *Meaning of Art* Supplement (Chap. 2, n. 84), p. viii.
30 cf. Read: *The Sense of Glory*, Cambridge U. P. 1929, pp. 145 et seq.; and Read (ed.): *A Sentimental Journey by Lawrence Sterne*, Scholartis Press, London 1929, pp. x et seq.
31 Read: *Wordsworth* (The Clark Lectures, Cambridge 1929–30), Jonathan Cape, London 1930.
32 Read's parallel thesis was that Wordsworth suffered an intense remorse, the result of an enforced separation from Annette Vallon, who had borne him a daughter in 1792. During the following decade he wrote his best poetry; but its quality diminished as his affection for Annette declined. Read saw a causative relationship between Wordsworth's growing resentment of revolutionary France (the instrument of separation) and the gradual extinction of poetic powers.
33 *Wordsworth*, p. 159.
34 See Woodcock (Chap. 2, n. 97), pp. 152–4.
35 *Wordsworth*, pp. 160–1.
36 ibid., p. 49.
37 ibid., p. 184.
38 ibid., pp. 180–2.
39 A theme on which Read had previously speculated: see n. 6.
40 *Wordsworth*, p. 195.
41 cf. Read: Introduction (1930) to J. Benda: *The Betrayal of the Intellectuals*, Boston 1955, pp. xxi–ii; and Read (ed.): *Surrealism*, Faber, London 1936, p. 22.
42 See Hulme: *Speculations* (Chap. 2, n. 18), pp. 138–40.
43 Read: Diary entry 2.6.1918 (*Contrary Exp.* pp. 131–2).
44 See Read: *Phases of English Poetry*, Hogarth Press, London 1928, pp. 102–6.
45 See Whitehead (n. 16), pp. 103–18. Significantly, this was the part most quoted by Read in his review (n. 17).
46 Whitehead, p. 108.
47 My insertion of 'individual' in the following quotation.
48 Read: *Meaning of Art* Supplement (Chap. 2, n. 84), p. viii. When this was republished, two years later, the quoted passage was omitted. See the extensive repetition of passages which preceded and followed it in the original version, in Read: *The Meaning of Art*, Faber, London 1931, pp. 29–33 and 154–8.
49 See Read: *The Place of Art in a University*, Oliver & Boyd, Edinburgh 1931, pp. 15–22.
50 Letter Read to Hausermann dated 6.8.37 (61/86 Vict).
51 *Surrealism* (n. 41), pp. 22–3.
52 Read (criticizing T. S. Eliot): *Form in Modern Poetry* (n. 27), pp. 7–9.

See also Eliot's review of *Reason and Romanticism* in *The New Criterion*, vol. IV, no. IV, Oct 1926, pp. 751–7.

53 *Psychoanalysis and the Critic* (Chap. 2, n. 87), p. 220.

54 Read was adversely criticized for introducing the term 'conscious' into this description. See H. W. Hausermann (n. 7), p. 73.

55 *Form in Modern Poetry* (n. 27), pp. 12–19.

56 cf. ibid., p. 32, an initial, cautious statement, and also the more forthright in *Surrealism* (n. 41), pp. 76–8.

57 *Form in Modern Poetry* (n. 27), pp. 38 and 35.

58 See ibid., p. 32 and Chap II. Note, however, an inconsistency in Read's argument here, which may only be attributed to careless proof-reading. His theme is elaborated precisely enough. Character is a disposition to inhibit instinctive forces (p. 15); and the 'difference between the conditions necessary for the formation of a character and for the formation of . . . a personality, corresponds precisely with the difference between rhetorical and lyrical literature, which is the difference often loosely implied in the terms "classical" and "romantic" literature' (p. 17). 'Character, in short, is an impersonal ideal which the individual selects and to which he sacrifices all other claims, especially those of the sentiments or emotions. It follows that character must be placed in opposition to personality, which is the general common denominator of our sentiments and emotions. That is, indeed, the opposition I wish to emphasize; and when I have said further that all poetry, in which I include all lyrical impulses whatsoever, is the product of the personality, and therefore inhibited in a character, I have stated the main theme of my essay' (pp. 18–19). The inconsistency, however, appears at the climax of this argument: 'Finally . . . may we not perhaps explain the dreary quarrel of romantic and classic as an opposition between two kinds of art, springing respectively from character and from personality?' (p. 33) This is clearly a reversal of the fundamental argument expressed throughout the whole of *Form in Modern Poetry*. (See also its repetition when the work was republished in Read: *Collected Essays in Literary Criticism*, Faber, London 1938, pp. 39–40.) It was eventually corrected when it was published for a third time in *Form in Modern Poetry*, 2nd Edn, Vision, London 1948: '. . . quarrel of romantic and classic as an opposition [of] . . . personality and . . . character' (p. 38). This corrected version was again republished in A. Tate (ed.): *Herbert Read: Selected Writings: Poetry and Criticism*, Faber, London 1963, p. 96.

59 See Hausermann (n. 7), pp. 73–4.

60 Read to Hausermann (n. 50). This was a response to Hausermann's submission of a draft essay (n. 7) which was first published in his book *Studien zur Englischen Literarkritik 1910–1930*, 1938. Read wrote: 'I am amazed at the closeness of your understanding; in no respect have you misrepresented me, and if at times you are puzzled, the fault is mine.'

61 *Form in Modern Poetry* (n. 27), p. 9.

62 Read: *Art and Society* (the Sydney Jones Lectures, University of Liverpool 1935–6), Heinemann, London 1937, p. 203.
63 ibid., p. 204: see also *Surrealism* (n. 41), p. 76.
64 See Read: 'Obscurity in Poetry' in *In Defence of Shelley and Other Essays*, Heinemann, London 1936, pp. 147–63. This essay is substantially a repub. of Read: 'Views and Reviews', *New English Weekly*, vol. VII, 1935, pp. 233–4.
65 Read: 'What is Revolutionary Art?'; in *Five on Revolutionary Art*, Wishart, London 1935 (pp. 11–22), p. 21.
66 *Surrealism*, pp. 22–36. The supreme example of a 'visual metaphor' Read described in his Foreword (1p unnumbered) to the catalogue *Surrealist Objects and Poems*, London Gallery, 1937: 'The chance meeting of the umbrella and the sewing-machine on a dissecting table is our classic instance . . . .'
67 *Surrealism*, pp. 38–40.
68 Read: Introduction to cat. *The International Surrealist Exhibition*, New Burlington Galleries, London 1936, p. 13.
69 *Surrealism*, pp. 43–4.
70 Read: 'The Faculty of Abstraction'; in Martin, Nicholson and Gabo (ed.): *Circle: International Survey of Constructive Art*, Faber, London 1937, p. 64.
71 See Read to Hausermann (n. 50) and Hausermann (n. 7), p. 79.
72 See Woodcock (Chap. 2, n. 97), p. 26.
73 Transcript in *Tribute* (Chap. 2, n. 25) p. 41.
74 *Surrealism*, pp. 30, 54–6.
75 Perhaps then best represented in England by David Gascoyne, both in his own writings and in his translations of Breton. See D. Gascoyne: *A Short Survey of Surrealism*, Cobden-Sanderson, London 1936 and D. Gascoyne (trans.): A. Breton: *What is Surrealism?* Faber, London 1936.
76 *Surrealism*, p. 90.
77 Read: *Education through Art*, Faber, London 1943, p. 25. This was written during Read's Leon Fellowship at London University, 1940–42.
78 ibid., pp. 26–7.
79 ibid., pp. 90–100.
80 ibid., pp. 34–5. Hausermann, however, at least three years earlier, had pointed out that Jung did not recognize such antagonism. See Hausermann (n. 7), p. 65.
81 *Education through Art* (n. 77), p. 174.
82 Freud quoted by Read: ibid., p. 177.
83 ibid., p. 176.
84 ibid., p. 177.
85 Jung quoted by Read: ibid., p. 194.
86 Read: 'Art and Crisis' (1944) in Read: *The Grass Roots of Art*, Lindsay Drummond, London 1947 (Chap. V), p. 77. See also Read: 'Art and Ethics' (1939) in Read: *A Coat of Many Colours*, Routledge, London 1945, pp. 205–7.

186

87 'Art and Ethics', p. 206.
88 'Art and Crisis', pp. 77–8.
89 ibid.; see also *Grass Roots* (n. 86), pp. 8–9.
90 'Art and Crisis', p. 93.
91 Read: 'The Moral Significance of Aesthetic Education' (1949) in Read: *Education for Peace*, Routledge, London 1950, p. 71.
92 ibid.
93 See Chapter 4 below, pp. 99 et seq.

Chapter 4 **Superrealism and abstraction**

1 See Read: 'Byzantine Art', *The Listener*, vol. V, 1931, p. 986; and Read: 'Turner Revived', *The Listener*, vol. VI, 1931, pp. 338–9.
2 Read: 'Bomberg', *Arts Gazette*, 13 Sept 1919, pp. 391–2.
3 See Parrington Jackson in *Tribute* (Chap. 2, n. 25), p. 68.
4 See Read: 'Beyond Realism', *The Listener*, vol. III, 1930, p. 679; and Read: *Art Now*, Faber, London 1933, p. 136.
5 See Read: 'Paul Klee': *The Listener*, vol. V, 1931, p. 509; and Read: 'Paul Klee': *The Listener*, vol. XI, 1934, pp. 108–9.
6 Read: 'Beyond Realism' (n. 4), p. 679.
7 ibid.
8 Read: 'Psychoanalysis and Art', *The Listener*, vol. III, 1930, p. 737.
9 *The International Surrealist Exhibition*, New Burlington Galleries, London, 11 June – 4 July 1936.
10 See Woodcock (Chap. 2, n. 97), p. 26.
11 Read: 'Max Ernst', *The Listener*, vol. IX, 1933, p. 899.
12 See Read: *Art Now* (n. 4), pp. 97–129.
13 ibid., p. 144.
14 Read: *Art Now* (2nd Edn), Faber, London 1936, p. 146.
15 ibid., pp. 149–51.
16 Read: 'Revolutionary Art' (Chap. 3, n. 65), pp. 18–19.
17 ibid., p. 21.
18 Read: *Art Now*, 2nd Edn (n. 14), p. 146.
19 *Form in Modern Poetry*: see Chap. 3, n. 27 and n. 58.
20 See Read: 'Pablo Picasso' (1934), published as Chap. VIII of *Defence of Shelley* (Chap. 3, n. 64), pp. 210–20.
21 Read: *Henry Moore, Sculptor: an Appreciation*, Zwemmer, London 1934, pp. 10–11.
22 Read: 'Art – the Situation Today'; *London Mercury*, vol. XXX, no. 180, Oct 1934, pp. 574–5.
23 See Woodcock's explanation (Chap. 2, n. 97), p. 183.
24 Read: 'Surrealism – the Dialectic of Art', *Left Review*, vol. 2, no. 10, July 1936 (Suppl. fac. p. 508), pp. ii–iii.
25 Read's Introduction to Read (ed.): *Surrealism*, Faber, London 1936, pp. 22–3.
26 See Read: 'A Nest of Gentle Artists', *Apollo*, vol. 76, no. 7, Sept 1962 (pp. 536–8). 'There is no denying that a tension was created between the two extremes represented by the Circle group and the

Surrealist group, and that I was in the position of a circus rider with his feet planted astride two horses. I tried to argue, and I still believe, that such dialectical oppositions are good for the progress of art, and that the greatest artists (I always had Henry Moore in mind) are great precisely because they can resolve such oppositions' (p. 538).

27 Read: Introduction to Surrealist Exhib. Cat. (Chap. 3, n. 68), p. 13.
28 Read: 'Faculty of Abstraction' (Chap. 3, n. 70), p. 64.
29 In *The London Bulletin*, the organ of the English Surrealist Group.
30 Read: 'An Art of Pure Form', *London Bulletin* 14, 1939, pp. 6–9. This was a repub. of pp. 124–5, *Art and Society* (Chap. 3, n. 62).
31 Read: 'The Development of Ben Nicholson', *London Bulletin* 11, 1939, pp. 9–10.
32 Read: 'Faculty of Abstraction' (Chap. 3, n. 70), p. 66.
33 See Woodcock (Chap. 2, n. 97), p. 26.
34 Letter Gabo to Read dated 4.1.53 (48/44 Vict).
35 Gabo to Read 9.4.42 (48/44 Vict).
36 Gabo to Read 14.5.41 (48/44 Vict).
37 Read: 'Vulgarity and Impotence: Speculations on the Present State of the Arts', *Horizon*, vol. V, no. 28, Apr 1942 (pp. 267–76), pp. 274–5.
38 Letter Hepworth to Read dated 8.4.42 (48/61 Vict).
39 Gabo to Read (1943), published in *Horizon*, vol. X, no. 55, Jul 1944, pp. 57–65.
40 ibid., p. 59.
41 ibid., pp. 59–60.
42 ibid., p. 61.
43 See Read: *Education through Art* (Chap. 3, n. 77), pp. 196 et seq.
44 Read to Gabo: *Horizon* (n. 39), p. 64.
45 Gabo to Read 8.9.47 (48/44 Vict).
46 Nina Gabo Williams (letter to the author 21.11.78) has pointed out the inaccuracy of the convention that Gabo and Pevsner jointly wrote this manifesto.
47 Read: Introduction to the cat. *Gabo and Pevsner*, Museum of Modern Art, New York 1948, p. 10.
48 ibid., p. 11.
49 ibid., p. 32.
50 ibid., p. 10.
51 ibid., pp. 10–11.
52 op. cit., n. 45.
53 Gabo to Read 31.10.47 (48/44 Vict). Read referred to this corres. in his essay 'Realism and Abstraction in Modern Art' (1948) published as Chap. 5 of *The Philosophy of Modern Art*, Faber, London 1952; and he permitted the slight misquotation (p. 94): 'We know only . . . what we construct; and . . . all that we construct, are realities.'
54 op. cit., Chap. 3, n. 3.
55 Gabo to Read 31.10.47 (48/44 Vict).
56 ibid.
57 Gabo to Read 8.9.47 (48/44 Vict).

58 See Read: 'Moral Significance of Aesthetic Education' (Chap. 3, n. 91).
59 See Read: *Education through Art* (Chap. 3, n. 77), pp. 126–37.
60 Read to Gabo 14.12.47. (49/10 Vict).
61 ibid.
62 Read: *Surrealism* (n. 25), p. 90.
63 Read: 'Realism and Abstraction' (n. 53), p. 95.
64 See Read: *Education through Art* (Chap. 3, n. 77), pp. 16–22.
65 This refers to Read's recommending the book H. Focillon: *Vie des Formes*, Paris 1934 (trans. *The Life of Forms in Art*, New York 1948).
66 Hepworth to Read 14.5.44 (48/61 Vict).
67 Read: *Grass Roots* (Chap. 3, n. 86), p. 78.
68 Read: *Education for Peace* (Chap. 3, n. 91), p. 83. My italics.
69 Read: 'Ben Nicholson and the Future of Painting', *The Listener*, vol. XIV, 1935, pp. 604–5.
70 Endorsed by Nicholson in a letter to Read dated 21.8.44 (48/101 Vict). It had not occurred to him before, and Read's observation was of the nature of a revelation.
71 Read: 'Ben Nicholson' (1948); published as Chap. 12 of *Philosophy of Modern Art* (n. 53), p. 224.
72 On one occasion Read went further and suggested that the abstract artist's social responsibility was to invest his sensed perceptions of nature in the practice of industrial design. See transcript *Aerial in Wartime; the Question of Abstract Art*, BBC Home Service 1.5.42 (BBC Written Archive).
73 Read: 'Ben Nicholson' (n. 71), pp. 220–1.
74 ibid. See also Read: 'Realism and Abstraction' (n. 53), p. 98. See also Nicholson's letter to Read, undated (1952) in which he conveys his enthusiastic reception of *The Philosophy of Modern Art* and agrees about his simultaneous love for realism and abstraction (48/101 Vict).
75 op. cit., n. 66. See also Read: 'Realism and Abstraction' (n. 53), p. 98. See also Read: 'Barbara Hepworth; a New Phase'; *The Listener*, vol. XXXIX, 1948, p. 592.
76 ibid. (*Listener*).
77 In a letter to Read dated 6.3.48. (48/61 Vict).
78 ibid.
79 Read: 'Realism and Abstraction' (n. 53), p. 99.
80 P. Nash: letter to *The Times* 2.6.33, repub in *Unit One* (Chap. 3, n. 2), pp. 10–22.
81 Nash to Read 21.1.39 (48/99 Vict).
82 Read: Introduction to cat. *Paul Nash*, Soho Gallery, London 1937.
83 Read: 'Paul Nash as Artist' in M. Eates (ed.): *Paul Nash*, Lund Humphries, London 1948, pp. 7 et seq. See also Read: 'Paul Nash', Chap. 10 of *Philosophy of Modern Art* (n. 53). This was written in 1944, and revised and extended in 1948.
84 Read: 'Ben Nicholson' (n. 71), p. 220.

85 Read: 'Paul Nash' (*Philosophy of Modern Art*) (n. 83), esp. pp. 179–82 and 185–8.
86 See H. Moore; untitled article in *Architectural Association Journal*, May 1930, pp. 408–13.
87 See H. Moore in *Unit One* (Chap. 3, n. 2), pp. 29–30. This was paraphrased by Read in his essay 'Henry Moore' (1944), published as Chap. 11 of *Philosophy of Modern Art* (n. 53), p. 206.
88 See Moore (n. 86).
89 See Moore (n. 87).
90 See Moore: 'Quotations'; contrib to *Circle* (Chap. 3, n. 70), p. 118.
91 Read: 'Henry Moore', in *Philosophy of Modern Art* (n. 87), pp. 213 et seq.
92 ibid., p. 212. See also Read: 'The Situation of Art in Europe at the End of the Second World War' (1948); Chap 2 of *Philosophy of Modern Art* (n. 53), p. 55.
93 ibid. (Art in Europe), p. 54.
94 Read: 'Henry Moore' (n. 87), p. 202.
95 ibid., p. 209.
96 Read: 'Realism and Abstraction' (n. 53), p. 94.
97 ibid., p. 99.
98 Read: 'Art in Europe' (n. 92), pp. 45, 47–9.
99 See n. 23.
100 Read: 'The Problem of Picasso'; *Journal of the Royal Society of Arts*, 18 Jan 1946, pp. 127–8: repub. as part of Chap. 8, *Philosophy of Modern Art* (n. 53), pp. 162–3.
101 Read: 'Art in Europe' (n. 92), pp. 48–54.
102 ibid., p. 47.
103 Read: 'The Dialectic of Art'; contrib. to F. C. Thiessing (ed.): *Erni: Elements of Future Painting*, Zurich 1948, p. 13; repub. in *Philosophy of Modern Art* (n. 53), p. 104.
104 Although the title of this essay is *Realism* and Abstraction . . . Read's temporary definition of 'realism' took account of superrealism. He wrote: 'By *realism* we (the common people) mean fidelity of representation, truth to nature. By *abstraction* we mean what is derived or disengaged from nature, the pure or essential form abstracted from the concrete details. // From this general point of view, realism will include, not only the attempt to reproduce with fidelity the images given in normal perception, but those distorted or selected images due to exceptional states of awareness which we call idealism, super-realism, expressionism, etc.' (Lecture Notes, Notebook 2) (27/4/3 Vict). In the published version, in *Philosophy of Modern Art*, the words here bracketed are omitted.
105 Read: 'Realism and Abstraction' (n. 53), p. 97.
106 These notes are part of Read's draft of 'Henry Moore' (*Philosophy of Modern Art*, Chap. 11). They throw light on a sentence which (due to typographical error?) in the published version makes little sense because of the absence of the words here bracketed. 'The terms of the debate need careful definition, but obviously the whole scope

of art is altered if you make it, instead of the more or less sensuous symbolization of intellectual ideals, the direct expression of an organic vitalism. No doubt intellectual elements will enter into the choice and elaboration of the (forms of this expression just as sensuous elements enter into the) images which the intellect selects to represent its ideals . . . .' See Read: 'Henry Moore' (n. 91), p. 207; and Read: Blue Notebook (13/2/3 Vict).

107 Read: Appendix (1951) to 'Realism and Abstraction' (n. 53), pp. 102–3.

108 Read was not quite sure whether Gabo's work was 'optimistic' or 'pessimistic'. Much of Gabo's description, given in the long correspondence with Read, was essentially pessimistic. However, Read tried to persuade him otherwise: he wrote to Gabo 'I have discovered another German philosopher, Woltereck . . . who is exactly in our line of thought. How near, you may judge from the following quotation: "This biological freedom and what becomes of it has an ontic significance quite different from the existential compulsion to free decision. The latter *cripples* our sense of vitality . . . the creative emergence from the minds of individuals of new forms, new norms, new ideas – all that is the possible result of man's *positive* freedom." That is nearer to my point of view, and I think nearer to yours than the existentialism of Sartre.' Read to Gabo 14.12.47 (49/10 Vict).

109 See Read: 'The Modern Epoch in Art' (1949); Chap. 1 of *Philosophy of Modern Art* (n. 53), pp. 20–2. See also 'Realism and Abstraction', and its 1951 postscript, in *Philosophy of Modern Art*, pp. 95–6, 103. See also Henry Moore postscript (1951), *Philosophy of Modern Art*, pp. 214–15.

110 ibid., n. 102.

Chapter 5 **Anarchy and order**

1 A. J. Penty: *The Restoration of the Guild System*, Swan Sonnenschein & Co., London 1906.

2 It is said that Orage initiated guild-socialism, and judiciously enhanced all contributions to this theory published in *The New Age* between 1912 and 1915. See W. Martin: *The New Age under Orage*, Manchester U. P. 1967, pp. 207–8.

3 His brother William had become apprenticed to a Leeds tailor who, though unrelated, also bore the name William Read. This man encouraged Herbert Read's very early poetry, and it was to him that the first volume of *Collected Poems* was dedicated.

4 He was awarded the Military Cross for his part in a night raid, in August 1917, which led to the capture of a senior German officer; and he gained the Distinguished Service Order for assuming command of a break-out and orderly retreat under heavy fire in March 1918. See 'The War Diary', published in *The Contrary Experience*, Faber, London 1963, pp. 70–146; and *In Retreat*, Hogarth Press 1925.

5 Read: 'The World and the Guild Idea'; *The Guildsman*, no. 5, April 1917, p. 6; and No 6, May 1917, p. 4. See also Read's criticism of Penty's 'intense spirit of localism' in his unpublished diary entry 10 Oct 1917 (28/5 Vict).

6 Op. cit., trans. R. Aldington, entitled *The Great Betrayal*, Routledge, London 1928. See Read's review of this in *The Criterion*, vol. VIII, no. XXXI, Dec. 1928, pp. 270–6.

7 His efforts directly to superimpose such arguments on a theory of plastic creativity (loc. cit. Chap. 2, n. 84) provoked a critical response from Eric Gill, and the beginnings of a correspondence eventually to help persuade him away from the view of the artist as abnormal individual. Gill protested that the artist had no desire to communicate an exceptional vision, but merely to make things well, and that in any case an ability to think in Platonic images was not an exceptional faculty. See corres. E. Gill to Read 19 Oct 29 and 27 Aug 34 (48/46 Vict).

8 Read: *Art and Industry*, Faber, London 1934, p. 33.

9 ibid., pp. 32–3.

10 He tended to use the term 'Marxian', instead of the more usual 'Marxist' to signify philosophical rather than practical Marxism.

11 That is, during his tenure of the Sydney Jones Lectureship in Art at Liverpool University 1935–6. See Read: *Art and Society*, Heinemann, London 1937, pp. 253, 265–6.

12 ibid., pp. 266–73.

13 Corres. Read to Wyndham Lewis dated 9 Dec 34 (48/82/14.01–.02 Vict).

14 See Read: 'Why I am a Surrealist', *New English Weekly*, vol. 10, March 4 1937, pp. 413–14.

15 *Art and Society*, p. 253. It was suggested, by T. A. Jackson, that Read's assertion that Surrealism would directly transform the world, without the benefit of some transitional state, was more Utopian or Pragmatist than Marxist. See their exchange of views in *Left Review*, vol. 2, no. 10, July 1936; supplement fac p. 508, pp. ii, iii; vol. 2, no. 11, Aug 1936, pp. 565–7 (Jackson); and vol. 3, no. 1, Feb 1937, pp. 47–8.

16 Not by original research, but by digesting the works of eminent anthropologists.

17 *Art and Society*, pp. 68–71.

18 ibid., p. 225.

19 ibid., pp. 97, 121 et seq.

20 See corres. Read to Frank Pick dated 19 Feb 41 (61/158/5.01–.03 Vict).

21 George Woodcock's account of Read's anarchism cannot be improved upon, and the attempt has not been made. See Woodcock: *Herbert Read: the Stream and the Source*, Faber, London 1972, Chap. 7.

22 Read: *Poetry and Anarchism*, Faber, London 1938, p. 16.

23 See Read: 'The Necessity of Anarchism', *Adelphi*, vol. 13, 1937, pp. 458–63; and vol. 14, 1937, pp. 12–18, 44–8.

24 Read: *Politics of the Unpolitical*, Routledge, London 1943, p. 160.

Read argued with H. G. Wells about the retention of money. To Wells it was a simple item of exchange, permitting free choice of reward for labour. Read objected to it in its role as commodity, and pointed out that every major prophet had condemned usury. Wells was persuaded to modify slightly his *Natural Rights of Man* (p. 5). See corres. between Read and Wells (48/151/1–11 Vict).

25 ibid., n. 22.

26 *Art and Society*, 1937, p. 223 (over-proliferation). *Art and Society*, 2nd ed., Faber, 1945, p. 107 (everyone an artist). See also Read: *To Hell with Culture*, Kegan Paul, Trench, Trubner, London 1941, pp. 36–8 (the emergence of this latter argument).

27 He was granted a Leon Fellowship of the University of London for this purpose. The revised draft of this thesis is at Victoria (13/2).

28 As long before as 1926 he had been criticized for this by J. Middleton Murry, who had argued for an identity of creative procedures in artists and ordinary people alike, the only difference being intensity of comprehension. Read had maintained, however, that whereas an 'ordinary' response to environment was empathetic (i.e. indiscriminate identification projected from within), highly perceptive individuals were capable of selection and abstraction, directly from without. See corres. between Read and Middleton Murry (48/96/1–15 Vict).

29 Read: 'The Truth of a Few Simple Ideas' (1967) repub. in *The Cult of Sincerity*, Faber, London 1968, pp. 44–5. 'Snake Around the World and a Boat' is reproduced in Read: *Education through Art*, Faber, London 1943, fac p. 96.

30 And also, as representative of the British Council, for a wartime exhibition of children's art. See his routine correspondence with the large number of teachers with whom he made contact (14/2 Vict).

31 'Few Simple Ideas' (n. 29), p. 43.

32 See, for example, the sequence of 'mind pictures' reproduced between pp. 184–5 in *Education through Art*.

33 Pages xvi, xix, xx, xxi, xxii, 141, 143, 144, 145, 146, and 147.

34 In Great Britain alone the first hardback edition of 2,000 was sold immediately, and first edition reprints totalled 8,500.

35 As joint editor of his collected works: see Chap. 1, n. 49.

36 Holographed MS (27/1 Vict). Jung's initial response was a brief note on a postcard dated 24.9.49 (48/72 Vict).

37 'Jung at Mid-Century', *Hudson Review*, vol. IV, 1951–2, pp. 259–68; 'Zum 85: Geburstag von C. G. Jung', Zurich 1960 (29pp); 'Carl Gustav Jung', *Sunday Times*, 11 June 1961; 'Carl Gustav Jung', Chap. VII of *The Cult of Sincerity* (n. 29).

38 Jung's only serious criticism concerned a quotation of Freud's about the Mother Complex, which Read had mistakenly attributed to him. See postcard (n. 36).

39 MS (n. 36), pp. 8–14. Read made great efforts to understand Jung's precise meaning of the concept 'archetype', a task made difficult because Jung did not usually engage in definition. R. F. C. Hull greatly assisted Read in this, scouring Jung's works, many of which were

untranslated, as well as numerous interpretations made by other scholars. See corres. between Read and Hull (48/67 Vict).

40 Stemming from this were several *invited* contributions: from 1950 he was a regular participant in the Eranos Tagung, a gathering over which Jung presided, held annually in Switzerland.

41 In a letter to the chairman of the Central Institute of Art and Design, published in *C.I.A.D. Bulletin*, no. 3, March 1942, p. 85.

42 Read: 'Culture and Education in a World Order' (1948), repub. in *Education for Peace*, Routledge, London 1950, p. 58.

43 Other members of the steering committee were F. Ashton, J. Beddington, J. B. Brunius, E. Clark, A. Comfort, M. St. Denis, E. C.(P). Gregory, G. Grigson, G. M. Hoellering, R. Melville, E. L. T. Mesens, R. Penrose, J. M. Richards, P. Watson, W. E. Williams.

44 Formative discussions began c. 1937 immediately after the International Surrealist Exhibition, and the publication of the International Survey of Constructive Art, which two events temporarily placed London at the focus of contemporary art. An original possibility was to establish a Museum of Modern Art in London, financed by the Guggenheim Foundation; but it did not materialize because of the war, the consequent further migration of prominent European artists to the USA, and thus the change of international focus. See the Gabo-Read corres., esp. 18 Nov 39 (48/44 Vict).

45 cf. the *Policy Statement of the Proposed Institute of Contemporary Arts*, Lund Humphries, London 1947, p. 3.

46 He wrote: Anarchists must participate in the activities and structure of the existing society, become functional units of that society. Anarchists should welcome modern art as an art of social protest. My poems are my acts of anarchism. Much research is needed to bring anarchist ideals up to date. Anthropology, social psychology, community experiments . . . all these are subjects for assessment in the light of anarchist principles. (Precis of unpub, undated memorandum: 35/72 Vict).

47 This is discussed at length in Chap. Six.

48 *40,000 Years of Modern Art*, ICA, London Dec–Jan 1948–9, held in the Academy Cinema Hall, Oxford Street.

49 For example, great store was set by Gauguin's journeys to Tahiti, and also the circumstances 'still to some extent obscure' which had prompted Matisse, Vlaminck and Derain to collect primitive sculptures at around the turn of the century. A culmination of such events was said to have taken place in Picasso's painting *Les Demoiselles d'Avignon* (1907), the first European work 'to resemble negro art in general style' and to afford it 'the supreme homage of imitation'. This work was given position of honour in the exhibition, and the manner of its presentation, artificially lit below ground level, aroused a sense of initiation into contemporary art. See commentary by W. G. Archer and R. Melville in the catalogue (n. 48), pp. 9–46: see also R. Melville: 'The Exhibitions of the ICA', *The Studio*, vol. CLXI, no. 697, April 1951, pp. 99–100.

50 Read: Preface to the catalogue (n. 48), pp. 6–7.
51 See J. P. Hodin's survey of events promoted by the ICA during the first three years of its occupancy of Dover Street: *Int. J. of Aesthetics and Art Criticism*, vol. XII, no. 2, Dec 1953 (pp. 278–83), p. 281. Hauser's talk was entitled 'Prehistoric Art and its Relation to Modern Art: the Sociological Aspect', and for a sense of his arguments it seems fair to refer to his contemporary publication *The Social History of Art*, Routledge, London 1951. Giedion's contribution was entitled 'Art and the Continuity of Human Experience', and similarly it seems fair to refer to his book *The Eternal Present (vol 1): The Beginning of Art*, Oxford U.P. 1962 (written during 1947–57: see p. viii).
52 Hauser (n. 51), pp. 23–4.
53 ibid., p. 30.
54 ibid., pp. 33–4.
55 ibid., pp. 35–7.
56 See Read's unpub. notes on Giedion's *Eternal Present* (24/7 Vict).
57 Giedion (n. 51), pp. 10–12.
58 ibid., p. 16.
59 ibid., pp. 16, 74–5.
60 Read's notes (loc. cit., n. 56).
61 Read: *Art and the Evolution of Man*; lecture given at the Conway Hall, London 10 April 1951, Freedom Press, London 1951, p. 23.
62 ibid., p. 31.
63 ibid., p. 40.
64 Read: *Art and Society* (n. 11), p. 71.
65 Read: *Icon and Idea: the Function of Art in the Development of Human Consciousness*, Faber, London 1955 (written during Read's tenure of the Charles Eliot Norton Lectureship, Harvard University 1953–54).
66 ibid., p. 5.
67 ibid., pp. 29–31.
68 ibid., pp. 38–50.
69 ibid., pp. 18–20.
70 ibid., pp. 83–4 (Greek harmonics) and pp. 65–6 (Gothic architecture). Read listed in a memorandum the seven evolutionary stages of human consciousness which seemed to him most significant, viz: '1. Paleolithic Art — animalism; 2. Greek humanism; 3. The Romanesque church — holiness; 4. The Gothic cathedral – transcendentalism; 5. Shakespeare and Racine – pure spirit of love – beauty (Mozart); 6. Cézanne – realization of the actual; 7. Picasso – dimensions of the unconscious.' Memo p. 50 of Read's holographed MS 'Art and the Evolution of Man' (27/9 Vict).
71 *Icon and Idea*, pp. 92–105. The seed of corruption was evident in the work of Michelangelo, he wrote to Adrian Stokes. Stokes agreed. See corres. A. Stokes to Read dated 13.8.55 (48/136 Vict).
72 *Icon and Idea*, pp. 130 et seq.
73 ibid., p. 137.
74 Read: *Anarchy and Order*, Faber, London 1954.

75 ibid., pp. 23–4.
76 ibid., pp. 25 et seq.

Chapter 6 Formlessness and form

1 Several were also teachers engaged (some briefly, others over a considerable period) in an 'organic' art teaching. I have attempted a detailed account of this in *A Continuing Process*, ICA, London 1981.
2 op. cit. pp. 191–4.
3 As, for example, it did following his remarks that a preponderance, in art, of those four-fold images classifiable as 'mandalas' might be due to some neural consequence of the quaternary molecular structure of carbon, the chief chemical component of the brain (ibid., pp. 190–2.) It was pointed out to him that physiologists considered cerebral anatomy more instrumental than chemistry upon the nature of neural activity, and that in any case most carbon atoms in organic matter were effective only in unsymmetrical arrangements (Alex Comfort; letter to Read dated 9 June 1946: 48/20/4–7 Vict.). Read excised the questionable passages from future editions of *Education through Art*: nevertheless, he said, an ambition had been served by the stimulation of a scientist's thinking (letter Read to Comfort dated 27 June 1946: 62/7/29–30 Vict.).
4 For Read's own summary of such supporting opinion see his Prologue (pp. 7–14) and Epilogue (pp. 263–8) in J. Brumwell (ed.): *This Changing World*, Routledge, London 1944.
5 D. W. Thompson: *On Growth and Form*, Cambridge U. P. 1917; revised, enlarged edn. 1942.
6 He had enjoyed Read's review in *The Listener* (n. 7 below), but expressed reservations, to which Read made the following responses. '. . . it was presumptuous of me to attempt (the review) but it is not necessarily the man inside the House of Science who has the best general view.' (PC dated 17 Nov 1942; D. W. Thompson Archive, St Andrews University.) 'Such references are inevitable – you have built the bridge between science and art. The danger lies in one's impulse to cross it too impetuously, without a proper understanding of the country on the other side.' (PC undated; D. W. Thompson Archive, St. Andrews University.) Thompson died in 1948, that is before his treatise became generally popular at the ICA.
7 In his review; *The Listener*, vol. XXVIII, 1942, p. 335.
8 Thompson (n. 5) 1942, p. 16. My italics.
9 A property, that is, of certain works of art. Anton Ehrenzweig was simultaneously discussing at the ICA the phenomenon 'Gestalt-free perception and creativity'. See his paper 'Unconscious Form Creation in Art', *British Journal of Medical Psychology*, vol. XXL, 1948, pp. 185–214.
10 Thompson (n. 5), 1942, p. 357. My italics.
11 This kind of organicism was typified in the work of Richard Hamilton; and we have his own brief description of what occurred when creative

activity was given momentum. Each of his works, he said, began with a point, the simplest mark, its position arranged in significant relationship (as were those of all subsequent marks) with elements already existing (in the first instance with the dimensions of the given surface). As the number of elements within the composition increased, so did the complexity of the problem of arranging each point or part in satisfying relationship with all the others. He said he took a blank canvas and after considerable thought placed a mark upon it: then he made another addition in considered relationship with the first and with the boundary. The marks in this way accumulated; but at each stage there had to be a significant contribution to the growth of an idea. See R. Morphet; cat. of the exhibition *Richard Hamilton*, Tate Gallery, London 1970, p. 18.

12 Victor Pasmore's work represents this second type of organicism. For a description see text below, pp. 146–7.

13 See V. Pasmore, R. Hamilton, T. Hudson and H. Thubron: *The Developing Process*, ICA, London and King's College, Durham, 1959. This exhibition at the ICA was in effect a homecoming of ideas which originated there.

14 Thompson (n. 5) 1942, p. 283.

15 See Read: 'The Notion of Organic Form: Coleridge' (1951), published in his collection of essays *The True Voice of Feeling*, Faber, London 1953, esp. pp. 16–21.

16 He was qualified in Law, Psychology and Art, but held no exclusively psychological degree; and it is perhaps preferable to consider him a theoretical psychologist.

17 He wrote to Read: 'When I call the process of creation "dialectical" I take up quite consciously a programmatic thought which you expressed in "Surrealism." When I read that passage in "Surrealism" where you state the conception of art should be dialectical, I thought at once "I could do that" and already then (some years ago) I felt the wish of writing to you, to find whether you would accept my interpretation of your thought. You will now understand how happy I felt when I got your letter, when it became apparent that our thinking really went on the same lines.' Letter Ehrenzweig to Read dated 5 Feb 1945 (61/58 Vict.).

18 Letter Ehrenzweig to Read dated 19 Jan 1945 (61/58 Vict.).

19 Letter Ehrenzweig to Read dated 17 Feb 1945 (61/58 Vict.).

20 Read had sought assurance that Ehrenzweig did not exclude a concept of *value* from his speculations. Ehrenzweig referred to this in his reply (17.2.45) without, however, offering a satisfactory response.

21 Ehrenzweig used the term '*biological* thinking': ibid., n. 17.

22 Originally planned to be a treatise, the eventual result of their collaboration was an ICA symposium entitled *Aspects of Form*. See below, n. 34.

23 Source: interview with J. P. Hodin, January 1977.

24 For an account of this research see J. P. Hodin: 'The London Institute

of Contemporary Arts', *Journal of Aesthetics and Art Criticism*, vol. XII, no. 2, Dec. 1953, pp. 278–82.

25 For a summary of his efforts to this particular date see L. L. Whyte: *The Next Development in Man*, Cresset, London 1944.

26 See Read: 'Goethe and Art', *The Listener*, vol. XLIII, 1950, p. 13.

27 A. N. Whitehead: *Science and the Modern World*, Cambridge U. P. 1926, p. 83.

28 ibid., pp. 103–4.

29 ibid., pp. 91–2.

30 ibid., p. 135.

31 See Whyte: *The Two Philosophies: Atomism and Pattern* (pamphlet for private circulation); copy Read Library Stonegrave, dated Oct. 1950.

32 He wrote to Read: 'The applications to history of thought, art etc. are at several removes, and therefore risky. Even biologists have misunderstood (or neglected) the fact that the theory of organism only applies *directly* to basic (physical) structures. But the fusion between physical and mental (as aspects of the phenomenon) which can be reached through the principle is remarkable. I'm all with you, *art extends awareness*.' (Letter Whyte to Read dated 19 Nov 1950; Read Library Stonegrave.) Whyte later came much closer to Read's standpoint, however. See his paper 'The Unity of Visual Experience', *Bulletin of the Atomic Scientists*, vol. XV, no. 2, Feb 1959, pp. 72–6.

33 This is the sense to be drawn from I. Progoff's definition of Jung's Archetype, a definition Read recommended as the best he knew (in a letter to R. Skelton dated 13 July 1954: 53/6 Vict.). See I. Progoff: *Jung's Psychology and its Social Meaning*, Routledge, London 1953, esp. pp. 221–35.

34 See Whyte (ed.): *Aspects of Form: a Symposium on Form in Nature and Art*, Lund Humphries, London 1951. Contributors were R. Arnheim (psychologist); H. B. Cott (biologist); A. Dalcq (human–anatomist); E. H. Gombrich (art historian); C. C. L. Gregory (astronomer); F. G. Gregory (plant physiologist); S. P. F. Humphreys-Owen (crystallographer); K. Z. Lorenz (psychologist); J. Needham (biochemist); C. H. Waddington (animal geneticist) and W. G. Walter (neurologist).

35 See, for example, Ernst Gombrich's argument about art as symbolic substitute for an original object or experience: *Aspects of Form* (n. 34), pp. 219 et seq.

36 ibid., pp. 9–10 (Humphreys-Owen).

37 ibid., p. 27 (C. C. L. Gregory).

38 ibid., p. 199 (Arnheim).

39 ibid., p. 197 (Arnheim).

40 ibid., p. 46 (Waddington).

41 ibid. (Preface), pp. v–vi.

42 Whyte, as editor, changed this phrase of Read's draft Preface to the as printed '. . . science can no longer neglect aesthetic factors.' See MS copy (37/144 Vict).

43 Read: *Art and the Evolution of Man*, Conway Hall, 10 Apr 1951, Freedom Press, London 1951.
44 ibid. (Whyte's Introduction), p. viii.
45 ibid., pp. 35–7.
46 ibid., pp. 38–9.
47 cf. Read: 'The Dynamics of Art' and Whyte: 'A Scientific View of the Creative Energy in Man'; contributions to Jung's *Eranos* conference 1952 (*Eranos Jahrbuch 1952*, Band XXI; Rhein-Verlag, Zurich 1953). See also Whyte: 'The Growth of Ideas' (1954), *Eranos Jahrbuch 1955*. Versions of these papers were also presented at the ICA. Together with their contributions to *Aspects of Form* (and also to the Conway Lecture evening), these indicate a considerable area of agreement.
48 See Whyte: 'Creative Energy' (n. 47), pp. 419–28.
49 Thus the workings of the human brain became a subject of discussion at the ICA. It was a subject pursued by Whyte in his paper 'The Growth of Ideas' (n. 47); and by J. Z. Young, who was invited to lecture on 'Creative Activities of the Human Brain' (17.3.53), with reference to his BBC Reith Lectures of 1950, published as J. Z. Young: *Doubt and Certainty in Science*, Oxford U. P. 1951.
50 Series entitled 'The Aesthetics of Sculpture' (Jan–Feb 1953), comprising (i) The Human Image; (ii) The Discovery of Space; (iii) The Realization of Mass; (iv) The Illusion of Movement. The whole of this sequence may be understood as an exploration of the pedigree of the organic, constructive tendency which was now preoccupying certain members.
51 Read noted with satisfaction that Ehrenzweig's principle would guide perception to the aesthetically best Gestalt, and to an appreciation of abstract form for its own sake. See Read: 'Psychoanalysis and the Problem of Aesthetic Value', *Int. Journal of Psychoanalysis*, vol. XXXII, 1951 (pp. 73–82), p. 80.
52 ICA, London, Jan–Feb 1953.
53 See letters Read to Gabo dated 19 Mar 1953 (49/10 Vict.); Gabo to Read dated 1 Apr 1953 (48/44 Vict.); and Gabo to Read dated 7 Oct 1953 (Beinecke Library, Yale University).
54 This was when the ICA's interest in science gave way first to science fiction and then to popular culture. See Chapter 7 below, p. 163.
55 Read: *The Art of Sculpture* (A. W. Mellon Lectures, National Gallery of Art, Washington, 1954), Faber, London 1956, pp. 102–3.
56 ibid., pp. 111–12.
57 ibid., pp. 113–14.
58 In a letter to R. Tapié dated 2 Sep 1952 (48/139/1.01-1.04 Vict.).
59 Letter Read to T. Munro (editor of the *J. Aesthetics and Art Criticism*) dated 16.11.54 (61/135/2.01-2.05 Vict).
60 Read: 'An Art of Internal Necessity', *Quadrum One*, Brussels 1956 (pp. 7–22), p. 7.
61 Read: 'A Blot on the Scutcheon'; *Encounter*, vol. V, no. 1, July 1955, pp. 54–7. Given as a lecture to the ICA 5 Jan 1956.
62 See Read: 'The Drift of Modern Poetry', *Encounter*, vol. IV, no. 1,

Jan 1955 (pp. 3–10), p. 10. 'There was one clear line of progress – the isolation and clarification of the image, and the perfecting of a diction that would leave the image unclouded by rhetoric or sentiment . . . . But now there is a failure of nerve . . . . Sentiment supersedes sensation, the poetic consciousness is corrupted.'

63 Read: 'Internal Necessity' (n. 60), pp. 8–14.

64 He had become familiar with the work of Francis and the New York School in an ICA exhibition bearing the peculiarly-Readian title *Opposing Forces* (Jan–Feb 1953).

65 Read: 'Internal Necessity' (n. 60), p. 14.

66 ibid., p. 16.

67 Kandinsky's late work proved to Read how difficult it was to maintain such a creative state, and how easily it might become calculation – a transition which would be degenerate in anyone without Kandinsky's highly developed eidetic vision.

68 Read: 'Internal Necessity' (n. 60), p. 22.

69 Read: *Art Now* (4th Edn), Faber, London 1960, pp. 119–20.

70 It was becoming apparent, to some, that American art was, to a degree, formulated. See Patrick Heron's articles on the British influence upon New York painting in *The Guardian* 10, 11 and esp 12 Oct 1974.

71 Read: typescript (35/88 Vict), undated, but see Read: *Letter to a Young Painter*, Thames & Hudson, London 1962, pp. 109–12.

72 See Read: 'Lynn Chadwick' (ibid., pp. 91–103), p. 101.

73 See Read: 'Great Britain', in M. Brion (ed.): *Art Since 1945*; Thames & Hudson, London 1958, pp. 221–50.

74 See A. Ehrenzweig: 'Victor Pasmore's Architectural Constructions', *Quadrum Four,* Brussels 1957, pp. 51–60. See also the catalogue raisonné *Victor Pasmore*, Thames & Hudson, London 1980, esp. pp. 56–85.

75 ibid., n. 73.

76 See Read: 'Victor Pasmore' in B. Dorival (ed.): *Les Peintres Célèbres,* Masenod, Paris 1964, repub. in cat. *Sao Paulo Biennale*, British Council, 1965.

Chapter 7 **Reconciliation**

1 Read: *The Origins of Form in Art*, Thames & Hudson, London 1965, p. 7.

2 Read: *Art and Alienation*, Thames & Hudson, London 1967, p. 7.

3 Read: *The Redemption of the Robot*, Trident, New York 1966 (Faber, London 1970).

4 Read: *The Cult of Sincerity*, Faber, London 1968.

5 Read: *Henry Moore*, Thames & Hudson, London 1965.

6 Read: *Arp*, Thames & Hudson, London 1968.

7 S. Langer: *Philosophy in a New Key*, Harvard U.P. 1942 (2nd ed. Oxford U. P. 1951).

8 Read: BBC Transcript; Tues 13 Mar 1951; Third Programme 8.30–8.50 p.m. See also *World Review*, Sept 1951, pp. 33–6.

9 Read: *Art and the Evolution of Man* (Chap. 6, n. 43), p. 40.
10 BBC Trans (n. 8).
11 ibid.
12 ibid.
13 Read: 'The Dynamics of Art', *Eranos Jahrbuch Band XXI, 1952*, Rhein Verlag, Zurich 1953, pp. 259–62 (repub. as Chaps. 3 and 4 of Read: *The Forms of Things Unknown*, Faber, London 1960, pp. 53–6).
14 Read quoted this phrase several times: see BBC Trans (n. 8); 'Dynamics', p. 263 (*Forms Unknown*, p. 56).
15 'Dynamics', pp. 263–4 (*Forms Unknown*, pp. 56–7).
16 ibid.
17 An argument he was still willing to express: see unpub ? notes on R. Penrose: *Picasso: His Life and Work*, Lund Humphries, London 1956 (35/22 Vict).
18 Read: 'Dynamics', pp. 275–8 (*Forms Unknown*, pp. 68–70.)
19 ibid.
20 ibid., p. 279 (pp. 71–2).
21 Read quoting C. Fiedler, *Forms Unknown*, p. 42.
22 Read quoting E. Neumann in letter Read to R. F. C. Hull, dated 3.3.52 (48/67/1.01 Vict).
23 Assisted greatly by R. F. C. Hull, one of the principal translators involved in the publishing of Jung's *Collected Works* (Read, Fordham and Adler, eds, Routledge, London 1953).
24 See Read: *The Psychopathology of Reaction in the Arts*, ICA, London 1955, pp. 6–7. Read considered himself to have been a recipient of reactionary abuse. When this booklet was republished (*Sewanee Review*, vol. LXIII, 1955; pp. 551–66), he appended an intentionally-ironic note: 'It may be no accident that these thoughts came to me after reading *The Demon of Progress in the Arts*, a somewhat scathing tract by P. Wyndham Lewis. I would not like it to be thought, however, that they have any reference to Mr. Lewis himself.'
25 Read: 'The Creative Nature of Humanism', *Eranos Jahrbuch Band XXVI, 1957*, Rhein Verlag, Zurich 1958, pp. 338–9 (repub. as Chaps. 11 and 12 of *Forms Unknown*, pp. 194–5).
26 Read: 'Nihilism and Renewal in the Art of Our Time', *Eranos Jahrbuch Band XXVIII, 1959*, Rhein Verlag, Zurich 1960, pp. 358–9 (repub. as Chaps. 9 and 10 of *Forms Unknown*, pp. 154–5).
27 Read: *Psychopathology* (n. 24), p. 6; and 'Creative Humanism' (n. 25), p. 340 (*Forms Unknown*, p. 196).
28 Letter C. G. Jung to Read, dated 2.9.60 (48/72 Vict); a response to Read's gift of a copy of *Forms of Things Unknown*.
29 And, in literature, James Joyce (ibid.).
30 ibid.: Jung wrote to Read 'I have just read the words of a *Man*, that is the statement of your views about my work. Courage and honesty have won out, the two qualities, the absence of which in my hitherto critics has hindered every form of understanding. Your blessed words

are the rays of a new sun over a dark sluggish swamp, in which I felt being buried.'

31 This, Read thought, was the way of Proust's *A La Recherche du Temps Perdu*; Joyce's *Ulysses*; and Eliot's late poems. See 'Creative Humanism', p. 341 (*Forms Unknown*, p. 197).

32 Read: 'The Problem of Aesthetic Consciousness'. *Proceedings of the Third Int. Congress on Aesthetics*, Instituto di Estetica, Università di Torino, 1956 (pp. 257–60), p. 259.

33 Read: 'Poetic Consciousness and Creative Experience', *Eranos Jahrbuch Band XXV, 1956*, Rhein Verlag, Zurich 1957; p. 370 (repub. as Chaps. 7 and 8 of *Forms Unknown*, pp. 121–2).

34 Letter Read to Kathleen Raine, dated 27.1.56 (48/111 Vict).

35 With Karl Jaspers.

36 Read: 'Creative Humanism', p. 335 (*Forms Unknown*, pp. 191–2).

37 ibid., pp. 340–1 (pp. 196–7).

38 See Read: 'Nihilism' (n. 26), pp. 361–70 (*Forms Unknown*, pp. 155–6).

39 Read: *Kandinsky*, Faber, London 1959 (repub. as Chap. X of *Art and Alienation* (n. 2)).

40 Read: 'The Origins of Form in the Plastic Arts', *Eranos Jahrbuch Band XXIX, 1960*, Rhein Verlag, Zurich 1961, pp. 203–5 (repub. in *Origins of Form* (n. 1), Chap. III, pp. 85–7).

41 Read: *Origins of Form*, p. 92.

42 ibid., p. 96.

43 R. Shattuck: *The Banquet Years*, Faber, London 1959.

44 Read: 'Avantgardism and Modernism' (review of 43), *London Magazine*, vol. 7, no. 3, March 1960, pp. 57–60. See also Read: 'Form in Architecture', Chap. V of *Origins of Form*, p. 111.

45 Shattuck: *Banquet Years*, pp. 256–7.

46 Shattuck slightly misquoted by Read in 'Form in Architecture' (*Origins of Form*, p. 111). Shattuck's words were 'The factotum word is *juxtaposition*: setting one thing beside the other without connective' (*Banquet Years*, p. 256).

47 Read: *Origins of Form*, pp. 50–1. He used the word 'pleasure', but substituted 'vitality' in subsequent arguments.

48 After A. Stokes (Read: *Origins of Form*, pp. 60–1).

49 cf. Read's definition of individual imagination: 'dissolution, dissipation, diffusion prior to recreation,' in 'Rational Society and Irrational Art' (1967), *Art and Alienation*, Chap. II, p. 37.

50 Read: 'Disintegration of Form in Modern Art' (1964), *Origins of Form*, Chap. IX, pp. 175–6.

51 ibid., pp. 179–82.

52 Read: 'The Limits of Painting' (1962), *Art and Alienation*, Chap. III, p. 46.

53 Read: 'Rational Society and Irrational Art' (1967), *Art and Alienation*, Chap. II, p. 31.

54 Read: 'Style and Expression' (1965), *Art and Alienation*, Chap. IV, p. 63.

55 ibid., pp. 74–6 (Read quoting H. Focillon: *The Life of Forms in Art,* 1948).
56 ibid., p. 74.
57 The main theme of his Eranos presentation 'The Creative Nature of Humanism' (n. 25).
58 Read: *Arp* (n. 6), pp. 87–8, 129.
59 Read: 'Naum Gabo: Before the Gates of the Vacant Future' (1966), *Art and Alienation,* Chap. XII, p. 162.
60 Read: *Arp,* pp. 132–3.
61 Read: 'Gabo' (n. 59), p. 164.
62 Read: 'Henry Moore: the Reconciling Archetype' (1965), *Art and Alienation,* Chap. IX, pp. 127–34.
63 Read: *Moore* (n. 5), p. 208.
64 Read: 'Creative Humanism', pp. 331–5 (*Forms Unknown,* pp. 188–92).
65 ibid., p. 319 (p. 177).
66 Read: *Moore* (n. 5), pp. 257–9; and 'Reconciling Archetype' (n. 62), pp. 124, 135–6.
67 See Read: 'A Nest of Gentle Artists', *Apollo,* vol. 67, no. 7, Sept 1962, pp. 536–8.
68 Read: 'T. S. Eliot: a Memoir', *Sewanee Review,* Winter 1966, repub. as Chap. VI of Read: *The Cult of Sincerity,* Faber, London 1968, p. 104.
69 See corres. Read to E. Dahlberg, published in Read and Dahlberg: *Truth is More Sacred,* Routledge & Kegan Paul, London 1961, pp. 209–10.
70 ibid., pp. 211–13.
71 ibid. (Dahlberg's consistent argument).
72 And Hilda Doolittle.
73 Read: 'Richard Aldington' (1965), repub. as Chap. IX of *Cult of Sincerity,* pp. 154–5.
74 ibid., p. 154.
75 Read: 'What is There Left to Say?' *Encounter,* vol. XIX, no. 4, Oct 1962 (pp. 27–31), p. 28.
76 Read: 'Apology for E.S.', Chap. IV of *Cult of Sincerity,* pp. 70–1.
77 Strickland was Read's mother's maiden name, and 'Eugene Strickland' was the pseudonym he used at the start of his literary career, when there was possible conflict with his occupation in the Civil Service. See letter J. Middleton Murry to Read, dated 11 June 1920, in which he praises a prizewinning essay of Read's which had been submitted to *The Athenaeum.*
78 Read: 'Apology for E.S.' (n. 76), pp. 63–6.
79 Read seems to have overlooked Hulme's reference to the notion of a collective unconscious (in a note to Bergson, which Read did not publish). See S. Hynes (ed.): *Further Speculations by T. E. Hulme,* Minnesota U.P. 1955, pp. 45–6.
80 See A. R. Jones: *The Life and Opinions of Thomas Ernest Hulme,* Gollancz, London 1960, esp. pp. 57–9.

81 Read: *Icon and Idea*, Faber, London 1955, p. 19.
82 Read published Hulme's outline Plan in *Speculations* (Chap. 2, n. 18), pp. 261–4. It would have featured Platonic theory and English Romanticism as predisposing influences; and would have interrelated Bergsonian and Crocean philosophy with German morphology and theories of empathy.
83 Read: *Moore* (n. 5), p. 259.

Index

205

Index

Index

Mondrian, Piet, 14–15, 79–80, 93–4, 96, 103, 121, 124, 155, 159, 168; *Neo Plasticism*, 88–90
Monument to the Unknown Political Prisoner (ICA), 139
Moore, Henry, 14, 15, 80–1, 95, 99–104, 115, 124, 141, 146–7, 153, 158, 165–8, 173, 175, 190–1; shelter drawings, 100
moral consciousness, 12
morality, 38, 73–4
morphology, 46, 132–6
Morris, William, 1, 2
Murry, John Middleton, 193
Museum of Modern Art, London (proposed), 16, 194
myth, 157, 163

Nash, Paul, 4, 14, 95, 97–8, 103, 168, 173, 176
natural creativity, 3, 73–4, 94, 99–101, 116, 133–4, 174
natural philosophy, 2–4, 33
naturalism, 71, 98, 118–19
neolithic art, 118–19
neo-realism, 27–32
neurosis, 55, 112
Nevinson, Christopher, 27
New Age (The), 5, 25–32, 39, 76, 105, 182
new reality, 62, 90–1, 102
Nicholson, Ben, 14, 79, 95–6, 98, 103, 168, 173, 189
Nietzsche, Friedrich, 2–3, 5, 18, 30–1, 169
nihilism, 155
Now, 17

objectified self-enjoyment, 42
On Growth and Form: see Growth and Form
Opposing Forces (ICA), 200
optimistic art, 103, 148, 191
Orage, Alfred, 5–6, 25–7, 37–8, 105–6, 177, 181
organicism, 19, 54, 57–8, 63, 73–5, 84, 86, 93–5, 99–101, 103, 126–30, 133–4, 151, 163, 165–6, 173–5, 196–7
origination, principle of, 72
Origins of Form in Art (The) (Read), 150
Ouspensky, P. D., 177

paleolithic art, 119–23
Pasmore, Victor, 146–7
pattern, 74, 122, 133–6, 138
Penty, Arthur, 25, 105–6, 108
personality, 11–12, 74, 79, 153–8, 165, 185
pessimistic art, 103, 148, 191
Pevsner, Antoine, 88, 188
Philosophy in a New Key (Langer), 150–2
Philosophy of Modern Art (The) (Read), 15; elaboration of, 85–104
Picasso, Pablo, 29, 80–1, 102–3, 153–9, 194–5; *Guernica*, 153
Platonic philosophy, 5, 25, 93, 202
poetic form, 4
poetic theory, 3–4, 6–9, 11–12, 56
popular culture, 163
positive and negative work (Thompson), 128
Pound, Ezra, 36, 169
preconscious, the, 11
prehistoric and primitive art, 17, 109, 112–13, 118–23, 160–1, 173
prevision, 8
primary imagination (Coleridge), 19
process dominance in art and science, 126–36
psychology of art, 8, 54–5, 64–73, 100–2, 109, 145–6, 168, 172–4
pure form, 4, 15, 83, 84, 109

quantum theory, 9, 47, 57

Read, Herbert: early life, 1–2; war service, 106, 191; employment at the Treasury, 4; employment at the Victoria and Albert Museum, 4; friendship with T. S. Eliot, 7–8, 168–70; start of literary career, 5–6, 168; early classicism, 59, 168–9; retention of romanticism, 171; early political thought, 105–6, 111, 170; rejection of communism, 109, 170; poetic theory, 3, 6–8, 11–12, 56; his 'futurist' paintings, 27; as surrealist, 12–14, 66–70, 81–2; Chair of Fine Arts at Edinburgh University, 10, 167; life in Hampstead, 167–8; own aesthetic preference, 10; art criticism in *The Listener*, 76–8; ed. *Burlington Magazine*, 169;